T0272192

LABOR RELATIONS IN THE AVIATION AND AEROSPACE INDUSTRIES

LABOR RELATIONS IN THE AVIATION AND AEROSPACE INDUSTRIES

STUDY GUIDE

Robert W. Kaps, J. Scott Hamilton, and Timm J. Bliss

Southern Illinois University Press
Carbondale and Edwardsville

Copyright © 2012 by the Board of Trustees,
Southern Illinois University
All rights reserved
Printed in the United States of America

ISBN-13: 978-0-8093-3044-7 (pbk. : alk. paper)
ISBN-10: 0-8093-3044-X (pbk. : alk. paper)
ISBN-13: 978-0-8093-9022-1 (ebook)
ISBN-10: 0-8093-9022-7 (ebook)

Printed on recycled paper. ♻
The paper used in this publication meets the minimum
requirements of American National Standard for Information
Sciences—Permanence of Paper for Printed Library Materials,
ANSI Z39.48-1992. ♾

Contents

Part Three. The Changing Labor Relations Environment

Preface

This study guide is designed for use with the textbook *Labor Relations in the Aviation and Aerospace Industries*. It is intended to assist students in comprehending basic terminology and principles of labor relations and the law, to relate those principles to unique features of the aviation and aerospace industry, and to prepare for the kinds of labor relations–related decisions students will make as aviation professionals, whether in private- or public-sector employment.

We have taught this course at the undergraduate and graduate levels in the traditional classroom setting, online, and a combination of both. This study guide is suitable in all of these contexts.

The supplemental readings may be used per the instructor's discretion for greater depth of the coverage of certain topics, especially for graduate course work.

The mock negotiation in chapter 5 provides an opportunity for the instructor to incorporate a simulation of collective bargaining.

Because this study guide is closely keyed to the text, we suggest that as soon as you have read a chapter in the text, and it's still fresh in your mind, you work through the discussion questions and any online work your instructor assigns.

LABOR RELATIONS IN THE AVIATION AND AEROSPACE INDUSTRIES

Part One. Foundations of Labor Law and Policy

1. Public Policy and Labor Law

1. The aviation industry consists of several distinct segments, including:

   a. _____

   b. _____

   c. _____

   d. _____

2. The _____ Act of 19____ established the regulatory framework for the labor-relations process in the airline industry. Congress amended that act to make it also applicable to the airlines in 19____.

3. What was Congress intending to accomplish by enacting that act?

4. What federal administrative agency administers that act?

5. What airlines' employee relations are governed by that act?

6. Define *collective bargaining*.

7. Define *self-help*.

8. Define *lockout*.

9. Define *craft union*. Give one example in the airline industry.

10. Define *craft unit*. Give three examples in the airline industry.

11. What act applies to labor-management relations in the aerospace manufacturing industry?

12. What federal administrative agency administers and enforces that act?

13. Define *unfair labor practice*.

14. Is the aerospace manufacturing industry's workforce extensively unionized?

15. Give one example of a major labor union active in the aerospace manufacturing industry.

16. What act governs labor-management relations in the general aviation industry?

17. Is the general aviation industry workforce extensively unionized? Why?

18. Give one example of a unionized group of employees in U.S. general aviation.

19. What act governs labor relations in federal government employment?

20. Identify a craft union of federal employees directly involved in aviation.

21. What federal agency is responsible for establishing the rules and regulations governing federal civilian employment procedures and practices?

22. What federal agency decides issues arising under those regulations?

23. What federal agency oversees the process of collective bargaining in the federal sector?

24. What is the main difference in collective bargaining between the federal government and private industry?

Online Assignments

1. Locate a source for the current full text of the Civil Service Reform Act online. Give the URLs for all online sources used.

2. For an aviation or aerospace company or government agency that you or your instructor selects, research online and prepare to present in class a brief biography of the CEO, including as much of the following information as possible:

    a. Name

    b. How long with the company or agency

    c. Previous major management experience

    d. Photo

    e. Reputation with company employees and unions

    f. Compensation

    g. URLs for all online sources used

2. The Violent Beginnings of U.S. Labor Law

Review Questions

1. Define closed shop.

2. Define good-faith bargaining:

3. Define strikebreaker.

4. What is the difference between a strikebreaker and a scab?

5. The most vigorous organization in pursuit of the national-union concept in the late 1800s was the
_____ (_____).

6. The leader of the organization in question 5 was _____, who is known as the "father of the American labor movement."

7. The main platform of the organization in question 5 insisted on _____ as the ultimate weapon to achieve its aims and goals.

8. Which political party did the organization in question 5 initially concentrate on establishing an alliance with?

9. List techniques and strategies used by employers in the late 1800s to prevent unionization of their work-forces and to prevent strikes from succeeding.

10. What legal argument supports use of these tactics?

11. What violent historical event triggered a media and public backlash against organized labor?

12. What violent historical event subsequent to the one of question 11 galvanized public opinion in favor of labor's position and led to a progressive era of reform?

13. What was the Sherman Act designed to do?

14. How was the Sherman Act used against organized labor?

15. Define sympathy strike.

16. How was a sympathy strike used in the Pullman strike? What was the result?

17. Define secondary boycott.

18. Are secondary boycotts legal now in the aerospace manufacturing industry? In the airline industry? In the general aviation industry?

19. Define yellow-dog contract?

20. Are yellow-dog contracts legal today in the aerospace manufacturing industry? In the airline industry? In the general aviation industry?

21. Did railroad (and airline) labor law and policy develop more rapidly or less rapidly than legislation affecting other industries? Why?

22. What effect did World War I have on unionization and collective bargaining in the railroad industry?

Online Assignments

1. For an aviation or aerospace company or agency that you or your instructor selects, research online and prepare to present in class the following information regarding unionization of the workplace:

   a. Identify three unions representing craft units in the organization and the craft(s) each represents.

   b. Identify which, if any, of those are affiliated with the AFL-CIO.

   c. Identify a current (or if no current, then the most recent) bargaining issue between your management and one of those unions.

   d. Give the URLs of all online sources used.

2. Research online and prepare to present in class a brief biography of the president of one of the unions you listed in online assignment 1, including as much of the following information as possible:

   a. Name

   b. Number of years with the union

   c. Previous major union experience

   d. Photo

   e. Reputation with union members

   f. Compensation

   g. URLs of all online sources used

3. Major Collective Bargaining Legislation

Review Questions

1. Is there a relationship between U.S. immigration policy and the bargaining power of American workers? If so, describe.

2. What is the oldest federal collective bargaining legislation in the nation?

3. Define *company union*.

4. Are company unions legal in the aerospace manufacturing industry? In the airline industry? In the general aviation industry? Why?

5. Define *union shop*. What is the difference between a union shop and a closed shop?

6. Define *agency shop*.

7. What shops—union, agency, and closed—are legal in the airline industry under the Railroad Labor Act (RLA)?

8. Define *right-to-work law*.

9. What effect, if any, do state right-to-work laws have on the airlines, under the RLA?

10. Prior to Congress bringing the airlines under the RLA, the National Labor Board (NLB), charged with enforcing the National Industrial Recovery Act (NIRA), issued its Decision 83, which is a supplemental reading to this chapter. What was that decision, and what effect, if any, does it have today?

11. What were the effects of the Norris–La Guardia Act of 1932 on labor-management relations?

12. What did Congress intend to accomplish by enacting the National Labor Relations Act (NLRA or Wagner Act) in 1935?

13. What are the key provisions of the NLRA aimed at accomplishing the goal in question 12?

14. What federal administrative agency administers and enforces the NLRA?

15. Does that agency have jurisdiction over the aerospace manufacturing industry? Over the airline industry? Over the general aviation industry? Over public sector aviation employment?

16. What three rights in Section 7 of the NLRA are guaranteed employees in industries covered by the act?

17. What employer behaviors in industries covered by the NLRA does Section 8 of the NLRA prohibit as unfair labor practices?

18. What was Congress's intent in enacting the Taft-Hartley Act (Labor-Management Relations Act of 1947)?

19. What changes did Taft-Hartley make to the unfair labor practices set forth in Section 8 of the NLRA?

20. What federal administrative agency did the Taft-Hartley Act create?

21. Does the agency in question 20 have jurisdiction in the aerospace manufacturing industry? In the airline industry? In the general aviation industry? In public employment?

22. Under Taft-Hartley, what is a National Emergency Board? When and how is one created? What are its powers? What is the role of the courts if such a board is empanelled?

23. What is the effect of Taft-Hartley on secondary boycotts?

24. What was Congress's intent in enacting the Landrum-Griffin Act, further amending the NLRA?

25. How does the Landrum-Griffin Act go about accomplishing that legislative intent?

26. How did the Airline Deregulation Act of 1978 affect the labor relations environment in the airline industry?

27. How did Texas Air Corp. chairman Francisco A. "Frank" Lorenzo use the corporate-reorganization provisions of the federal bankruptcy act to the airline's advantage in collective bargaining?

28. What measures did Congress take to preclude other airlines from following suit?

29. Whatever became of Texas Air Corporation?

30. How can airline pilots be forced out of work at age sixty-five, considering the requirements of the Age Discrimination in Employment Act?

31. You are an executive in management of a general aviation aircraft manufacturer with six hundred employees. Due to reduced customer demand resulting from a global economic recession, the company is cutting back production and plans to lay off a quarter of the workforce. Are there legal requirements applicable to implementation of this plan? If so, describe.

32. You are the chief pilot for an airline. Outraged by terrorist attacks on America, a group of your captains feel it is their patriotic duty to join the air force and apply their talents to the war on terror.

    • Is the airline required to reemploy them when they return from military service?

    • If so, will they have lost their seniority?

    • Can the airline then rehire them as first officers, instead of captains?

    • If during their absence, the airline has adopted a two-tier pay scale (one for senior employees and a lesser one for new hires), can the airline rehire these pilots at the lower rate?

    • Why?

33. Describe *featherbedding*.

34. Is featherbedding prohibited in the airline industry? In the aerospace manufacturing industry? In the general aviation industry?

35. Give an example of alleged featherbedding in the airline industry.

36. In your observation, do the racial and gender demographics of U.S. airline flight crews closely match those of the population at large?

37. Are airlines required to take affirmative action to address underutilization of minorities and women in filling those jobs? Explain.

38. In the supplemental reading "Detailed Examination of the Events Leading to Rule #83 Decision," at the end of this chapter, identify similarities between the situation described in the reading (in 1932) and today.

39. What did David L. Behncke, a United Air Lines pilot and the principal organizer of the Air Line Pilots Association (ALPA), present as the most insistent rationale for the creation of that union?

40. In 1932, what justification did the airlines give for proposed cuts in pilot pay?

41. In 1932, how did ALPA determine what its members wanted?

42. Why did the pilots prefer seniority, rather than merit, as the sole factor in promotion?

43. Did David L. Behncke trust airline management? Did most pilots? Do you? Why?

44. Define *wildcat strike*.

45. What famous politician (for whom a major airport is named) eagerly honored David L. Behncke's plea for support of ALPA?

46. What famous media magnate's newspapers featured editorials supporting ALPA? Was this out of character for him?

47. What may have been a major factor that made the airlines reluctant to take a pilots' strike in late 1933?

48. Define *picketing*.

49. Define *secondary picketing*.

50. Does the RLA permit secondary picketing in an airline labor dispute?

51. Does the NLRA permit secondary picketing in a labor dispute in the aerospace manufacturing or general aviation industry?

52. What feature of the RLA is highlighted as contributing to the demise of Eastern Airlines?

53. How did the Professional Air Traffic Controllers Organization (PATCO) strike of 1981 affect public opinion toward unions?

54. What difference does it make whether an employee is exempt or nonexempt? What are the differences between those two categories?

55. Do railroads and railroad-employee unions seem to favor amending or doing away with the RLA? Why? Does ALPA? Why?

Online Assignments

1. Conduct an online search for the Employee Free Choice Act to determine its objective(s), arguments for and against the act, and its current status.

2. For an aviation or aerospace company or agency you or your instructor selects, research online and prepare to present in class:

   a. Identify those U.S. states in which the organization has employees. (A map is the best way to present this information.)

   b. Identify which of these states are right-to-work states. (A map is the best way to present this information.)

   c. Determine whether the state's right-to-work law applies to your organization's employees in those states and state the reason.

   d. Give the URLs of all online sources used.

Supplemental Readings

Detailed Examination of the Events
Leading to Rule 83 Decision

AUTHORS' NOTE: The following is reprinted, by permission of the publishers, from George Hopkins, *The Airline Pilots: A Study in Elite Unionization* (Cambridge, MA: Harvard University Press, 1971), 112–41.

The vagaries of Washington politics caused considerable turmoil in the air transportation industry during the early New Deal. The Century strike generated wide public awareness of the role subsidies played in airline operations, but the drama of the pilots' strike temporarily overshadowed the issue of government paternalism. Even though E. L. Cord temporarily got out of the air transportation business after losing his dispute with the pilots, he left a residual legacy of mistrust and suspicion hanging over the nonmail operators. However, the independent operators found many willing listeners among New Deal Democrats for their tales of fraud and malfeasance, and just prior to the end of the Herbert Hoover administration, the Senate created a special committee, chaired by Alabama's Hugo L. Black, to investigate Walter Folger Brown's air-mail policies. But even before the Black committee began its work, the aviation trade journals were predicting severe cuts in the subsidy, since candidate Franklin D. Roosevelt's "balanced-budget" campaign rhetoric in 1932 about the early New Deal had forced Hoover to publicly promise new economies in government spending in the last days of his term. When the U.S. Post Office Department reduced the subsidies late in 1932, the temporary alliance between the major airline operators and Air Line Pilots Association (ALPA), which was predicated only on their mutual fear of Cord, collapsed.[1] Indicating the irritation of airline executives over high pilot salaries, *Aviation* magazine expressed dismay over the disparity between the high pay of pilots and the low pay of ground personnel. The implication was clearly, however, that pilot salaries should be lower, not that ground personnel salaries should be higher.[2]

Shortly after the lower subsidies became effective in December 1932, the operators announced their intention to decrease pilot salaries an amount compatible with the percentage of subsidy reduction. Eastern began with a 16 percent reduction, Northwest announced a flat 10 percent cut, and all the other airlines indicated that they, too, would reduce salaries in the near future. One of Behncke's most insistent rationales for the creation of ALPA was that a union would prevent pay reductions. Early in the depression, it was the threat rather than the fact of pay cuts that alarmed pilots; and even on lines where the hourly system of pay prevailed, such as TWA, pilot salaries remained fairly high. But late in 1932, reality stared the pilots in the face—the rhetoric and scares were over, the operators fully intended to cut pay, and ALPA would have to produce positive results in order to justify its existence.

At the same time, serious problems of technological unemployment faced the profession, since the airlines were rapidly introducing more-modern aircraft, such as the Boeing 247, which, because it was larger and faster, vastly increased pilot productivity and resulted in some pilot layoffs. The Century strike proved there was no shortage of pilots, and Lyman D. Lauren, the aviation writer for the *New York Times*, estimated that there were over 7,000 licensed transport pilots in 1933, but he placed the total number of pilot jobs at 1,500.[3] Faced with these dismal statistics and the obvious financial difficulties of their respective airlines, a surprising number of pilots were willing to acquiesce in the pay reduction.

Behncke, however, had to deal with a credibility crisis among the remainder of his membership, and he desperately petitioned his newfound friends in Washington for help.[4] At his request, Congressman James M. Mead of Minnesota intervened directly on ALPA's behalf. He asked Northwestern General Manager to withhold action on the pay cuts until Congress and the Post Office Department had time to study the whole situation.[5] Mead also intervened with Captain Thomas Doe, the President of Eastern Air Transport. Many Congressmen were becoming increasingly suspicious of the air-mail subsidies, and the situation at the time was very tense. As an indication of the antagonism the subsidy issue aroused in Congress, the Senate deleted the entire air-mail section in the Post Office appropriation, and a conference committee only barely succeeded in restoring it. The times were uncertain as the country awaited Roosevelt's inauguration, and nobody could be sure of the direction of aviation policy in the forthcoming New Deal. While expecting and preparing for the worst, most operators saw no advantage in prematurely alienating an important member of the House Post Office Committee. Brittin and Doe, therefore, reluctantly acceded to Mead's request.[6]

"Welfare Capitalism" and the anti-union activities of American businessmen during the prosperity decade of the 1920s had decreased the strength of the American labor movement, and the downward trend in union membership accelerated with the depression. But the confidence and enthusiasm which the early New Deal generated proved very helpful to union organizers, and the thrust of its policies seemed to offer organized labor a golden opportunity to write guarantees of maximum hours and minimum wages into federal law. The prestige of the entrepreneur in American society had sagged along with the index of industrial production, and many aggrieved and embittered people who formerly looked suspiciously upon unions were now willing to countenance them. While ALPA was already an organized union, it still had need of federal guarantees of the right to bargain collectively, and the new prestige of organized labor, particularly among influential legislators, gave Behncke cause for optimism.[7]

In the interim, however, before anybody could be sure of the shape of the New Deal air transportation and labor policies, Behncke and the operators warily sparred over the pay issue. During the 1932 convention, Behncke told the delegates that the House Post Office Committee had promised to await ALPA's recommendations before passing any new air-mail legislation, and early in 1933 Congressman Mead asked the pilots for their views on a variety of aviation issues, including pay, hours, and air safety. Behncke undercut the stereotype of the individualistic aviator when he triumphantly informed the delegates that the pilots could "look forward to being adequately protected by some regulation or legislation during the coming session of Congress."[8] He wanted a firm commitment from his membership as to what they wanted, and, prior to the convention, he had polled all twenty-nine of ALPA's locals asking for their ideas on such things as salaries, hours, hazard pay, foreign-duty pay, vacations, and sick leave.[9] From the composite questionnaires he determined that the pilots preferred a base pay, plus mileage pay, with increased factors for the size, speed, and weight of the aircraft, and, of course, hazard pay for night, over water, and mountainous terrain flying. At Behncke's insistence the convention established a National Basis of Pay Committee to aid him in the effort to have Congress write federal guarantees which would apply to all airline pilots but especially to pilots working for airlines which had air-mail contracts.[10]

The matter of a federal limitation of flying hours per month provoked some of the hottest exchanges of the 1932 convention. There was already a good deal of talk about limiting the hours of all workers to thirty hours per week, and William Green had endorsed the idea as early as 1930. The month following ALPA's convention, the AFL formally endorsed the thirty-hour week on the theory that it would spread the available work.[11] Pilot interest in reduced hours of flying preceded such economic theorizing, deriving mainly from the fact that too many pilots spent three nights out of four away from their homes. While some pilots preferred the hefty paychecks they received for flying long hours, most pilots opted for a more relaxed routine even at the risk of lessened pay. The Department of Commerce set a maximum limit of 110 hours per month, but during busy seasons the airlines habitually exceeded this total on the theory, which the department never tested, that the maximum was meant to be an annual average rather than an arbitrary total for any one month. But to complicate matters for the pilots, many of the smaller airlines declared that they could not continue to operate if pilot hours per month were too low, and the pilots were genuinely worried about it. There was fundamental agreement, however, that the operators should not be allowed to exploit pilot labor, and John Huber spoke for the majority when he declared that "the idea behind all this is to set a regular scale . . . so there will not be any competition between the lines." The general discussion slowly yielded an understanding, for most of the delegates, that unless they stuck together and refused to fly more than other pilots, there would be anarchy within their ranks which would eventually destroy the union.

Many pilots evidenced a managerial mentality, and at times they seemed more concerned with their line's profit margin than with their own salaries. While there was some merit in this view, Behncke worried lest it dominate ALPA policy, and he insisted that ALPA must necessarily adopt a hard posture in favor of a uniform national scale. Despite this disagreement, it was apparent to almost all of the pilots that seniority should be the only factor in promotion. They openly derided the merit system, declaring that it was almost always used to favor management's cronies. They knew that they would eventually have to secure contractual agreements with the operators to use the seniority system exclusively, but Behncke persuaded them that it was better to seek federal protection before entering direct negotiations with the employers. The tricky problem of job security would necessarily involve a combination of federal guarantees and direct union-employer collective bargaining agreements. Still, until they got these agreements, federal rules governing their hours and wages would do them little good if, as one delegate put it, management could "fire an old man with a high base and start in a young fellow with a low base."[12] The times seemed propitious for a concerted effort in Washington, however, and Behncke persuaded a majority of the delegates that ALPA should delay action on direct collective bargaining.

At one point in the discussion the delegates seemed to be on the verge of adopting a variable scale on maximum hours and minimum pay which would allow for regional variations, the size of the airline, and the type of aircraft. Behncke adamantly opposed this idea, insisting on a single standard that would apply to all airline pilots everywhere. After a delegate offered a formal resolution that the hourly limit be subject to a "plus or minus fifteen hours" variation, Behncke blurted: "No! No! That is all wrong, that fifteen hour business. That leaves the sky for the limit." Since Behncke would not countenance a variable hourly limit, the convention seemed willing to adopt the Commerce Department's limit of 110 hours per month, until a delegate moaned that such a high hourly total would "just about drive us crazy on our line. With the run I'm on we would have to fly, well about damn near every day. And on account of the cancellations for weather we would just have a merry time."

Behncke favored an 80-hour-per-month maximum, which was about what most pilots were then flying, and he stressed the fact that the Aeromedical Association, a private group of physicians interested in aviation medicine, endorsed his view. He had written to Frederick C. Warnshuis, the Chairman of the association, asking for a "scientific" determination of the maximum number of hours which would be compatible with safety. Warnshuis replied that, in his opinion, the Department of Commerce limit of 110 hours per month was too high, and he recommended 90 to 100 hours for day flying, 60 to 70 for night flying, with a standard figure of 80 hours per month for a combination of both types.[13] Behncke had a telling and effective point in the doctor's opinion, and the convention finally agreed to support him in his effort to make 80 hours per month the federal maximum.[14]

Behncke intended to make the Pay Committee his vehicle for Washington lobbying activities. The committee met for the first time on December 22, 1932, and promptly endorsed a pamphlet which Behncke had previously written entitled "The Truth about Pilot Pay." He subsequently circulated the pamphlet among all members of Congress, and he sent dozens of copies to newspaper editors.[15] Behncke knew the

operators would not delay their pay cuts much longer, and he wanted to publicize the pilots' views as widely as possible. At this time he abandoned all idea of a strike, if and when the pay cuts became effective, partly because he felt that ALPA's structure was too weak to survive a major strike, but mainly because he wanted to pursue the issue in Washington.[16]

The uneasy truce which had existed between ALPA and the operators since Congressman Mead intervened to win a delay in the pay cuts ended abruptly on February 25, 1933, when a committee of executives from the nation's five largest airlines announced in New York that they were instituting a new, uniform system of hourly pay. All five lines declared that their decision to terminate mileage pay was irrevocable, and they set copilot pay at a flat $225 per month, regardless of the number of hours they flew. Three of the "Big Five" were already using the hourly system, but American and United, the two largest, were still paying their pilots on the old mileage basis. The new pay system raised pay very slightly on T&WA, Eastern, and Western Air Express, which were already paying on the hourly scale, but the impact of the new pay policy on United and American was to reduce salaries. United, which always treated its pilots gingerly, announced that there would be no lost pay the first year as a result of the new system of pay computation because it would pay the pilots a "bonus" equal to the amount they would have made on the old mileage system. But United's management adamantly insisted that the new hourly method of computing pay was in effect and permanent.[17]

Behncke promptly objected to the new pay method, and he condemned the operators for deceptively calling it a "pay raise" when in fact it was a pay cut. He took a few days off to go to Washington in the hope of enlisting the aid of his friends on the House Post Office Committee, and William Green issued a statement from AFofL headquarters condemning the operators. Green insisted that it was folly for the government to cut the pay of its own employees, thus reflecting Behncke's notion that the airline pilots were "quasi-governmental" employees.[18] The operators had lent credence to this idea by citing cuts in the mail subsidy as their reason for reducing pilot pay. The President of the AFofL seemed genuinely to like Behncke, and the two were on very friendly terms. Green went out of his way to be helpful to ALPA from the very beginning of its connection with the Federation, perhaps because ALPA was one of the few unions to affiliate with it in the bleak years between 1929 and 1933. Green and Behncke shared a common Horatio

Alger story background, since both had risen in the world from rural, working-class backgrounds, despite their lack of formal education.[19] But there was little the House Post Office Committee, William Green, or anybody else could do to prevent the operators from changing the basis of pay in the uncertain period before Roosevelt's inauguration. Green promised Behncke that he would use whatever influence he had with the new president,[20] and owing to his efforts Behncke received an invitation to attend a presidential "Industrial and Labor Conference" in Washington on March 31.[21] In the frantic atmosphere of Washington, however, where ardent New Dealers were already busily planning their assault on the depression, there was no place for the leader of a small union to present his case. Other far larger issues were on the minds of officialdom, and Behncke realized that he would have to swim with the tide of events for the time being.

The labor provisions of the National Industrial Recovery Act (NIRA), which the president signed on June 16, 1933, were enormously important for organized labor, but for ALPA the vital aspect of the measure lay in its basic assumption that cooperation between labor, capital, and the government offered the best solution to the problem of economic collapse. The heart of the Blue Eagle crusade was its insistence that agreements between the various participants in an industry, as stated in an industry-wide "code," could restore prosperity.[22] The Air Transportation Code, which became effective on November 27, 1933, had no effect on pilot laborers because they were not in it—they wanted no part of it and they fought furiously to avoid any definition of their maximum hours and minimum wages under the code.[23] Ordinarily it might seem that the code offered an ideal vehicle for ALPA to achieve its goals. But Behncke distrusted airline management more, perhaps, than any other pilot in America. He never evidenced any sign of the managerial mentality which characterized so many pilots, and he stubbornly insisted that ALPA adhere to its original objective of specific federal laws covering wages and working conditions of airline pilots. He refused to depend on the good will of airline managers for the simple reason that he did not expect to have their good will very long.[24]

Initially, however, Behncke had to go through the motions of cooperating in the effort of the National Recovery Administration (NRA) to draft a code for the air transportation industry. While many people in the NRA regarded it as a straightforward method for introducing

government planning into the economy, another faction worried that the charge of "czarism" might discredit their work. General Hugh Johnson, the head of the NRA, was in a difficult position when it came to the harsh realities of actually hammering out workable codes for each industry. He had grave doubts about the constitutionality of the NRA, and quite early he decided that, in order to avoid court tests, labor and capital would have to voluntarily assent to a code before the NRA could approve it. The NRA, then, simply provided a forum at which the bargaining between labor and management could take place.[25]

Prior to coming to Washington for the final approval of a code, both labor and management were supposed to engage in preliminary discussions with the assistance of an N.R.A. functionary. General Johnson began the codification process almost as soon as the basic framework of the N.R.A. was operable in June 1933.[26] The June 15, 1933, meeting of ALPA's Central Executive Council was devoted exclusively to discussing the kind of labor provisions the pilots wanted in the Air Transportation Code. Many of the members believed the code could guarantee the kind of wages and working conditions they wanted. Behncke, while not overly critical of the idea, was skeptical, and he tried to tone down the enthusiasm of the council members. He warned that ALPA must exercise extreme caution before committing itself to support of the code.[27] In order to present a united front of all airline labor, Behncke suggested to the July 6 meeting of the Central Executive Council that ALPA take the lead in forming a "Directorate" of all airline labor groups. Only a few airline workers were fully organized at the time, but Section 7(a) of the NIRA was stimulating the growth of unionization among several groups of unorganized air workers, and Behncke wanted ALPA, as the senior air transport union, to occupy a dominant position. After an exceedingly lengthy meeting, however, the Central Executive Council for once failed to act as a rubber stamp for Behncke and ordered him to concentrate strictly on the part of the code affecting pilots. The council decided that if the results of the code discussions with the various operating companies were satisfactory, Behncke could then pursue his rather visionary idea of creating an Air Line Labor Executives Association similar to the organization of executives of railroad labor groups.[28]

The code conference which United held with its pilots on July 25 at the Edgewater Beach Hotel in Chicago produced an unexpectedly satisfactory result. United's management was always inclined to be lenient in its dealings with ALPA. The president of United, William A. Patterson, personally represented his company, while J. L. Brandon headed the United pilots' committee, although Behncke was a member. United's various division managers had previously held a series of meetings with their pilots in which they pointed out that changes in working conditions would be necessary with the introduction of the new Boeing 247. While there would be pilot layoffs in the future owing to the greater speed and consequent decrease in the need for pilot crews to fly the new aircraft, Patterson agreed to reemploy his old pilots as soon as possible and to abide by the rule of seniority in doing so. The old basic conflict between pilots and management over who should gain the benefits from improved technology underlay these meetings, however, and Patterson could not agree with the pilots' notion that only by retention of the mileage pay factor could they be fairly recompensed for their increased labor productivity. Patterson necessarily insisted that since the companies took the risk by investing in new aircraft, they, and not labor, should reap the rewards. The conference was tense and at times strained, but Patterson's genuine desire to retain good relations with his pilots eased the situation. To prove his good will, Patterson overrode his lower-echelon managers and partially gave in to the pilots on the mileage pay question by agreeing to support some kind of mileage pay increment in the final code.[29]

Although ALPA's victory on United was significant, it was isolated. The Eastern pilots got no satisfaction from their employer, and the Chairman of the Eastern pilots' committee, Wallace S. Dawson, informed Behncke that the company had openly irritated ALPA members by hiring two Century scabs the week before the conference.[30] A few Eastern pilots favored a wildcat strike of short duration to protest the hiring of the two scabs, but Behncke counseled against it because he thought it would make ALPA appear irresponsible just when NRA officials were studying the industry as a whole.[31] The Eastern pilots accomplished very little in the way of influencing the labor provisions of the code during the conference, which was held from July 28 to August 2, despite the presence of an NRA official to smooth the proceedings. All the other "Big Five," with the exception of United, copied Eastern in refusing to retreat on the hourly pay issue.[32]

Shortly after the code conferences with United and Eastern were completed, Behncke formally requested similar conferences with the remaining airlines. Most of the operators proved reluctant to meet with ALPA, and they suggested

that Behncke take his request to their agent, the Aeronautical Chamber of Commerce. The NRA's policy of dealing mainly with the employers and slighting labor in the initial codification process alarmed Behncke, and he grew increasingly uneasy about the kind of labor provisions the code would eventually contain. Furthermore, he realized that management would undoubtedly dominate the Code Authority which would administer the code. Fearing disaster, Behncke dropped all idea of further negotiations with the individual airlines and instead resorted to the approach he originally favored of taking his case directly to Washington.[33]

In the intervening period, Behncke concentrated on lining up a battery of supporters to testify at the code hearings. He wanted William Green to appear in ALPA's behalf, but the AFofL President was too busy, and as a substitute he arranged for Victor Olander of the Illinois State Federation of Labor to be present.[34] Olander was a lawyer, and Behncke hoped that by having him there ALPA's depleted treasury could be spared the expense of hiring legal help.[35] At Behncke's request, the August 15 meeting of the Central Executive Council named a committee of prominent airline pilots to attend the hearings, among them E. Hamilton Lee, the veteran United pilot who had been one of the principals in the air-mail pilots' strike of 1919, and Mal B. Freeburg of Northwest, who had won the first "Air Mail Pilot Medal of Honor" by saving his aircraft and passengers after a spectacular in-flight explosion and fire.[36] In addition, Dr. Ralph Green, former Chief Medical Examiner for the Department of Commerce and current head of the Aeromedical Association, agreed to testify on behalf of the eighty-hour-per-month maximum.[37] A covey of congressmen would speak for ALPA, but Behncke's star witness was to be the nimble and vibrant Fiorello La Guardia, who, despite his liberalism, had been defeated in the Republican debacle of 1932 and was then running for Mayor of New York on a fusion ticket. The hearings promised La Guardia some badly needed public exposure, and he eagerly honored Behncke's plea for help. Behncke secured yet another leave of absence from United, and he was on hand at Washington's National Airport, along with a committee of pilots, to meet La Guardia when he took time out from the mayoralty campaign to fly down. They went into an immediate conference with William Green at AFofL headquarters to plan their strategy during the hearings, which would begin the following day.[38]

When the code hearings convened in the ballroom of the Hotel Mayflower under the supervision of Deputy

NRA Administrator Malcolm Muir, Behncke's urgency in assembling his all-star cast of witnesses received immediate justification. The rumors which had been circulating in the aviation trade journals that the operators intended to impose ridiculously high hour and low minimum-wage provisions proved to be true, thus confirming Behncke's worst fears.[39] La Guardia responded with his usual pugnacity when he discovered that Title III of the operators' proposed code established 140 hours per month as the maximum, and $250 per month as the minimum pay. The industry's spokesman was Frederick W. Coburn, a former President of American Airways, but there were four current airline chiefs in attendance as well. Lester D. Seymour of American denied that management intended to decrease the status or wages of pilots, and he cited Title V of the code, which guaranteed the right of collective bargaining, as proof. The hour and wage provisions, he insisted, were simply minimums and maximums, and he ridiculed the idea that the major operators would ever pay their pilots so little or work them so hard. The particular figures, Seymour maintained, were "fixed with consideration for the smaller operators, at least one of whom now pays his pilots as low as $100 per month." La Guardia displayed his usual histrionics when he attacked Seymour's contentions, and he had a telling argument when he pointed out that, in the codes so far adopted, the working conditions and wages specified usually corresponded very closely to actual conditions.[40] La Guardia's argument struck a responsive chord with most air travelers.

There was a rather general uneasiness among airline patrons that the operators might unduly reduce pilot salaries, and the New York Times expressed this fear when it pointed out that in the first six months of 1933 the airlines had flown over twenty-five million passenger miles with only two fatalities. The newspaper attributed this safety record to pilot skill, and it believed that the industry's profit level was secondary in importance to preserving "the highest type of pilot morale."[41] Indicative of the public's support for high pilot salaries, even during the depression, the following day the New York Times printed a letter which declared: "If the captain of an ocean greyhound can be called a 'glorified ferryboat skipper,' . . . if an eagle can be called a 'glorified sparrow,' then a scheduled air transport pilot can be called a 'glorified chauffeur.'"[42]

Deputy Administrator Muir, harried and tired and with more important industry codes demanding his immedi-

ate attention, was inclined to approve the code despite the various objections to it. As this fact became increasingly clear to Behncke and La Guardia, they decided to press for total exemption of the pilots from the code, rather than take a chance on the hour and wage provisions becoming industry-wide standards. The thrust of their argument was that the pilots were professional workers whose wages and hours were subject to the regulation of the Department of Commerce, and hence they did not belong in the code. In his testimony, Behncke suggested that rather than writing arbitrary standards, the code should instead provide for a "planning, coordinating, and conciliating" committee to study the question of pilot labor. He believed that the committee should have one member each from the NRA, the Aeronautical Chamber of Commerce, and the AFofL. He preferred that the committee's recommendations be the subject of direct negotiations between the operators and the pilots. Clearly, Behncke's motive in suggesting this cumbersome arrangement was to obfuscate the issue, to use some last desperate ploy to delay approval of the Code's provisions for pilot labor.[43]

NRA head Johnson, in the meantime, was in a quandary over the Air Transportation Code. It presented curious problems to begin with, because of the close association of business and government, and the pilot labor sections were even more obtuse since the Department of Commerce actually had the statutory power to regulate such things, regardless of what the code said. Malcolm Muir recommended that he accept the code despite the pilots' objections, but Johnson, with his deep fear of court challenges of the NRA's constitutionality, insisted that both sides agree to the code before it received final NRA approval. Since the pilots adamantly refused to accept the code as it was, Muir had no alternative but to accede to their demands and exempt them from the code altogether.[44] Behncke had demonstrated once again that his appeals to government agencies and officials could be very effective, and the decision to omit the pilots from the code was one of the stepping stones which led to complete victory for the pilots later on.

One of the factors which aided the pilots in this victory was the editorial support of the Hearst newspapers. Hearst was generally anti-labor, but aviation fascinated him and for some reason he liked the pilots.[45] Before the code hearings in Washington began, Behncke wrote to the sage of San Simeon to ask for his help. Although Hearst never answered the letter, the Hearst newspapers responded with a series of editorials favorable to the idea of exempting the pilots from the code, notably in the *Washington Daily News*. Behncke always believed that Hearst had personally intervened with Hugh Johnson to help ALPA, and he later told the 1942 convention: "I got in touch with Mr. Hearst, and I don't know to this day what happened, but the next day the air carriers' code . . . was withdrawn and General Johnson announced that the airline pilots were taken out of the Code because theirs was a profession and not just a job."[46]

With ALPA out of the code and the situation highly nebulous, there was no reason for the operators to delay the institution of a national, uniform basis for computing pilot pay on the hourly system. Early in September they formally announced that the new system was in effect and permanent. Behncke had about exhausted his resources of appeal among government officialdom, he had been in Washington continuously for almost two weeks, and he knew his job with United was in jeopardy owing to his absenteeism. The last thing he wanted was another strike, since he knew that it would, in all probability, fail and discredit ALPA in the process. Behncke reassessed his position, frantically telephoned local chairmen around the country, and concluded that while some locals could endure a strike, the majority would collapse. He told the 1934 convention: "I believe that American Airways was the best balanced of all operating companies. . . . They were pretty much together and I believe that [they] . . . would have walked out to a man. T&WA would have collapsed completely and I know that on United everything south and east of Chicago would have gone out, and west of Chicago it would have been just a little bit better than half."[47] Still, he could see no alternative to an old-fashioned strike confrontation with the operators over the new pay scale. While hoping that the operators would not call his bluff, he decided to threaten a strike. Behncke set October 1 as the deadline for the operators to restore the mileage system, and in order to dramatize his contention that the strike would be nationwide; he prepared a set of color charts and graphs for use in his news conference showing the geographic extent of the national airline network.[48]

At this point, the kid gloves were off, and the bare-knuckles battle between ALPA and the operators was in earnest. A national strike of airline pilots was heady stuff to the press, and it faithfully reported the charges and countercharges which Behncke and the operators traded. Each side declared that the other was trying to force a national strike, and the

operators even went so far as to take out full-page advertisements in several newspapers accusing ALPA of trying to wring the neck of the Blue Eagle. Behncke was rapidly developing into a major league polemicist, and he gave as well as he got in the exchanges with airline public relations men. But in one area Behncke was highly vulnerable, he was still only an employee of United, and there were limits to the patience of W. A. Patterson. Disquieting rumors began to reach Behncke that his future with United was in deep jeopardy, and at this time he began to seriously think about devoting full time to ALPA.[49]

Behncke's threat of a national strike moved Secretary of Labor Frances Perkins to arrange a thirty-day truce, which was a godsend for ALPA since it allowed time for maneuver. In the meantime, Behncke tried desperately to get ALPA's case before the National Labor Board (NLB) of the NRA. He believed the board would take the case because a clause in the NIRA stipulated that no industry operating under a code could reduce pay levels below the pre-code level, and he argued that the operators had done precisely this. In formally requesting that the NLB take jurisdiction, Behncke told the board's secretary, W. M. Leiserson, that the operators were "gradually cutting down on salaries. Now they want us to accept starvation pay."[50]

The function of the NLB, composed of three members each from labor and industry, was to iron out disputes which arose over the interpretation of the codes. But as Arthur M. Schlesinger Jr. said of the NLB: "Its mandate was vague, its procedures were undefined, and its direct power of enforcement, beyond the appeal to public opinion, was nonexistent."[51] On this curious body, however, Behncke staked the entire future of his organization. Fortunately, only he knew that the threat of a strike was a hollow bluff. During the 1934 convention, Behncke told the delegates, "The only way you can keep a striking element in line is to keep them informed. . . . I figured it would cost $1,000 a day to conduct the strike . . . and our treasury had $5,000 and we would have lasted about five days. After that our communications would have been cut, we would have been completely broke." Furthermore, he admitted that the strike would have caused "a perfect split in our organization that would probably have never been able to mend back together."[52]

In fact, the mere threat of a strike was enough to unravel some of ALPA's locals on T&WA. ALPA's strength on T&WA was always weak, and management had considerable success when it embarked on yet another of its efforts to wreck the union. This time, the company persuaded the Master Executive Council to declare itself independent of the National on the strike issue, and former Master Executive Council Chairman W. A. Golien led the move. While a few ALPA members held out against the company union idea, most of them went along, and ALPA's strength on the line collapsed. There was also considerable restiveness among Eastern pilots because of the proposed strike, and although a company union drive there failed, Behncke had to resist pressure to withdraw the strike decree.[53] But nothing would sway Behncke at this point—the whole ALPA idea was a long desperate shot, he was determined to play the game out, and he exhibited the fanaticism of the confirmed gambler who had nothing to lose. One favorable omen for him was that the major airlines were again making a profit by late 1933, general revenues were up an average 20 percent despite the mail pay cuts, and the operators were, consequently, very reluctant to engage in a ruinous shutdown.[54] Still, they were in a better position to weather the strike than ALPA. Behncke's only real hope, then, was to get the shaky NLB to accept jurisdiction so he could call off the strike before the October 1 deadline revealed ALPA's weakness.

But persuading the NLB to take ALPA's case proved a difficult task, for it was inundated with code disputes and strikes in industries that were far more important than air transportation. During late September, the NLB held all its meetings behind closed doors in order to keep the swarm of persistent leaders of small unions from interfering with its deliberations. William Green was on the NLB, but he was ill at the time, and the remaining labor members were either too busy or too tired to bother with ALPA. As the strike deadline neared, and Behncke still had not established contact with the board through conventional methods, he decided to adopt a direct approach and personally seek out one of the members he vaguely knew. Professor Leo Wolman of Columbia University was a member of the NLB whom La Guardia had once introduced to Behncke, and he seemed the likely candidate for a personal contact.[55] Because of the pressure on board members, most of whom had other jobs, their home addresses were kept secret. By following the professor home after he emerged from a twenty-four-hour NLB session, however, Behncke learned his address. Wolman as well as other prolabor board members had been dodging Behncke for two weeks, and needless to say he was unhappy to see the dogged aviator burst into his living room at ten o'clock at night with a wide-eyed tale of a national pilot

strike. But he sat down with Behncke and, after listening to his side of the dispute, agreed to use his influence to get the case before the board. In exchange, Behncke promised to cancel the strike. The exhausted academic then retired, but Behncke spent most of the remainder of the night calling ALPA's local chairmen on his living room telephone.[56] Professor Wolman subsequently persuaded Senator Wagner to contact the "Big Five" with a request that they voluntarily withhold the pay cuts until the NLB could study the situation.[57] Once again, under what had seemed impossible odds, Behncke had staved off defeat.

The NLB began its hearings on the airline pay dispute on October 4, 1933. Behncke, Hamilton, and American's Master Executive Council Chairman Clyde Holbrook represented ALPA, with Victor Olander present to give them legal advice. The presidents of all the "Big Five" plus several executives from smaller lines attended the hearing, bringing with them complete batteries of corporation lawyers. The disparity between the overblown management group and the spare ALPA delegation gave the pilots an underdog's psychological advantage which outweighed the merits of the miles versus hours argument. Hamilton gave most of the oral presentation for ALPA, trying to build a case that the pilots were quasi-governmental employees and, hence, deserving of government protection. With a bow to the ghosts of Grover Cleveland and Richard Olney, Hamilton declared that even should the pilots' strike, they would "not be a party to retarding the U.S. Mail" but would only refuse to carry passengers and freight. He also used the rhetoric of class warfare in a tub-thumping anticapitalist harangue against the "powerful financial interests that are behind these . . . big operating companies" who were trying to crush "this splendid corps of airline pilots who are . . . going through all kinds of dangers losing one of their number . . . every twenty-nine days, and who incidentally are the first line of defense material in time of war." While he conceded that pilots frequently made more money than airline executives, he maintained that they were nevertheless a group of "mass wage earners" and that they needed special protection in order to retain the high state of morale which was essential to air safety.[58]

Things went poorly for the operators from the beginning, when Senator Wagner and Victor Olander, who were old friends, exchanged just enough banter to make them feel like they were sitting before a hanging judge. In fact, Wagner's predisposition to favor the underdog pilots and his sharp criticism of the airline executives for bringing lawyers to the hearing meant that the pilots were almost certain to receive a favorable verdict from the NLB. To make matters worse, the operators allowed their lawyers to begin with the legalistic argument that since the pilots were not in the Air Transport Code, the NLB had no jurisdiction. Wagner replied that the labor policy of the New Deal was to play fair with unions and he rather pointedly hinted: "You are doing government work and I thought you would be first in line." Sensing Wagner's rising irritation at the operators' lawyers, Olander interjected: "If we find ourselves in a position . . . where the opposition presents its case through some distinguished lawyers who are trained in the technique of merely defending their clients, we will not get very far." The Senator agreed and promptly condemned any further "legalistic quibbling." "I am a member of the law profession myself," he said, "but we are always looking for technicalities and we can do better when these technical gentlemen are not around at all." A lawyer representing American quickly succeeded in antagonizing Wagner further by beginning his presentation with the courtroom pleasantry that he regretted "bothering gentlemen like you and asking for your intervention in a matter like this when there are so many other affairs . . . which should be taken care of." Wagner virtually exploded: "Nobody's rights are too small to be taken care of. I do not know whether you understand that! . . . Nothing is greater than the individual's rights and the smaller he is . . . the more he needs our help."[59]

The nervous airline executives squirmed as their lawyers, who were supposed to keep them out of trouble, only succeeded in getting them in deeper. In an effort to discredit ALPA, T&WA's lawyers declared that most of their pilots had resigned from the union and that it could not, therefore, speak for them. Behncke was prepared for this argument, and he called attention to a petition which a majority of T&WA pilots had previously signed designating ALPA as their bargaining agent. He denounced T&WA's labor policies and declared that the line's executives were intimidating pilots and pressuring them to resign from ALPA. He asked Senator Wagner to consider the case of T&WA pilot Wayne Williams, who was present in the room, who had been fired when he refused to cease his organizational work on behalf of ALPA. Senator Wagner was immediately interested in Williams' case because it personalized the issue, and he asked the T&WA lawyer, whose name was Henry M. Hogan, to explain his position in the light of Behncke's

signed petition. Hogan declared that many of the T&WA pilots had resigned from ALPA since signing the petition, and the subsequent exchange between Senator Wagner and the lawyer ruined the operators:

WAGNER: How did you happen to see them?

HOGAN: Because I have seen copies of some letters of resignation.

WAGNER: How did you happen to see them?

HOGAN: Because I represent the company . . . and the letters were sent to us . . .

WAGNER: You are not an officer of the Association. Why should they send letters to you? How did they know the company was interested in them . . . ?

HOGAN: I imagine if you were a pilot you could answer that.

WAGNER: What? No. It might indicate that the company was evidencing a little interest in their resigning.

THOMAS B. DOE [President of North American Aviation]: We are interested in everything they do, Senator.

WAGNER: That is something you ought not to be interested in because it is none of your business. When a man working for a concern is a member of a union and he resigns from that union and then hurries to tell his employer—well now, I am not a child. . . . Wayne Williams was discharged for no other reason than his activity in organizing the pilots. . . . That sort of thing must stop. . . . If certain rights are given to them under the law, to organize, the government should not permit employers to discriminate against them. . . . You must understand that this is a new era. There is an equality of rights that we must take into consideration. We are not living in an old century.[60]

The operators were beaten at this point, and all they could do was try to minimize their losses. Almost in chorus the airline representatives began to sing the praises of their pilots. Ernest R. Breech, a lawyer for Eastern, declared: "I for one will never subscribe to paying these fellows chauffeurs' wages because they are the greatest salesmen we have." J. Bruce Kremer, a managerial spokesman for United, added: "Candidly, knowing their fearless spirit, I think a man shows a great deal of temerity who tries to intimidate any one of them." Unimpressed, Wagner replied that it did not take much courage to fire a man, and he insisted that the pilots must receive fair treatment or he would see to it that the airlines received no more "liberal mail subsidies." He ordered T&WA to reinstate Wayne Williams immediately, and he appointed a special fact-finding board, to be composed of Behncke, Lester D. Seymour of American, and Judge Bernard L. Shientag of the New York Supreme Court, to study the pay question. He required that the committee report its findings to the NLB within three weeks, and he asked the airlines to voluntarily retain the mileage pay system until then. Considering the Senator's irate mood, the airline executives would probably have agreed to anything just to get out of the disastrous hearing.[61]

The fact-finding committee was essentially a device whereby Behncke and Seymour could present their views to a neutral, Judge Shientag, who would then make a decision. Each side could call witnesses, and the operators scored an initial victory when Eugene Vidal, Director of the Bureau of Air Commerce, agreed to testify in behalf of the hourly pay system.[62] There were a number of complex factors in the hearing, which was held on October 27 and 28 in New York City, but the essential conflict came over ALPA's contention that increased speed meant increased hazard, and that accidents were a function of the number of miles flown, rather than the number of hours flown. From this notion, Behncke could argue that the pilots should be paid on the mileage system because of the risks involved.[63] Vidal demolished this argument in his testimony, correctly pointing out that most accidents occurred on takeoff or landing and that the new aircraft, while they flew faster when cruising at altitude, actually had lower landing and takeoff speeds than the old tri-motored aircraft.

Before Judge Shientag, the operators were at last able to take advantage of their expensive legal talent. They presented an exhaustive series of charts and legal briefs showing that airline stockholders were sacrificing current profits in order to invest in the new aircraft and that the stockholders, rather than the pilots, deserved the productivity gains which accrued from investing the risk capital. The presidents of all five major airlines assured Judge Shientag that they "considered their pilots in a class at least semi-professional and out of self interest wished to maintain their morale at a high level." They argued that pilot pay would average $6,000 per year under the hourly system and might go as high as $9,000 per year in some cases. To bolster their contention that this amount was satisfactory, they produced the startling information that the master of the largest ocean liner in America's merchant fleet, the twenty-six-hundred-passenger *Leviathan*, earned only $6,000 per year. To refute ALPA's contention that the new aircraft were more difficult to fly, the operators submitted letters from famous aviators Wiley Post and Captain Frank M. Hawks declaring that the new aircraft were easier to fly. Post said that he accomplished a ten-hour flight in a Boeing 247 "without noticeable mental or physical fatigue."[64] The pilots looked bad in the exchange, and Behncke later ruefully admitted: "hey really ganged up on us that time."[65]

Fearing that Seymour was winning the argument, Behncke asked that a "scientific study" be made of the safety factor by the Department of Labor. He had a naive faith in "statistics," and he believed that the Department of Labor would render a "good report because they would only deal with the facts, there would be no politics . . . it would be submitted to their statisticians . . . and they would make a report."[66] Judge Shientag leaned to the operators' side, but he decided he could not make a final decision on the available facts, so he returned the controversy to the NLB suggesting that "the rates proposed by the operators should continue without prejudice to the contentions of the respective parties, pending a prompt, thorough, and scientific investigation . . . to be made by a government agency to be designated by the NLB."[67]

The Shientag decision was a blow to Behncke, but Senator Wagner reprieved him by rejecting the report. The Senator wanted a clear-cut decision, once and for all. He was tired of studies and investigations and inconclusive disputation. He allowed the operators to begin paying on the "new standardized scale," retroactive to October 1, but he warned them that the final decision, regardless of the fact-finding committee's views, would rest with the NLB itself.[68]

Thinking they had won, the operators did not mount a second major offensive to influence Judge Shientag. Only Lester D. Seymour of American came to the second meeting, held in mid-November, and he left the floor largely to Behncke. Behncke later remarked that he felt ALPA had scored well in the second hearing because "I could argue and Eddie [Hamilton] could figure." But Behncke's forensic talents were a dubious advantage, and Judge Shientag was less impressed with the substance of the debate than with the obvious fact that he would have to arrive at some kind of compromise in order to satisfy the NLB. He was in poor health, suffering from heart disease, and he wished to rid himself of the troublesome case. In order to resolve the question he simply combined the basic hourly pay (which would increase with the speed of the aircraft), with a very small mileage increment, and called it a compromise.

In similar fashion, the judge resolved the hours per month question by splitting the difference between the operators' preference for a ninety-hour limit and ALPA's preference for an eighty-hour limit. Needless to say, Seymour, representing all the operators, was horrified at this turn of events. What had originally shaped up as a sparkling victory for the operators had inexplicably turned into something quite different. Shientag's report represented a clear retreat from his first position in favor of straight hourly pay, and Seymour refused to sign it. Although the report established an hourly component, Behncke was willing to accept it because it was geared to the speed of the aircraft and therefore gave pilots a share of the increased productivity. Principles aside, Behncke later admitted that he liked the report because "the amount [of money] was not so bad and that is the controlling factor in a thing like that."[69]

The NLB subsequently spent about two weeks converting Judge Shientag's report into a definite wage formula, and when Senator Wagner summoned all interested parties to Washington for a conference on December 14, the reluctant operators had no alternative but to attend. Wagner, however, still operating under the Johnsonian policy that labor and management must, if at all possible, voluntarily assent to all NRA decisions, insisted that the pilots and the operators meet one last time to iron out their difficulties. The meeting which took place on December 15 in the Mayflower Hotel produced no general agreement, except that both sides acknowledged that there had to be *some* limit on the number of miles a pilot could fly each month, regardless of whether an hourly or mileage system of pay prevailed. The operators were well aware of the problems involved in Judge Shientag's complicated system of pay computation, but there was little they could do about it. After the meeting broke down, Behncke formally requested binding arbitration by the NLB because he believed that it would favor ALPA.[70]

Behncke had been in either New York or Washington almost continuously since August, and he had not flown enough for United to remain "current," according to Department of Commerce regulations. When he returned to Chicago for the Christmas holidays, United fired him, claiming that his repeated absences had made it necessary to fill his position. Whatever good will once existed between

Behncke and Patterson had long since disappeared in the heat of repeated confrontations. While Patterson probably expected to face Behncke across the bargaining table for years to come, he was not particularly anxious to continue to paying his salary while doing so. Behncke did not intend to lose his job without a fight, and he lined up support from Green, Olander, and several Congressmen in an effort to have the NLB reinstate him. Mayor Edward J. Kelly of Chicago, who owed the Chicago Federation of Labor a great deal, also offered to come to Washington to testify in his behalf. Simultaneously with United's dismissal of Behncke, T&WA raised the absurd claim that ALPA was connected with the Chicago underworld. As proof, T&WA complained to the NLB that pro-ALPA "elements" had assaulted one of its anti-ALPA pilots in the parking lot of the Newark Airport. Despite this climate of recrimination, however, Behncke successfully presented his case to the NLB, and, on January 18, Senator Wagner ordered his reinstatement.[71]

Judge Shientag's compromise report eventually emerged as Decision 83 of the NLB and it was, as a leading expert on airline labor relations has said, "without doubt . . . the most far-reaching ruling ever issued in the air line labor field."[72] Because it embodied both mileage pay and an hourly pay rate which increased as the speed of the aircraft increased, it guaranteed the pilots a huge share of the productivity gains associated with improved aircraft technology. The essentials of this pay formula still apply to airline pilots today.[73] But perhaps even more importantly, for the first time the airline pilots had persuaded an agency of the federal government to grant them special protection. In a sense, Behncke won his argument that the pilots were "quasi-governmental employees." Although Behncke would later score a stunning victory in keeping Decision 83 in the Air Mail Act of 1934, the fight over pay scale would always remain the classic example of his effectiveness in obtaining his goals through appeals to Washington.

Two Labor Laws Are One Too Many

AUTHORS' NOTE: The following is reprinted from March 20, 1989, *Business Week* by special permission from McGraw-Hill Inc.

The Machinist strike at Eastern Airlines may touch off a big labor battle in Congress—but over an issue that is much narrower than the real problem. If the International Association of Machinists (IAM) sets up picket lines at railroads and other airlines, President Bush will demand that Congress amend the Railway Labor Act—which covers airline and railroad employees—to outlaw secondary picketing. The government's concern about widespread travel disruptions is understandable. But a better solution would be to dismantle the RLA, along with its obsolete strike-avoidance procedures, and transfer airline and railroad employees to the National Labor Relations Act, which covers all other private-industry employees.

The fact is that this dualism in federal labor law creates two classes of workers and employees, with different rights and duties. Under the NLRA, workers are prohibited from engaging in secondary picketing, while the RLA allows it. But an equally significant difference arises out of the provisions governing collective bargaining. The 1935 NLRA encourages "good faith" bargaining but for the most part stands aside and lets the two sides fight it out. The government intervenes only in cases of national emergency. The purpose of the RLA, on the contrary, was to use the powers of the government to prevent strikes by union members. Back in 1926, when the Act was passed, big rail strikes could disrupt the national economy. But the RLA's cumbersome provisions, including conciliation by the National Mediation Board and numerous meaningless deadlines, permitted endless stalling. These procedures are largely responsible for the mess at Eastern and actually impede collective bargaining. Thirteen months lapsed before the NMB declared an impasse in the IAM-Eastern talks, and some bargaining rounds have lasted much longer. The protracted negotiations at Eastern allowed by the NMB also have been criticized by Frank Lorenzo, chairman of Eastern's owner, Texas Air, but his confrontational tactics in dealing with unions only serve to damage the process.

Even after the NMB's procedures have been exhausted, the president may delay a strike for sixty days by appointing an emergency board to recommend a settlement, which either side may reject. At that point, Congress normally steps in and mandates the settlement terms. The undesirable result then becomes collective bargaining by edict.

Call to Revisit RLA Receives Mixed Reactions from Parties

AUTHORS' NOTE: The following is reprinted, with permission, from "Daily Labor Report," no. 147, C-12–C-6, July 30, 1992, Bureau of National Affairs Inc.

National Mediation Board member Patrick Cleary's recommendation that a panel be created to consider possible changes in the Railway Labor Act has drawn mixed reactions, but most observers agree that labor and management are far from a consensus on changes in the law that they might support.

Major interest in revisiting the law appears to be confined to the railroad industry, although the statute governs collective bargaining in the airline industry as well. Discontent with the prolonged process for settling contract disputes under the RLA has come to the fore as Congress has been forced to intervene to end railroad shutdowns twice in the last year. In both instances, the disputes involved efforts to resolve contracts that had been open for renegotiation since 1988.

Noting that the RLA came into being in 1926 only after representatives of both labor and management agreed on its framework, several practitioners said that it may require a similar consensus before any proposed changes are given serious consideration. Even though congressional leaders grumble about the RLA when faced with a rail strike and calls for intervention on Capitol Hill, they are not considered likely to propose changes in the system unless labor or management representatives themselves put forward some recommendations.

In a July 12 speech to railroad industry officials, Cleary, who served as NMB chairman until July 1 and remains a board member, urged formation of a panel to consider whether changes should be recommended. That panel, said Cleary, should include representatives of labor and management, as well as academics and lawmakers (135 DLRA-11, 7/14/92). He said that such a group would ideally be formed on the initiative of labor and management and urged Congress to consider only those changes on which both parties have agreed. Cleary's recommendations were expressions of his personal viewpoint, and other members of the three-member board have not taken a position on his suggestions.

Representatives of railroad associations called Cleary's recommendation premature since railroad negotiations that were the subject of back-to-work legislation adopted by Congress in June are still underway. That process will be concluded by early August with either voluntary agreements or an arbitrator's selection of final proposals for settlement.

Several railroad union representatives, meanwhile, viewed the recommendations with skepticism. Although rail union leaders would like to see changes in the law to clearly define the right to strike and provide a means for bringing negotiations and mediation to a speedier conclusion, they see little prospect for agreement with the carriers over how to change the law.

The Air Line Pilots Association (ALPA), on the other hand, sees nothing wrong with the RLA and maintains the view that "if it ain't broke, don't fix it." Even convening a group such as Cleary suggested would be considered a "waste of time" by ALPA, a spokesman for the union said.

Railroad Union's Priorities

Although rail union leaders appeared willing to participate on a panel to review the law, they considered the veto power over proposed changes a vital condition for union participation.

Thomas DuBose, president of the United Transportation Union, remarked that if someone "can't recognize [the RLA] is broke, than their eyesight is bad."

He said that the UTU, which claims to represent 90 percent of the operating employees in the railroad industry, would favor reexamination of the law provided that such a review is not aimed at "providing relief for the industry" or at forcing the parties to begin paying arbitration costs and eliminating the government-financed system of grievance adjustment provided under the RLA.

"If it's in the public interest to prevent railroad strikes, it is also in the public interest to pay arbitration costs" to resolve disputes," DuBose said.

He said the UTU would not dismiss recommendations for compulsory arbitration as a means for reaching contract agreements since "Congress is never going to let railroad unions exercise Self-Help." DuBose added, however, that the UTU would agree to such a system only if several other issues were addressed as well, such as adequate funding for arbitration of major and minor disputes, creation of a neutral, nonpolitical body to encourage agreements, and protection for workers whose jobs are eliminated in railroad line sales.

Robert J. Irvin, president of the American Train Dispatchers Association and secretary-treasurer of the Railway Labor Executives' Association, said that compulsory arbitration is among the changes that he would oppose. Irvin said he would also oppose amending the RLA to prohibit secondary boycotts or revise the current union-shop rule.

Although Irvin said he would favor revisions in the law to prevent the president and Congress from intervening in rail labor disputes, he said he thinks that "the gains labor might get would not be worth the price of the trade-offs" management would demand in exchange.

Jedd Dodd, general chairman of the Pennsylvania Federation of the Brotherhood of Maintenance of Way Employees and a frequent critic of the current bargaining structure, suggested that the right to call a secondary boycott under RLA could be exchanged by the unions for protection against permanent replacement of strikers. That change should be coupled with defining the strike "as an absolute right," putting a cap on the duration of mediation, and providing full cost-of-living adjustments for the period in mediation, Dodd said. Dodd said the law "definitely needs to be reexamined." He added, however, that he is doubtful that his concept of how it should be changed would be shared by the carriers or others outside of the labor movement.

"It is difficult to envision" how labor and management could reach agreement on revising the law, Irvin said, observing that "they can't agree on anything else."

Railroad Association Views

"I think everyone is asking is there a better way," said Edwin Harper, president of the American Association of Railroads, who agreed with chief railroad industry negotiator Charles Hopkins that it is premature to seek formation of a group to examine the law. "Our first priority is to complete the 1988 round of negotiations," he said.

Harper suggested that informal discussions between labor and management would be a better approach to examining the law than appointment of a formal commission. Cleary's proposal, he noted, recognizes that "if labor and management don't both subscribe" to any potential revisions, "it probably is not worth pursuing."

Officials of CSX Corp. think that the process could be reexamined, said a spokesman for the carrier, where a strike by the International Association of Machinists touched off a two-day nationwide rail shutdown in June when other carriers locked out workers.

"If you measure the RLA's success in preventing strikes, it has been pretty effective," said spokesman Lynn Johnson, who said that CSX has experienced just three days of strikes in the last ten years. "When viewed from the perspective of how quickly the process works; however, CSX officials believe the process needs some changes. The process takes too long, Johnson said, "negotiations can't be very productive after four or five years of posturing for a fight." He said that CSX officials who have considered the issue are less certain about how they would change the law, but added that binding arbitration is not an approach they prefer.

Officials of Burlington Northern Railroad have also said that reexamination of the law may be warranted.

Many other carriers are believed to share the sentiments expressed by Robert Schmiege, chief executive officer of the Chicago and North Western Transportation Company, in a letter following a one-day rail strike in 1991. In the letter to then-AAR President Michael Walsh, Schmiege disputed the notion that "more economically advantageous settlements" could be achieved if the RLA were revised and the unions' right to strike made easier.

The RLA, Schmiege wrote, "is remarkably effective at preventing unions from achieving the legal right to strike." He argued that the current law "remains the best alternative as a legal framework to govern railroad labor relations."

No Push from Air Carriers

Robert DeLucia, vice president of the Air Conference, sees "no push to change the act" coming from the airline industry. He added, however, "If they start the ball rolling, we may get swept up in it." It would be premature to speculate about whether the airline industry would want changes in the law, he said, but the industry "will want to be a player" if a reexamination of the law gets under way. In any event, no group such as the one envisioned by Cleary is likely to be convened until after the November election, DeLucia said.

Cleary suggested that any panel convened to examine the law might consider whether railroads and airlines should continue to be covered under the same labor law given the "vast differences in the operations of these two modes of transportation." DeLucia and several others who commented on Cleary's recommendation, however, said negotiations in the airline and railroad industries currently are treated differently under the law. There has been no presidential emergency board appointed to resolve a contract dispute in the airline industry since 1966, DeLucia said. He explained that different structures for bargaining in the industries are responsible for their different experiences under the law. In the airline industry, said DeLucia, unions and carriers bargain individually, while industry-wide negotiations involving multiple carriers and multiple unions are common in the railroad industry.

The appointment of presidential emergency boards to recommend settlement of disputes has been common in the railroad industry, and that opens the door to congressional intervention after cooling-off periods expire and the unions become free to strike. Under the RLA, the NMB can recommend appointment of an emergency board when a bargaining impasse threatens "substantially to interrupt interstate commerce to a degree such as to deprive any section of the country of essential transportation service."

Congress' Role in Rail Bargaining

Herbert R. Northrup, professor emeritus of management at the University of Pennsylvania's Wharton School, and a longtime critic of the RLA, said that "getting Congress to intervene has become part of the system" of railroad negotiations under the law.

The procedures established under the act, including the requirement that the parties maintain the status quo, the NMB's power to indefinitely hold the parties in mediation, and the potential for further government intervention through presidential emergency boards and congressional action, prevent real bargaining, Northrup said.

"To prepare for bargaining and to prepare for intervention require quite different approaches. If one expects intervention . . . it is often wiser to ask for more than expected and to yield nothing," Northrup wrote in the *Harvard Journal of Law and Public Policy* in the spring of 1990.

Northrup, who said he has been pointing out the flaws in the RLA for fifty years, held out little hope that they will be remedied by agreement of the parties, as Cleary suggested. "It is always going to be premature" to reexamine the law in view of the leaders of rail unions and carrier associations, Northrup said. They have a "vested interest in the status quo." "Something should be done" to change the system, according to Northrup, who contends that there is no justification for a separate law, to cover labor relations in the two transportation industries. It is "special privilege" legislation, he added.

Robert O. Harris, a former NMB member appointed during the Carter administration, said that in the airline industry, the RLA functions much as the NLRA does in other industries. One major distinction between the two statutes, he said, is the NMB's power to hold airline negotiations in mediation for an indefinite period beyond the reopening of the contract. That difference, however, benefits the airline industry because a finite date for a strike would bring a significant drop in advance bookings with each contract-expiration date, Harris said.

Reexamination Requires Nudge

Although "there is a historical basis for hoping" that leaders of labor and management "would be able to step forward" and agree on a reexamination of the law, it was doubtful that would happen that right away, said Robert B. McKersie of the Sloan School at Massachusetts Institute of Technology.

"I think it will have to be nudged" if a coalition is to be formed to consider changes in the law, McKersie said. Initiatives by government agencies, such as a staff-level examination underway at the Department of Transportation, will be "needed to stir the pot." "If somebody else gets things going," McKersie said he would not rule out rail labor and management coming to an agreement on changes they would like to see made.

Harris said that Cleary's initiative fails to consider the possibility that a Democratic president could be elected this year. Union dissatisfaction is the product of "who is president, not the workings of the law," said Harris. A Democratic president, he said, would be more likely to apply pressure for a settlement before a dispute reaches the point of impasse. "If there was somebody in there pushing for settlement, things would have been different" in the recent rail disputes, said Harris, who chaired the presidential emergency board convened last year to recommend settlement of union contract disputes with major freight carriers. He also headed the special panel that ultimately imposed those recommendations as new contract terms after a one-day strike in 1991 that ended with congressional intervention.

With the exception of the Carter administration, no Democrat has reached the White House for more than twenty years, Harris said. He likened the current situation facing rail labor and management to a "boil growing for more than 20 years and finally lanced." "After the wound heals" is time enough to examine the issue, he said, suggesting that the parties should take a look at it in 1993. If they still feel the "system is no longer functioning," then a reexamination of the RLA might be warranted, he said. Making recommendations that the law be reexamined "before the dust has settled" from the current railroad disputes was not "terribly wise," Harris said.

Emergency Board Agreement

He noted that creation of the emergency board appointed last year to recommend settlement of the unions' contract dispute with major freight carriers was unprecedented because rail labor and management representatives agreed in advance to send the unresolved issues to an emergency board. In addition, the parties agreed on an extended period for the panel to consider the issues and even on who would serve on the board, Harris said.

The International Association of Machinists refused to join in the agreement, leaving that union's negotiations for a new contract with the major freight carriers still to be resolved this year and setting the stage for the recent strike by IAM against CSX.

Combining the unresolved issues in talks with all the rail unions and sending them to a single presidential emergency board in 1991 "was a terrible mistake," Harris said. He said that the initial agreement on forming the board was reached with the understanding that only the common health and welfare issues would be considered, but later all unresolved contract issues were put to the three-member board. The agreement to let the board make the decisions on those issues, he said, "was abrogation of responsibility by the unions and the carriers."

Walter Wallace, a Reagan administration NMB appointee who left the board in 1990, made a similar assessment, calling the agreement on sending the open issues to the Board premature: "They agreed too quickly to go to an emergency board, and they shouldn't have done that," said Wallace, who defended the RLA as a process that promotes collective bargaining. About 98 percent of all contracts coming open under RLA are settled, Wallace said, but it's the exceptions to that rule that "get all the headlines."

Wallace said he was appalled that Cleary would make recommendations calling for review of the RLA because NMB members traditionally have maintained a low profile on the principle that you cannot be an effective mediator while also taking positions on legislative issues. Suggesting that the underpinnings of the RLA need to be examined destabilizes the bargaining process, said Wallace. "Any thought about such changes," Wallace said, is particularly inappropriate when Congress has just adopted a process to resolve the final railroad disputes.

Harris agreed that an NMB member should refrain from making recommendations about labor policy, but several members of the academic community found Cleary's recommendations appropriate. DeLucia, of the Air Conference, said the suggestions are consistent with Cleary's actions as NMB chairman calling for studies of various board procedures. "I don't see any reason he shouldn't at least raise the issue," DeLucia said.

Review of Rail Industry Suggested

Examining the railroad industry and the structure of the unions that represent its employees may be more important than revisiting the RLA, McKersie said. Too many unions are competing with one another in the industry, he said, and employee morale is so poor that it's difficult to introduce new cooperative programs that could improve labor-management relations. "Perhaps a commission to examine the bedrock of the industry" should be convened, he said. Such a group could also look at basic public policy concerns under the RLA, including the threat of secondary boycotts and the "very important Self-Help issues," he said.

Suggesting that "we have passed the phase where the unions' right to strike can be allowed" on the nation's freight railroads, McKersie said that "if we can't tolerate strikes," perhaps we should build a procedure into the law so Congress doesn't have to fashion a remedy each time there is a strike.

Morgan Reynolds, a professor at Texas A&M University, greeted Cleary's recommendation enthusiastically. The RLA "has outlived its usefulness if it ever had any," Reynolds said. He recommended that it be scrapped with the industries it covered brought under the National Labor Relations Act.

"It is absurd to call the RLA structure free collective bargaining," Reynolds said. Railroad management does not know how to win a strike, and the rail labor unions are frustrated by their inability to strike under the current system.

Short of repealing the law, he said, secondary picketing should be "explicitly banned," and a statement of "government neutrality" should be added to the RLA with a prohibition against the president or Congress intervening in labor disputes. Reynolds also said that parties to the collective bargaining agreements in the railroad industry should be required to pay for the administrative services they receive.

While Reynolds and Northrup called for repeal of the RLA and placing the railroad and airline industries under the NLRA, Wallace warned that such a move would "create a period of instability" that could be especially damaging to the airline industry. Dodd of the BMWE remarked that switching to the NLRA "would be preferable to the situation unions face under RLA. Under the NLRA, the parties would have to bargain in good-faith!"

Part Two. Principles, Practices, and Procedures in Collective Bargaining and Dispute Resolution

4. Elections, Certifications, and Procedures

1. At Lockheed-Martin, do supervisors in a flight service station have the legal right to unionize and bargain collectively? Why?

2. At United Airlines, do foremen in the aircraft sheet-metal shop have the right to unionize and bargain collectively? Why?

3. Give an example of a craft or class of airline employees under the RLA.

4. Define *bargaining unit* under the RLA.

5. Before the NMB will begin the process leading to certification of a union to represent a group of airline employees who are not presently represented, union authorization cards must be signed by at least ____ percent of those employees.

6. Before the NLRB will begin the process leading to certification of a union to represent a group of employees of a major aerospace manufacturer who are not presently represented, union authorization cards must be signed by at least ____ percent of those employees.

7. Who decides which employees of a bargaining unit (craft or class) get to vote in a certification election at an airline?

8. Who decides which employees of a bargaining unit get to vote in a certification election at a major aerospace manufacturer?

9. How many employees qualified to vote in the bargaining unit must cast ballots in order for a certification election to be valid? Does your answer depend on whether the NLRA or RLA controls?

10. How many qualified votes must the union receive in order to be certified as the representative of a bargaining unit? Does your answer depend on whether the NLRA or RLA controls?

11. What is the principal difference between the ballots used by the NLRB in certification elections in the aerospace manufacturing industry and those used by the NMB in the airline industry?

12. You are an airline employee who is qualified to vote in a certification election. You are opposed to being represented by a union. How do you vote "No"?

13. During the time leading up to a certification election for aircraft sheet-metal workers at a southern California facility, management of a major aerospace manufacturer notifies the employees that if the union wins, the company will close the plant and move the work to its facility in Malaysia. This is an _____ under Section ____ of the _____ Act. What recourse is available?

14. During the time leading up to a certification election for aircraft mechanics at its San Francisco maintenance base, management of a major airline notifies the employees that if the union wins, the company will close its maintenance base and contract out the aircraft maintenance. What recourse is available?

15. If a group of employees of a major aerospace manufacturer represented by a union becomes dissatisfied with the union's representation and desires to decertify that union and either replace it with another or return to an unrepresented status, ____ percent of the employees are required to indicate their desire in writing before the NLRB will begin the process leading to a decertification election.

16. If a group of employees of an airline represented by a union becomes dissatisfied with the union's representation and desires to decertify that union and either replace it with another or return to an unrepresented status, how do they go about it?

17. After a union is certified to represent a group of airline employees, for how long will the NMB refuse to begin the process leading to an election to replace that union with another? Does it matter whether the union has negotiated a collective bargaining agreement with the airline?

18. After a union is certified to represent a group of employees of a major aerospace manufacturer, for how long will the NLRB refuse to begin the process leading to an election to decertify or replace that union? Does it matter whether the union has negotiated a collective bargaining agreement with the manufacturer?

19. If that group of airline employees replaces the union representing them, what happens to the contract (collective bargaining agreement) negotiated by their previous union?

20. American Airlines is acquiring Ace Airlines, a regional carrier, and merging it into American. American's aircraft mechanics are represented by a union and work under a collective bargaining agreement negotiated by that union. Ace's aircraft mechanics are not represented by a union and have no contract. When Ace's mechanics are merged into American's workforce, what will happen to their representation status?

21. United Airlines is acquiring Mogollon Air, a regional carrier, and merging it into United. United's flight attendants are represented by a union and work under a collective bargaining agreement negotiated by that union. Mogollon Air's flight attendants are represented by a different union and work under a collective bargaining agreement negotiated by that union. What will be the representation status of these employees when the workforces merge?

22. What is the principal difference between collective bargaining agreements (union contracts) in the aerospace manufacturing industry under the NLRA and the airline industry under the RLA?

23. Define *employee stock-ownership plan* (ESOP).

Online Assignments

1. What would the Workforce Fairness Act, renamed the Cesar Chavez Workplace Fairness Act, do if enacted by Congress? What was the outcome or is the present status of the act? Give the URLs of all online sources used.

2. For an airline, aerospace, or other company or agency you or your instructor selects, identify a union-organizing campaign and describe:

   a. The location involved

   b. The craft or class of employees involved and approximate number of such employees at that location

   c. The union involved

   d. The current status or outcome of the organizing effort

   e. If resolved, reasons you believe account for the outcome

   f. URLs of all online sources used

Supplemental Reading

Strike by Trans World Airlines Flight Attendants: Contract Continuity under the Railway Labor Act

More than any other case in recent history, the strike action taken against Trans World Airlines by the Independent Federation of Flight Attendants (IFFA) in 1986 points out the perpetuity of relationships that exist under the Railway Labor Act. These events clearly point out that unilateral action on the part of a party to a dispute does not deny a striking union the right to represent the class or craft remaining on the premises.

Introduction

Trans World Airlines was one of the nation's largest and oldest air carriers. It was founded in 1926 and has endured the tests of years, including mergers, takeovers, deregulation, strikes, and corporate spinoffs. In its history, with all the profits and losses taken into consideration, the airline has virtually made no money.

Late in 1985, Carl Icahn invested $300 million in the company for controlling interest. He became chairman of the board in January 1986, at which time the airline was losing money at the rate of $1 million per day. At the time, Icahn was trapped, with his prospects riding on a marginal company in a viciously competitive industry.[1]

Recognizing, as have all corporate leaders involved in marginal companies, that the only major variable cost he could attack to reduce his costs was that of labor, he knew that he would have to obtain pay concessions and increased productivity from his employees. His expectations were to receive concessions of $300 million in wage and benefit costs, which would reduce TWA's labor costs approximately 20 percent and its total costs before taxes to about 8 percent. The airline's total losses for 1985 were approximately $150 million.

The members of the Air Line Pilots Association (ALPA) and the International Association of Machinists and Aerospace Workers (IAM) provided the wage concessions Icahn sought. The pilots agreed to roughly 30 percent, approximating $100 million; the machinists provided 15 percent, or approximately $50 million. In reaching agreements with these unions, Icahn promised a profit-sharing plan and the eventual employee stock-ownership plan (ESOP). Additionally, Frank Lorenzo of Texas Air Corporation, who was reputed to be a "union buster," had recently attempted to purchase the airline. The unions desired and received an agreement from Icahn that he would not sell the airline to Lorenzo for at least three years.

Halfway to his goal, Icahn expected to get the remainder of the needed concessions from the airline's flight attendants, management, and other nonunion employees. Icahn was obliged by his agreement with the pilots to seek pay cuts of 20 to 22 percent from the flight attendants. The pilots had resented the 15 percent cut the machinists had finally settled for and did not want the flight attendants to "get off" so easily. The pilot's association said that in addition to the pay cut in January, the pilots had taken one of 11 percent in 1983. Another important element of the pilots' contract was that they agreed not to honor the picket lines of other unions. The machinists refused to make a similar commitment.[2]

The head of the flight attendant's union, Victoria Frankovich, said they would not accept pay cuts greater than the machinists. Frankovich and Icahn could not reach an agreement before the takeover. Frankovich's lawyer, William Jolley, suspected that Icahn was somewhat sexist. According to the lawyer, Icahn argued that the flight attendants were not breadwinners in the same sense that the mechanics were and could therefore afford to take deeper pay cuts.[3]

Responding to these allegations, Icahn stated, "I never said they weren't breadwinners; that's completely untrue. What I do say is that we can't compete with airlines that are paying half what we are for flight attendants. Our average cost is $35,000 to $40,000. Peoples Express and Continental are paying around $18,000. I tell you categorically that TWA would have gone into Chapter 11 if I hadn't come along and gotten wage concessions. They're losing $150 million this year even with a Pan Am strike helping them."[4]

Icahn insisted that the flight attendants had to make $100 million in concessions if TWA was to become competitive. He originally asked for a 22 percent pay cut but finally agreed to settle for 17 percent. He also demanded a 2-hour increase in the workweek, which at that time consisted of 20 in-flight hours per week. The IFFA agreed to 15 percent wage reductions but refused to work as many hours as TWA demanded. Both sides were determined to get what they wanted. Frankovich replied to Icahn's demand of work-rule changes, "Mr. Icahn says all he wants is a few more hours a week of flying time from us. But he doesn't understand that every added hour of work means six hours away from home. My members already are away 60 hours a week."[5]

Icahn stuck to his position, saying he had trimmed his demand for a 22 percent wage cut to 17 percent but that he would stick to his demand for changes in work rules: "For TWA to exist, we must have this. We're asking for a TWA that can be competitive."[6] Work rules deal with the most fundamental labor-related issues, such as how long an employee must work, how much rest he or she receives between work assignments, and how many hours he or she must put in during the standard workweek or, in this case, work month.

If TWA received all the work-rule changes it demanded, the airline would need far fewer attendants; the number employed could decline by more than 41 percent. From TWA's standpoint, the new rules would make its flight attendant workforce more productive and the airline more cost competitive with other carriers. At this time, the airline needed 6,000 attendants, but under the new regimen, they would need only 5,000.

The attendants were therefore fighting for their livelihoods, and according to the union, it was also "a fight to preserve the occupation as one suitable for mature adults." The union contended that the new rules were too physically demanding and that only extremely healthy people could live up to them, and even they could do so for only a short period of time.[7] According to the union, most of the flight attendants were in their thirties and had families who depended on them as breadwinners; 45 percent had dependent children. If the new work rules were put in effect, these people would be forced from work.

In 1985, the average attendant worked 16 or 17 days a month. To work those days, an attendant spent about 75 hours a month actually working flights (hard time) and about 240 hours away from home (trip time). Trip time is time spent waiting at airports between flights and time spent staying overnight in cities away from their domicile. It does not include hard time.

Under the existing contract, the work rules precluded TWA from scheduling attendants for more than 75 hard hours a month. Employees could work more if they wanted to and were paid overtime after the sixty-fifth hour. Now, TWA was demanding more flexibility. The company wanted to be able to schedule people for anywhere from 70 to 85 hours and would pay overtime for the last 10 hours only.[8] The union said that an 85-hour schedule would translate to about 21 days a month and would force members to be away as much as 320 hours a month.

TWA also wanted to be able to schedule attendants for longer days, with shorter rest periods. The airline wanted to be allowed to schedule people on its domestic system to work 13 hours at a time, which was thirty minutes more than the present rules. And the airline wanted to reduce the minimum rest time from 8 hours to about 6½ hours.[9] The union stated that the rest period demanded by TWA was not enough because of the unhealthy conditions under which the flight attendants work. They argued that flight attendants work, sleep, and eat at irregular hours, are exposed to large numbers of people, and breathe the stale air of airplanes day in and day out.[10]

In addition to the time demands, TWA desired to reduce the number of flight attendants it used on various aircraft. It sought to cut vacation time by 20 percent so that employees with 8 to 24 years of service would have a maximum of 24 days of vacation a year. The airline also wanted to drop the 8-in-24 rule, which required the company to provide extra rest if an employee worked more than 8 hours hard time in any 24-hour period.

The Strike

The National Mediation Board (NMB) declared a thirty-day cooling-off period in February 1986. On March 6, the cooling-off period ended, and the negotiators for the IFFA declared a strike. In separate press conferences, Frankovich and Icahn both blamed each other for provoking the strike. "We're going to shut this place down," Frankovich said after final talks ended. "We went as far as we could . . . far beyond what other groups on this property were required to do." In response, Icahn declared, "We intend to stay in business. Within three or four days from now, we hope to be up to full capacity."[11]

As a result of the work stoppage, TWA had to cancel all sixty of its early-morning flights from St. Louis, the domestic hub of the airline. This occurred on March 6. The company did manage to start flying again around noon of that same day. Systemwide, the airline had to cancel about half its domestic flights and four of its twenty-three international routes. Icahn estimated that the strike would cost the company $45 million to $50 million. TWA had already expected to lose $125 million in the first three months of 1986, even without the strike. Nevertheless, stockholders did not appear to be frightened. Instead, confidence in TWA stock seemed to grow. The day after the walkout, the trading on the New York Stock Exchange raised an eighth of a point to $16.25 per share.

In anticipation of the possibility of a strike, TWA had been training new flight attendants at its training facility in Kansas City, Missouri. TWA had operated a training school, charging tuition to learn to become a flight attendant, without offering any assurance that the assumption of a position would actually take place. TWA had 1,500 immediate replacement attendants who had paid TWA for the opportunity to become flight attendants. Additional recruits were provided by ticket agents and other employees of the airline who had been trained in flight attendant safety procedures.

The International Association of Machinists and Aerospace Workers

The IFFA had a better chance of winning the strike if the IAM, which represented mechanics, stores clerks, and baggage handlers, would honor their picket line. TWA lost its first major battle when a federal judge in Kansas City, Missouri, denied the airline's request for a temporary restraining order that would bar the machinists from honoring the attendant's picket lines throughout the country. U.S. District Judge Howard Sachs did, however, set a date for another hearing on a similar TWA request for a preliminary injunction against the union's sympathy action.[12] Airline analysts claimed that the absence of the machinists could shut the airline down and that the strike would not succeed without their support.

In the interim period, the machinists were acting independently around the country. Some locals were honoring the picket lines and some were not, but as time continued, more and more support was being gained. By March 11, 1986, about 80 percent of the union's 10,000 members were respecting the line. Support was very strong in St. Louis and Kansas City, where TWA had located its major hub and overhaul bases.

In an attempt to scare the machinists and attendants into returning to work, Icahn threatened to dismember the airline and sell the individual pieces. He stated, "We need to have these cuts. We must be competitive. If we don't, we will sell the airline. The only way they [IFFA] can win is with the machinists. But then it's a no-win situation for both of them because I'd be reluctantly forced to sell the airline."[13] Analysts said that the airline's domestic system, international routes, and computer reservation system could all be sold separately. Icahn claimed that he could make a $200 million profit if he sold the airline that way.

Icahn's threat was not necessary, because Sachs issued the preliminary injunction, and the machinists were ordered back to work on March 12. The attendants were then

expected to settle promptly, but the stoppage continued. After the injunction was issued, Frankovich stated, "It's our battle. It's something we have to win with or without the support of other unions."[14]

Sachs's decision was based on his interpretation of the language contained in a contract the machinists had signed on January 3 of the same year of the attendants' strike. The language of the three-year contract provided, "The union will not authorize or take part in any work stoppage, strike, or picketing of company premises during the life of this agreement, until the procedures for settling disputes involving employees covered by this agreement, and as provided by the Railway Labor Act, have been exhausted."

The machinists argued that this language applied only to direct strikes by the machinist's union and that it had no bearing on sympathy strikes. TWA argued that it did have a relationship to sympathy strikes. Sachs believed that TWA would prevail in a grievance it had filed against the machinists with the System Board of Adjustment, the arbitration panel set up under the Railway Labor Act.

Sachs ordered the machinists back to work until this issue could be arbitrated because a continuation of the strike would harm TWA. The order stated that the machinists would be subject to discipline by the airline if they disobeyed the return order. It also established penalties if the machinists attempted to thwart TWA with lethargic or poor work.

Replacement for Striking Attendants

Since the beginning of the strike, TWA had been drafting into service hundreds of newly hired attendants. The replacements were being paid approximately $12,000 per year and were working under the rules Icahn was demanding of the IFFA. As of March 12, 400 attendants, out of a force of 6,000, had crossed the picket line. Along with the 1,200 replacements, TWA needed only another 2,300 to enforce its new work rules, which would leave approximately 3,300 of the striking attendants out of work if the union did return because Icahn promised to keep the new attendants on the payroll.

Talks Resume

On March 13, 1986, talks were held in Philadelphia for the first time since the walkout. The talks were under the supervision of an NMB mediator and a board commissioner. The talks lasted for three and a half hours, after which Meredith

Buel, a spokesperson for the National Mediation Board, said, "We will call for further talks when appropriate. The parties expressed their current positions and we see no basis for further discussions at this time."[15]

The flight attendants would not change their position. They argued that they could not be fired—that this was a legal strike and the union could call it off whenever they wanted and go back to work. Icahn also would not change his demand of a 17 percent pay cut and an 18 percent productivity increase. He reiterated that he would retain the now 1,750 new nonunion flight attendants hired since the strike began. By April, TWA was operating at or near 100 percent and was in the process of replacing all the unionized attendants.

New Attitudes on Labor Strikes according to the Media

In response to the IFFA strike, the news media reported the development of new national attitudes toward labor strikes, which were in general harsher toward union organizations. One such report appeared in the *St. Louis Post Dispatch* on April 13, 1986:

> The strike by the Independent Federation of Flight Attendants against Trans World Airlines demonstrates the new and harsher labor environment in which airline unions have been operating since deregulation. It also demonstrates the negative turn which the nation as a whole has taken towards unions in recent years.

Earlier that year, on January 12, the *Minneapolis Star Tribune* reported that

> strikes in general have become so difficult to win that labor leaders are reluctant to wage them. Ever since the strike by the Professional Air Traffic Controllers Organization in 1981, what was once taboo has become an increasingly common management tactic. The government fired the strikers, hired replacements and barred the former union members from getting their old jobs back. Employers have had the legal right to replace strikers in contract disputes since 1983, when the U.S. Supreme Court interpreted the federal labor law to say that employers could replace strikers as long as the employers did not discriminate against union activists.

Finally, on July 27, 1986, the *Akron (Ohio) Beacon Journal* reported on the increasing costs incurred by airline strikes after deregulation:

Before deregulation, struck airlines routinely shut down. In 1973, a strike by TWA flight attendants caused the airline to halt operations for 43 days. But in those days, a shut down was not as worrisome to management as it is now. The airlines had Mutual Aid Pacts that funneled the excess revenue received by competing carriers back to the strike-bound airline. Regulation stopped new carriers from jumping in and taking over business.

Also, before deregulation, organized labor's overall strength and popularity restrained airlines and other industries from exercising their legal rights to hire strikebreakers.

Now with the dissolution of Mutual Aid Pacts and the new era of cutthroat competition, the airlines find it crucial to stay in business during a strike. There is also a definite declining popularity of organized labor, which hurts the union's positions. The public does not care as much as it used to.

After deregulation, there was a high potential for strikes in the airline industry because of the pressure put on airlines to cut labor costs. During the 40-year period when the government regulated airlines, the union would bargain for a better contract and the airlines would pass the costs along in higher rates. If TWA mechanics received a raise, United mechanics would receive a better raise in their next round of negotiations and so forth. To offset these added costs, the airlines would go to the Civil Aeronautics Board (CAB) and ask for an across-the-board fare increase, which generally would be granted. Costs, today, can not be passed on to the customers as easily as before because of the high competition that the airlines are in with each other.

A Lost Battle?

Analysts claimed that the IFFA was in an especially weak position because flight attendants were the group that airlines could most easily replace. TWA said it was training new flight attendants in eighteen days and graduating nearly 20 a day. But by the end of April, TWA had stopped hiring replacements. The union thought that may have been a sign that the airline was interested in settling the dispute, but TWA stuck to its proposals. The carrier did say that it expected to have 4,000 flight attendants to replace the strikers and to staff its flights by May, which would be all that were required at that time of the year. For the peak summer months, they estimated they would need a maximum of 5,000 attendants.

The Fight to Regain Union Status

TWA filed suit in late April to stop union flight attendants from forcing the carrier to identify or collect union dues from nonstriking flight attendants or discharge nonstriking attendants for lack of dues payments because of the union-security clause in effect between the carrier and the IFFA. TWA took the position that the union was trying to enforce security provisions of an expired contract. Shortly before the strike, the union had filed a lawsuit asking Sachs to rule that the company had not negotiated in "good faith." The union contended that the period in which neither side could change the contractual obligations had not expired. Sachs denied the request but set the union's case for trial on June 30, 1986, at which time TWA requested that its suit also be considered; their position was that the union-security clause had expired March 7, 1986, and that the airline had no obligation to the union under those provisions.[16]

On May 17, 1986, the union unconditionally volunteered to return to work. By this time, TWA had already filled many of the striking employees' positions with replacement employees. They did, however, accept 198 of the senior union members, who returned with a 22 percent pay cut and an increase in working hours. In the previous month, 1,284 IFFA members had unilaterally decided to return to their former positions and were flying under the same terms and conditions. The remainder of the striking employees was placed on a waiting list until positions opened in the company. Icahn reiterated that he would keep the replacement employees, but he said that he might attempt an early retirement buyout for more than 1,000 of the veteran strikers.

On June 30, 1986, Sachs ordered all of TWA's 4,500 attendants to begin paying dues to the striking union, the IFFA. TWA sought to block the order in the U.S. Circuit Court of Appeals. Sachs, however, would not stay his order pending appeal: "The flight attendants must begin paying dues to the union by the beginning of September 1986. Also, TWA must, within two weeks of the order, implement a system for withholding dues from the flight attendant's paychecks and forwarding the money to the union." Addressing the perpetuity of agreements in the airlines, Sachs ruled that the union-security clause, like other contract provisions that were not subject to prestrike bargaining, continued in

full force. He stated, briefly, "The portions of the contract not subjected to renegotiation still exist."[17]

Sachs's decision was based on a 1966 U.S. Supreme Court decision written by Justice William O. Douglas in a case concerning the amendability of an airline contract under the Railway Labor Act (RLA). Douglas had written that collective bargaining agreements are "the product of years of struggle and negotiations and are not destroyed by a strike that represents only an interruption in the continuity of the relationship. A strike is not the occasion for the carrier to tear up and annul the collective bargaining agreement.... To do so, labor-management relations would revert to the jungle."[18] Sachs said that the RLA prevented parties to a contract from destroying a contract by simply proposing changes.

The order of June 30, 1986, meant that the newly hired flight attendants would be forced to pay dues to the union that had been trying desperately to replace them. The nonunion members would have to pay $100 initiation fees and $36 a month in dues. Union members who had crossed the picket line and returned to work would be required to pay the monthly dues.

This ruling had no effect on pay cuts and work-rule changes implemented by management or the fate of the former strikers who had not been recalled. About the ruling, Frankovich stated, "This is a first of a string of victories that we will win in court. We are very, very pleased. This will give us some money to operate on."[19] But on August 6, Sachs's decision on union dues was appealed. The airline asked the circuit court of appeals to stay Sachs's ruling and to hear the arguments on the appeal the week of September 8, 1986. The appeal said that under the order, TWA would have to collect approximately $161,000 a month in union dues. The airline felt that the money would be available to the union in support of its economic boycott of TWA.[20]

By the end of August, Sachs made another important ruling. He ruled that strikers with seniority could replace the 1,284 union members who had crossed the picket lines: "In my judgment all permanent employees working during an economic strike [strike held to pressure an employer to give in to economic negotiating demands] are safe from replacement."[21]

IFFA held fast to its belief that its members with seniority were entitled to be placed in the active workforce. It again filed suit, challenging the job status of three groups. Union members who did not strike, 1,200 new attendants who were prospective employees before the strike and placed on the payroll after the walkout, and 463 trainees hired after the union unconditionally agreed to return to work.

The central issue of the dispute was whether TWA clearly told new employees that they were permanently replacing the strikers. TWA maintained that under federal labor laws it had the right to hire replacements. The company contended that there were no jobs available for the former strikers. The union contended, however, that labor law allows strikers to be reinstated if a company can afford it and that TWA was unfairly refusing to hire former strikers. A ruling made by the Supreme Court during a recent strike by the International Brotherhood of Teamsters (IBT or Teamsters) had stated that an employer was liable for two payrolls if it told replacements they would be permanent and then offered union members their jobs back in settlement.[22]

During the first week of September 1986, Sachs ruled that TWA did not have to replace 2,500 of its flight attendants with the former strikers. But he also ruled that the airline had to reinstate 463 senior union members whose positions had been filled by trainees after the union had agreed to return. This reinstatement was required within thirty days, with back pay and interest retroactive to May 17, 1986. According to this ruling, TWA could either replace 463 new attendants or add 463 union members to its workforce in other than flight attendant positions, as long as striking employees were available to return. The judge agreed with the union that once the union made an unconditional offer to return to work, its members should have been recalled to fill any remaining openings. The 463 new flight attendants should not have been put on the payroll, he said. In deference, TWA offered the 463 other positions within the company. With regard to the 1,280 flight attendants who refused to strike, Sachs ruled that they could not be bumped by those who did strike. The previously placed 198 senior union members were not affected by the decisions.

All the striking flight attendants returned to the payroll. No agreement afterward existed between the parties other than the old agreement and the new implemented changes made by management, which was free—once the cooling-off period expired—to implement any change they had proposed in negotiations. Interestingly, because the parties were unable to reach an agreement, there was not a negotiated settlement, nor was there a contractual expiration date. One can only conclude that under this situation, any attempt to modify the present "limbo" agreement would have required a Section 6 notice, obligating the parties to renegotiate the present terms and conditions.

The outcome of the IFFA strike against TWA provides evidence that contracts are amendable under the Railway Labor Act. The provisions of the parties' old agreement that had not been a subject of bargaining—or that, in labor parlance, were not "openers"—remain in full force. One of these provisions, the seniority provision of the scheduling policy, awards those returning from a strike better bid opportunities based on seniority. The IFFA was the designated sole bargaining representative of all the employees, which would remain so until the majority of the employees seek a change to another representative.

Conclusion

Conditioned by the days of regulation in the airline business, the IFFA and other unions have failed to recognize that times have changed and the old rules no longer apply. In round after round of negotiation in which author Robert W. Kaps has been involved, the unions have steadfastly maintained the positions that they were protected by the Railway Labor Act and virtually could not be replaced and that if economics did play a part in the possible demise of a company, the government would stop a certified airline from going out of business or a merger would take place to work to the benefit of the union.

These attitudes were not confined to the unions alone but were also harbored by management. The airlines were an island by themselves, sheltered by the Civil Aeronautic Board, bolstered by the security of the Railway Labor Act, and secure in the belief that this atmosphere would last. Those in the business, Kaps included, believed that the attitudes, the approaches, and the legislated sparring would always be a part of our personal industry and that despite them, Camelot would not die. Vickie Frankovich must have believed that and, in some way, probably still wonders what happened to change the ground rules established over the years. It's unfortunate that, like King Arthur, we must eventually atone for our shortcomings.

Rarely in the modern history of the American labor movement has a union walkout backfired so powerfully against its participants. IFFA suits have variously charged TWA with bad-faith bargaining and with sex and age discrimination. The union also reported to the Federal Aviation Administration (FAA) many incidents of alleged safety violations by inexperienced attendants. The FAA had said it had found no unusual problems with the airline.

Harry Hoglander, former president of TWA's pilots' union, said about the IFFA, "The cabin attendants are seen by labor to be out to lunch. They really aren't dealing with the realities of the airline business."[23] Many people in the industry believe that Frankovich mismanaged the negotiations from the beginning and may not have kept the union members fully informed. F. Lee Bailey, the lawyer who advised all unions at the outset of talks in 1985, commented, "Their bargaining power was minimal. They were replaceable. Any experienced negotiator would have told them this was not the time to strike."[24]

Despite all the epitaphs written about the end of the IFFA, the union still existed because of the perpetuity of representation recognition under the terms of the RLA, on the premises of TWA until the company's demise, and the union's future was secure until another union would have sought to take the IFFA's place through a reelection procedure under the auspices of the NMB. Many believe the perpetuity aspect of the RLA is obsolete and deserves to be reconsidered. The industry has seen profound changes and has been totally deregulated in almost every aspect of its existence save one, the labor law. In the recent past, many calls have been made among industry officials to seek alternate legislation because they believe the act to be anachronistic and prolabor. This attempt seems to be gaining greater momentum than ever before.

Fortune Magazine highlighted the prolabor aspects of the NMB:

Easily the strangest federal agency in our country's capital these days is the National Mediation Board. Nobody can explain this animal to us. For openers, nobody can make clear how it has managed to remain totally, unabashedly pro-union after more than eight years of Reaganism. Both members of the board were appointed by Ronald Reagan (a third position is vacant), the guy who made his day by gleefully breaking a strike by the air traffic controllers. But the NMB members and staffers go right on acting as though nothing has changed since Frances Perkins was Secretary of Labor. The board members even had the liberal *New York Times* calling for their skin a while back, based on their obvious

commitment to the Machinists Union, which itself was bent on destroying the Lorenzo regime at Eastern Airlines.[25]

The other side of the picture is best related by middle-of-the-roaders and staunch supporters of the act. The following excerpts from letters to the editor of the *Wall Street Journal* highlight those positions:

Your suggestion to strike down the anachronistic Railway Labor Act may not be the thing to do. There is a lot more at stake and more to this law than the Supreme Court decision [concerning secondary picketing]. This is not to say that critical reexamination is out of order. It is appropriate to ask whether, in our contemporary, deregulated transportation environment, the law promotes or encumbers public interest considerations; whether nothing more is needed than to transfer the two industries to the other law; or whether, in an attempt to change, the collision of special interests in Congress might reshuffle the deck in some unpredictable way that would not serve either the public or the industries. For people who have invested their careers in one or the other of the Railway Labor Act industries, these are profound questions that deserve more than a throwaway line in what is otherwise a constructive editorial.

Charles I. Hopkins Jr.
National Railway Labor Conference
Washington

The Railway Labor Act has provided a legislative base for maintaining labor peace and stability in the railroad and airline industries during periods of severe stress and crises—namely deregulation and fare/rate wars. Despite a relatively few instances of interrupted service due to strikes, the law has achieved settlements without strikes in 97 percent of the cases handled in the airline and railroad industries. Neither the railroad carriers nor the labor organizations seek to abandon the law in favor of the National Labor Relations Act.

Walter C. Wallace, Member
National Mediation Board
Washington[26]

5. Negotiating the Collective Bargaining Agreement

1. Define *opener*.

2. Is there a difference between mediation and conciliation?

3. In the airline industry, what is the first step a union or airline must take to reopen negotiations to change the rates of pay, work rules, or working conditions in an existing collective bargaining agreement?

4. What must happen next in question 3's situation and when?

5. What usually results from an airline and/or one of its unions bringing lengthy "wish lists" to the negotiating table?

6. Define *pattern bargaining*.

7. The existing collective bargaining agreement between an airline and the union representing its aircraft mechanics is open for renegotiation, and the airline has filed a Section 6 notice requesting a change in the pay scale. At the first negotiating session, the airline's negotiator presents a proposal for a 15 percent reduction in the mechanics' pay scale, stating: "This is the best the company can do. I have no authority to negotiate this. Take it or leave it." Is this legal? Why? If not, what can the union do about it?

8. If the union and the airline are unable to reach an agreement, what must happen before the union can strike and the airline can fire and permanently replace the strikers?

9. Under the RLA, mediation is:

   a. Optional

   b. Mandatory

10. Mediation under the RLA is conducted by mediators employed by the _____.

11. How long can a mediator hold an airline and union in mediation?

12. If the mediator declares an impasse, are the union and the airline free to resort to self-help?

13. What is the difference between mediation and arbitration?

14. Under the RLA, if mediation fails, arbitration is:

    a. Optional

    b. Mandatory

15. If a dispute goes to arbitration under the RLA, the arbitrator's decision is:

    a. Binding

    b. Nonbinding

    c. Either of the above

16. If either the union or airline rejects an offer of arbitration, are they free to resort to self-help?

17. Can the president of the United States further delay the parties' right to resort to self-help? If so, under what circumstances?

18. Can Congress become involved in the dispute? If so, how?

19. The vast majority of self-help in the airline industry has centered on the _____, rather than the lockout, primarily because _____

_____

_____ .

20. Define *mutual aid pact*. How has it been used in the U.S. airline industry?

21. Is the mutual aid pact legal in the airline industry today? Why? Was it ever?

22. The existing collective bargaining agreement between a major aerospace manufacturer and the union representing its aircraft electricians is expiring in three months. The union wants to negotiate labor-protective provisions that would limit the company's ability to close U.S. plants and outsource work overseas, and the company wants the employees to agree to some wage concessions. What is the first step each must take to open negotiations and when? What if one of them misses the deadline?

23. At the first negotiating session, the manufacturer's negotiator, addressing the company's proposal for a 15 percent reduction in the mechanics' pay scale, states: "This is the best the company can do. I have no authority to negotiate this. Take it or leave it." Is this legal? Why? If not, what can the union do about it?

24. Meanwhile, the company unilaterally adopts and implements a better health-care plan for the aircraft electricians, effective immediately, without consulting the union or bargaining over the details. Does this present a legal issue?

25. If the company and union are unable to reach agreement over the items in dispute (wages and health care plan), are they free to resort to self-help?

26. Under the NLRA, mediation is:

    a. Optional

    b. Mandatory

27. A mediator employed by the _____ conducts mediation under the NLRA.

28. How long can a mediator hold the parties in mediation under the NLRA? Is that different from the RLA?

29. Under the NLRA, if mediation fails, arbitration is:

    a. Mandatory

    b. Optional

30. Arbitration under the NLRA is:

    a. Binding

    b. Nonbinding

    c. Either of the above

31. At what point in the process under the NLRA are the parties first free to resort to self-help?

32. Under what circumstances can the president of the United States intervene in a labor dispute under the NLRA to prevent or delay the parties from resorting to self-help? How and for how long?

33. Under the NLRA, is it legal for a company that has locked out employees to unilaterally hire temporary or permanent replacement workers without first consulting the union?

34. Under the NLRA, is it legal for a company whose employees are on strike to unilaterally hire temporary or permanent replacement workers without first consulting the union?

35. According to the textbook, "Under the NLRA, _____ are the 'crown of thorns' for unions."

Online Assignment

Research online and prepare to present in class a current, recent, or impending collective bargaining agreement negotiation or renegotiation involving an aviation or aerospace company or agency that you select or your instructor assigns, including:

    a. Union and bargaining unit involved

    b. Major issues

    c. Your assessment of the relative strengths and weaknesses of the union and company bargaining positions

    d. Which approach to bargaining does it appear they took, are taking, or appear likely to take?

    e. How did it work, is it working, or does it appear likely to work?

    f. What do you see as obstructions to an outcome that was, is, or would likely be mutually acceptable?

    g. How do you believe those obstacles might be overcome?

    h. URLs of all online sources used

Supplemental Readings

How to Cost Out Your Contract: The Mathematics of Collective Bargaining

Introduction

In negotiations, the union proposals and the company proposals will not be the same. This requires a method to estimate and compare the costs of union proposals and company offers. The way to do this is by both parties costing out the contract.

There are good reasons to go through the costing out process:

- You can make decisions about which benefit demands best meet the needs of the union's members and the company.
- You can evaluate the total economic welfare of the union's membership and make comparisons with other groups of workers.
- You can evaluate the cost impact on the employer of any set of wage and fringe-benefit demands.
- You help keep bargaining table nonsense to a minimum.
- Management can tell the union membership what the new contract is worth in dollar terms.
- The company will take the union proposal and "cost it out," so advance calculations by the union can keep the company from using its cost figures as a negotiating weapon.

Data Collection

Long before negotiations begin and throughout the bargaining process, data for costing should be collected. Information on the company can often be found in the business reference section of public college libraries, online, and corporate annual reports.

When the union notifies the company of its desire to begin negotiations, the union should soon after request the following data in order to intelligently negotiate a contract.

1. Total hours worked and total hours compensated for all represented workers

2. Projections for the next three years, annually, of total hours worked and total hours compensated for represented workers

3. Active employment (number of workers who receive pay for work)

4. Average active employment in the last year of the contract and to date for current year

5. Detailed average labor costs breakdown and a current job classification/wage breakdown of the number of workers in each classification

6. Life, medical, and dental insurance data (i.e., enrollment by plan and total enrollment; total premiums paid by plan; and total for all plans)

7. For nonrepresented workforce, average active employment, total hours worked and total hours compensated, detailed breakdown of total payroll costs

8. Income statements for the last three full years

9. Current outstanding contracts, including agreement terms and projected delivery dates, and expected contracts over the next three years

10. Extraordinary, unusual, or nonrecurring costs, write-offs, or income occurring in any of the last three years

11. Balance sheets for the latest available month and the prior year-end

12. Operating plans, budgets, forecasts, or any other documents dealing with projected sales, costs, and operating results, together with a list of the major assumptions used in preparing such information

NOTE: If the union asks for numbers 1, 3, 4, 5, and 6 above, it should receive this data. The remaining requests are excellent to have but harder to get.

Useful Definitions

base period. The reference point against which changes in costs are measured (usually the final year of the terminating contract).

base rate. The wage employees earn for all regularly scheduled straight-time hours. Shift, overtime, incentive, and longevity payments are excluded from the base rate.

end loading. Postponing major portion of a wage increase until the later years of a multiple-year contract; provides less take-home pay.

fringe benefit. Any provision of the collective bargaining agreement that improves the welfare of the bargaining-unit member and is provided at a cost to the employer (for example, vacations, holidays, sick leave, funeral leave, pensions, health insurance, disability insurance, life insurance, overtime, shift premiums, and the like).

Differences in fringe values:

- Some fringes have dollar benefits that are directly related to changes in wages (paid vacations and holidays, personal leave, for example).

- Other fringes are not tied to the employer's pay structure; they have negotiated formulas (pensions, health care, tuition reimbursements, employer provided personal safety equipment, tools, and the like, for example).
- Other fringes can be figured either way; a shift bonus can be a percentage of a worker's wage rate or a flat cents-per-hour amount.

front loading. Larger portion of the wage increase is paid during the early years of a multiyear agreement; provides more take-home pay for employees.

notice requirements. Party seeking to reopen (renegotiate) or terminate a labor agreement required by federal labor law to give the other party sixty-days' notice and FMCS and the state or territorial mediation service thirty-days' notice. (The notices are ninety and sixty days, respectively, in the health-care industry.)

total compensation. For costing purposes, consists of direct wages and fringes.

weighted average. Determined by multiplying the number of employees in each pay bracket by the applicable wage rate, adding the results for each bracket together, and then dividing the final dollar figure by the total number of employees in the bargaining unit. Weighted average used since most companies have many base-wage-rate brackets or classifications. NOTE: Employer may use another measure (arithmetic average, median, or mode) because it shows a higher average wage rate and makes the company look better; however, the weighted average is more representative because the distribution of employees within the pay categories is taken into account.

work year. Wages of employees are typically paid on the basis of a work year averaging 2,080 hours (40-hour week ÷ 52 weeks).

Be aware of the concept of paid-versus-productive hours. Sometimes, you will hear an employer talk about "productive hours." Wages/salaries of employees are typically paid on the basis of a work year averaging 2,080 hours. Actual hours worked are fewer because of holidays, vacations, coffee and lunch breaks, jury duty, and the like. Sometimes, employers will view the time employees spend off the job as nonproductive hours and will not include them when calculating the hourly cost of a fringe benefit. This inflates the employer's cost. The union should resist any unreasonable number for the sake of good costing. All of the following examples use the 2,080-hour figure.

First Steps

There can be a certain amount of anxiety when confronted with the economics of bargaining, but it is really a matter of taking some easy steps after relevant data is supplied by the employer. The arithmetic involved is quick and simple, usually requiring only a pencil, paper, and calculator.

In contract bargaining, cost can be reflected in at least three different ways:

- Total annual cost (TAC). The total cost to the employer in a given contract year
- Annual average cost per employee (AACPE). The total annual cost divided by the number of employees in the bargaining unit
- Average cost per hour worked per employee (ACPHWPE) or average hourly cost (AHC). Derived by dividing the annual average cost per employee (AACPE) by the average number of hours worked per year per bargaining-unit member

The most systematic and probably speediest way to cost any given benefit is to determine the total annual cost of the benefit and carry out two divisions—first by number of employees and then by average number of hours worked.

Task 1. Estimate the Cost/Value of a Wage Proposal

The proposal is for a 5 percent wage increase in each year of a two-year contract; three hundred employees are in the bargaining unit. You will want to know what this offer amounts to in dollars. Take the following steps.

Step 1. Calculate the weighted average in each wage classification.

Employees	Rate per hour ($)	Wages paid per hour ($)
55	5.75	316.25
80	6.25	500.00
25	6.75	168.75
40	7.00	280.00
60	7.50	450.00
40	8.00	320.00
300		2,035.00

Total wages paid per hour ÷ total employees = weighted average base rate

$2,035.00 ÷ 300 = $6.78 (weighted average base rate)

Step 2. Calculate proposed increase and new weighted average, year 1.

weighted average base rate × percentage of proposed increase

$6.78 × .05 = $0.34 (first-year increase)

new weighted average = $6.78 + $0.34 = $7.12 an hour
Total annual cost (TAC) to the employer is calculated by multiplying $0.34 times the number of bargaining-unit employees times 2,080 hours (the accepted number of hours in a work year).

TAC = $0.34 × 300 × 2,080 = $212,160

Step 3. Calculate proposed increase and new weighted average, year 2.

The second-year wage increase is calculated using the first-year hourly base rate of $7.12 (6.78 + 0.34 = 7.12) and is $0.36 per hour (7.12 × .05 = 0.36).

It looks like the total wage increase for two years is $0.70 (0.34 + 0.36 = 0.70); however, since the first-year increase is paid again in the second year, it is included in the two-year total. Thus, the combined hourly cost is $1.04 (0.34 ×2 years + 0.36 = 1.04).

Try it yourself:

The proposal is for 8 percent in the first year; 3 percent in the second year of a two-year contract; 200 workers; weighted average base rate is $11.50 an hour; average number of hours worked is 2,080.

Task 2. Estimate the Cost/Value of a Pension

Use the following:

TAC = Total employer contribution to pension plan over the past year.

1. AACPE = TAC ÷ number of employees
2. Average hourly cost = AACPE ÷ average number of hours

Relevant data: the employer contribution is $1,750,000; the number of employees 1,000; and the average number of hours worked equals 2,080. So:

1. TAC = $1,750,000
2. AACPE = TAC ÷ number of employees = $1,750,000 ÷ 1,000 = $1,750
3. Average hourly cost = AACPE ÷ average number of hours = $1,750 ÷ 2,080 = $0.84

Try it yourself:

There are 1,000 employees; average number of hours worked is 2,080. The cost of the current pension program is $1,750,000 per year, and from your discussions with the union's pension consultant, your proposals for improving the current plan will increase the cost of the plan by 10 percent. You want to know the cost of the improvement in cents per hour. Start by figuring 10 percent of $1,750,000 to get the new annual cost: $1,750,000 + $175,000 = $1,925,000. Continue as above:

1. TAC =
2. AACPE = TAC ÷ number of employees =
3. Average hourly cost = AACPE ÷ number of hours worked =

Task 3. Estimate the Cost/Value of a Hospital/ Medical Insurance Proposal

The formulas are:

1. TAC = average monthly premium × 12 months × number of employees
2. AACPE = TAC ÷ number of employees
3. AHC = AACPE ÷ average number of hours worked

Relevant data: The average monthly premium equals $135; there are 1,000 employees; and the average number of hours worked is 2,080.

1. TAC = $135 × 12 months × 1,000 = $1,620,000
2. AACPE = $1,620,000 ÷ 1,000 = $1,620
3. AHC = $1,620 ÷ 2,080 = $0.78

Try it yourself:

Within the past few months, a health-maintenance organization (HMO) opened in your community. The monthly average premium for medical and hospital coverage is $125 per month. The monthly premium on your current health-insurance program is $130 per month. Assuming all the cost savings would go into increased wages, how much could wages be increased if your local switched to the cheaper plan?

Additional information needed: 950 employees; average hours worked per year are 2,080.

Start by doing the calculations for the $125 per month cost; then for the $130 per month cost.

Task 4. Estimate the Cost/Value of a Holiday (or Paid Leave Time) Proposal

The basic equations are:

1. TAC = Total paid holiday hours
   × average hourly wage
   × number of employees
2. AACPE = TAC ÷ number of employees
3. AHC = AACPE ÷ average number of hours worked

In this example, there are ten, eight-hour paid holidays; the average hourly wage is $9.50; there are 1,000 employees; average number of hours worked are 2,080.

1. TAC = 10 × 8 hours × 1,000 employees × $9.50
   = $760,000
2. AACPE = $760,000 ÷ 1,000 = $760.00
3. AHC = $760 ÷ 2,080 = $0.36

Try it yourself:
You currently have ten holidays, and your local would like to negotiate one additional holiday per year. What is the cost of this proposal in cents per hour? The average hourly wage is $10.00; there are 750 members; average hours worked per year are 2,080.

Task 5. Estimate the Cost/Value of a Vacation Proposal

What is the cost of a fifth week of vacation for all employees who have completed twenty years of service? You will need to know the number of prospective beneficiaries of this contract improvement. That can be found by examining a list of employees and their hiring dates.

In this case, twenty-two employees are eligible for the extra forty vacation hours during the first year of the new agreement; the weighted average hourly rate is $10.53. The total number of employees is 95; average hours worked are 2,080.

The calculations are:
TAC = $10.53 × 22 beneficiaries × 40 hours of benefit
   = $9,266.40
Next, divide total cost by total annual hours for the bargaining unit:
   95 × 2,080 = 197,600 (total annual hours)
   $9,266.40 ÷ 197,600 = .047 or 4.7 cents

NOTE: The weighted average wage for the twenty-two affected employees would have been more representative to use.

Try it yourself:
Listed below is the basic data regarding the vacation program contained in your current contract. Figure out the cost of this contract provision in cents per hour. Assume each employee works an average of 2,080 hours per year.

Vacation time	Number of employees	Average hourly wage
1 week (40 hours)	23	7.00
2 weeks (80 hours)	85	8.10
3 weeks (120 hours)	35	8.65
4 weeks (160 hours)	10	9.50

Task 6. Estimate the Cost/Value of Benefits Applicable to a Portion of the Membership

General formula:
1. Figure the cents per hour cost of the benefit as though all of the membership receive it.
2. Multiply the above cents-per-hour cost figure by the percent of employees who do receive this benefit.

For example, to calculate the cost of 10 percent night-shift premium with an average hourly wage of $9.50 and 15 percent of employees receiving shift premium, you would proceed to calculate:

1. Cost per hour if 100 percent received premium
   = $9.50 × 10% = $0.95
2. Actual cost = $0.95 × 0.15 = $0.143

Try it yourself:
Your local would like to negotiate a twenty-day paid leave for members who must be absent from work for childbirth. What is the cost of this proposal in cents per hour? Additional information needed:

- Cost of one paid-leave day per employee
  = $0.02 per hour worked
- Number of members in bargaining unit = 100
- Expected number of members absent for reason of childbirth = 4

NOTE: Employers tend to be overly generous when making assumptions about the utilization of benefits.

Try it yourself:
In costing out a wage-and-benefit package proposal, the cost/value of the money package is obtained by combining all of the individual pay and fringe items.

Facts: XYZ Company has three hundred people in the OCAW bargaining unit; negotiations are in progress. The OCAW local union is prepared to make its proposal as follows:

- A one-year contract
- 10 percent wage increase
- 2 additional holidays
- $10 per month increase in the company contribution for medical/hospital insurance
- Increased life insurance coverage of $5,000 per employee

Current benefits are:

- Vacations: average of 2 weeks per employee
- Holidays: 8 days
- Sick leave: 5 days
- Medical/hospital insurance: company pays $50/month per employee
- Life insurance:

Employees covered	Amount of coverage	Cost per $1,000
165	$25,000	75 cents
135	$30,000	85 cents

- Pensions: Noncontributory (company pays $35/month per employee)

1. Costing out the wage-increase proposal

The proposal is for a 10 percent increase. The weighted average rate for the 300 people in the unit is $6.78 an hour. Calculate proposed increase and new weighted average:

$6.78 × 10 percent increase = $.68

New weighted average = $6.78 + $.68 = $7.46/hour

2. Costing out the additional holidays proposal (two additional days, from eight to ten)

The method for costing out additional days uses this formula:

Step 1. To calculate the current cost,

weighted average wage × hours worked × number of holidays = annual cost per employee

Step 2. To calculate the new cost,

annual cost per employee ÷ annual hours paid = cents-per-hour cost

For our example,

Step 1. Calculation of current cost.

$6.78 × 8 × 8 = $433.92

$433.92 ÷ 2,080 = $0.209 per hour

Step 2. Calculation of new cost.

$7.46 × 8 × 10 = $596.80 per employee

$596.80 ÷ 2,080 = $0.287 per hour

Step 3. Calculation of increase.

Increase per employee = $596.80 − $433.92

= $162.88 per year

Increase per hour = $162.88 ÷ 2,080

= $0.078 or $0.287 − $0.209 = $0.078

3. Costing out vacation-increase proposals

The method for costing out vacations is:

average hourly wage × hours worked/week × number of weeks = annual cost per employee

annual cost per employee ÷ annual hours paid = cents-per-hour cost

For our example, there is no increase proposed, employees receive two weeks of vacation:

Step 1. Calculation of current cost.

$6.78 × 40 × 2 = $542.40 per employee

$542.40 ÷ 2,080 = $0.261 per hour

Step 2. Calculation of new cost.

$7.46 × 40 × 2 = $596.80 per employee

$596.80 ÷ 2,080 = $0.287 per hour

Step 3. Calculation of increase.

Increase per employee = $596.80 − $542.40

= $54.40/year

Increase per hour = $ 54.40 ÷ 2,080

= $0.026 or $0.287 − $0.261 = $0.026

4. Costing out sick-leave proposals

The method for costing out sick leave is:

average hourly wage × hours per day × number of days = annual cost per employee

annual cost per employee ÷ average number of hours = cents-per-hour cost

For our example, employees receive 5 sick days per year, and no increase is proposed:

Step 1. Calculation of current cost.

$6.78 × 8 × 5 = $271.20 per employee

$271.20 ÷ 2,080 = $0.130 per hour

Step 2. Calculation of new cost.

$7.46 × 8 × 5 = $298.40 per employee

$298.40 ÷ 2,080 = $0.143 per hour

Step 3. Calculation of increase.

Increase per employee = $298.40 − $271.20 = $27.20/year

Increase per hour = $27.20 ÷ 2,080

= $0.013 or $0.143 − $0.130 = $0.013

5. Costing out increases to life-insurance coverage

For our example, the proposal is to increase coverage by $5,000 for each employee.

Step 1. Look at current coverage and proposed coverage.

Employees	Covered amount of coverage ($)		Cost per $1,000* (¢)	
	Current	Proposed	Current	Proposed
165	25,000	30,000	75	80
135	30,000	35,000	85	90

*The union must usually rely on these figures as furnished by the company in order make this calculation. In situations like this, the negotiating committee should attempt to verify, through independent sources, that the rate levels are reasonable. The OCAW research and education department can be contacted for this purpose.

Step 2. Calculate a weighted average to arrive at the cost for each employee.

> number of employees in group × coverage per employee ÷ 1,000 × 12 months × cost per thousand per month = total annual cost
> total annual cost ÷ total employees = annual cost per employee
> annual cost per employee ÷ annual hours paid = cents-per-hour cost

For our example, calculation of current cost is:

$165 × \$25,000 ÷ 1,000 × 12 × .75 = \$37,125$
+
$135 × \$30,000 ÷ 1,000 × 12 × .85 = \$41,310$

300	$78,435
	total annual cost

$78,435 ÷ 300 = $261.45 annual cost per employee
$261.45 ÷ 2,080 = $0.125 per hour

Calculation of new cost:

$165 × \$30,000 ÷ 1,000 × 12 × .80 = \$47,520$
+
$135 × \$35,000 ÷ 1,000 × 12 × .90 = \$51,030$

300	$98,550
	total annual cost

$98,550 ÷ 300 = $328.50 annual cost per employee
$328.50 ÷ 2,080 = $0.158 per hour

Calculation of increase:

increase per employee = $328.50 − 261.45
= $67.05/year
increase per hour = $67.05 ÷ 2,080
= $0.032 *or* $0.158 − 0.126 = $0.032

6. Costing out increases in medical/hospital insurance

The method for costing out changes in contributions to medical/hospital insurance is:

Step 1. Monthly cost per employee × 12 months × number of employees = total annual cost

Step 2. Monthly cost per employee ÷ monthly hours paid (2,080 × 12 months) = cents-per-hour cost

For our example, the union has proposed an increase of $10 per month per employee in company contribution (from $50 to $60):

Step 1. Calculation of current cost.
$50 × 12 × 300 = $180,000 per year
$50 ÷ 173.3 = $0.288 per hour

Step 2. Calculation of new cost.
$60 × 12 × 300 = $216,000 per year
$60 ÷ 173.3 = $0.346 per hour

Step 3. Calculation of increase.
increase per year = $216,000 − 180,000 = $36,000 in total
increase per hour = $10 ÷ 173.3 = $0.058

or

$0.346 − 0.288 = $0.058

7. Costing out a pension proposal

Method:

Step 1. Calculate annual cost per employee.
monthly cost × 12 months = annual cost per employee

Step 2. Calculate total annual cost.
annual cost per employee × total number of employees = total annual cost

Step 3. Calculate cents-per-hour cost.
monthly cost per employee ÷ monthly hours paid = cents-per-hour cost

For this example, the union has not proposed any increase in the pension benefit; however, the company claims that the proposed wage increase would cause its payment into the pension fund to increase from $35/month to $40/month for each employee due to effect of the wage increase on pension formula. (NOTE: The union has to rely on cost figures furnished by the company. See comment in life-insurance section.)

Step 4. Calculation of current cost.
$35 ÷ 173.3 = $.202/hour

Step 5. Calculation of new cost.
$40 ÷ 173.3 = $.231/hour

Step 6. Calculate increase per hour.
$5 ÷ 173.3 = $.029

Summary, Wage-and-Benefit Package

	Current cost ($ per hour)	New cost ($ per hour)	Amount of increase ($ per hour)	Percentage increase
Wages	6.780	7.460	0.680	10
Holidays	0.209	0.287	0.078	37
Life insurance	0.126	0.158	0.032	25
Medical insurance	0.288	0.346	0.058	20
Pension	0.202	0.231	0.029	14
Sick leave	0.130	0.143	0.013	10
Vacations	0.261	0.287	0.026	10
Total package	7.996	8.912	0.916	11

Mock Negotiation

Spitfire Aviation Manufacturing Corporation and Aviation Mechanics Brotherhood of America

Procedures

1. The instructor divides the class members into labor and management negotiation teams. Each team selects/elects one member to act as the chairperson.

2. Each team member is assigned a particular function and is required to do the necessary research for that specific area. Additionally, each team member is expected to represent such area at the bargaining table, acting as the chief spokesperson for that particular subject matter.

The chairperson coordinates team planning, decides on the time and place for planning sessions, and assigns work to each group member. The chairperson, however, is not to do all the talking during the actual negotiation session. To maximize the learning situation, each member of the team must positively participate in the negotiation session, particularly in his/her defined area of responsibility for which he/she is the major spokesperson.

3. Each team is to establish six (minimum) to eight (maximum) proposals for discussion. The subject matter of the proposals are to be taken from the assigned case. Wage demands and fringe-benefit demands are considered one proposal.

4. Actual negotiation activities are permitted and include compromises, counterproposals, trading, and the dropping of demands to secure a contract. Each team should strive sincerely and honestly to do the best job possible in the

representation of its employee group, investors, stakeholders, and other interested parties.

5. Because of class size, more than one management or one labor team may be formed; no consultation is allowed with any other like team; for example, if the class has two management teams, they may not be in contact in any way with each other. Consultation, collaboration, or collusion with another team, whether labor or management, is subject to grade alteration. Each team must depend entirely upon its own resources and initiative.

6. The parties may reach an agreement at any time during the allotted negotiation time frame, which ends with the strike deadline, set by the instructor. However, no strike, lockout, or concerted self-help effort may begin until the strike deadline is reached. When this deadline arrives, if no agreement is reached, the union is free to use the strike weapon, and the company may authorize a lockout or take whatever actions either deems appropriate. No time extension of the existing contract is permitted.

7. Each team chairperson, with or without team members, will make a brief statement to the class, concerning the goals and objectives of his/her team, the proposals and or contract modifications desired, the final outcome, and the perceptions of the process. Because of this final summation, someone on each team should maintain a record of the settlements reached. Should a strike or lockout take place, the parties must indicate how they expect to continue operation or support the strike activity.

8. Determine which bargaining interests (issues) are most important, and develop specific bargaining proposals and counterproposals to achieve desired bargaining outcomes, using the following criteria.

   a. Before the first scheduled bargaining session, each team is required to complete the bargaining-position analysis form and give a copy to the instructor. Begin by focusing on issues your own team plans to raise and then include additional major issues the opponent may raise.

   b. Depending on time limitations that the instructor imposes for formal negotiations, the number of bargaining subjects raised may need to be restricted. In no case should a bargaining team attempt to engage in serious negotiations over no more than eight separate bargaining issues.

9. Each team gathers and prepares to present information to support or refute proposals on each specific bargaining issue.

10. Each team develops and implements appropriate bargaining strategies and tactics designed to achieve preferred bargaining results on important issues.

11. Each team reformulates bargaining proposals and strategies as conditions and information exchanged during negotiations require.

12. Each team engages in a good-faith effort to reach a mutually acceptable settlement of bargaining issues in dispute.

The Case

Representatives of the Spitfire Aviation Manufacturing Corporation of Ft. Wayne, Indiana, and Local 5000, Aviation Mechanics Brotherhood of America, are in the process of renegotiating their collective bargaining contract. The current contract expires on the date and time established by your instructor. The negotiations cover only the Ft. Wayne plant, although Spitfire Aviation also owns a plant in Pigget, Arkansas. The southern plant is neither organized nor a part of the current negotiations. The current Ft. Wayne contract was negotiated for a three-year period. The time of the negotiation is the present, and accordingly, current elements of the economy, patterns of collective bargaining, labor relations law, and other globalize implications condition the parties.

The Ft. Wayne plant has been in business for over one hundred years, beginning as a bicycle manufacturer and progressing to the aviation industry. It has steadily grown in size. At present, 3,800 production and maintenance employees are in the bargaining unit for the plant.

Except for the depression years, 1929 to 1936, the financial structure of the company has been relatively good. For the current year, the corporate sales amounted to $211.87 million. Sales totaled $169.25 million in the preceding year and $113.83 million for the first year of the current contract period. During the last fiscal year, the corporation's profits were $7.9 million after taxes; profits were $6.9 million the preceding year and $7.7 million in the first year of the labor agreement. Over the three-year period, the company distributed 75 percent of its net income in dividends, 20 percent was held as retained earnings, and 5 percent was used to improve and expand facilities in the Ft. Wayne plant. The company's stock is listed on the New York Stock Exchange. It has no bonded indebtedness; although last year it borrowed $8.3 million from the Hoosier National Bank. The rate of interest on the loan is 6.9 percent. The loan, which was used to expand the Pigget plant, is scheduled for liquidation in ten years.

The company manufactures a variety of aviation accessories and in recent years has expanded into the area of carburetors, fuel injection, and repairs. The list of accessories manufactured is large and includes aircraft heaters, oil pumps, magnetos, actuators, fuel pumps, and deicing components, and in the last year the company has started the production of small-aircraft air conditioners. About 65 percent of its sales are to the general aviation aircraft manufacturers (Cessna, Piper, and others), 25 percent are to aviation-repair facilities, and the rest to government agencies. Additionally, the company has been awarded Federal Aviation Administration approval as a repair station. The plant operates on a two-shift basis. A 3-cent-per-hour shift premium is paid to employees who work the second shift. At present, the shifts are equally matched with 50 percent of both skilled and unskilled employees.

The employees of the company were unionized in 1937, as a result of the Congress of Industrial Organizations campaign to organize the mass-production industries. In August of that year, the union was victorious in a NLRB election. As a result of the election, certification was awarded on March 17, 1937, to Local 5000, and since then, Local 5000 has represented the production and maintenance workers of the company. The first collective bargaining agreement between the company and Local 5000 was signed on November 14, 1937.

Only one contract strike has taken place since the union came into the picture. It occurred in 1940; the issues were the union's demands for a union shop, increased wages, and six paid holidays. The union failed in its attempt to obtain any arrangement requiring membership in the union as a condition of employment. The contract also contains no provisions for "check-off." At the time of the present negotiations, all except 400 workers in the bargaining units are in the union, but only a small percentage (15 percent) has signed up for dues check-off.

The average wage for the production workers in the Ft. Wayne plant is $8.85 per hour. The 3,800 employees include 175 skilled maintenance employees (50 electricians, 60 aircraft mechanics, 15 carpenters, 25 mechanics, and 25 tool-and-die makers), and their average rate is $18.75 per hour. The payment schedule is in the table below.

The payment schedule is as follows:

Unskilled workers

Classification	Years of seniority	Pay/hour
Unskilled	Start through first year	8.00
Unskilled	Year 2 through year 5	9.50
Unskilled	After 5 years of seniority	12.00

Skilled workers

Classification	Pay/hour
Electrician	17.66
A&P mechanic	20.25
Carpenter and mechanic	17.25
Tool-and-die maker	19.72

Some friction between the skilled classifications has occurred, as both the carpenters and the mechanics believe the union is not adequately representing their interests at the table. They believe they should garner a salary approximating 10 percent above the other skilled workers.

The existing contract contains an "escalator" clause providing for the adjustment of wages in accordance with changes in the Consumer Price Index. It provides a 1-cent increase in wages for each 0.5-point change in the CPI. During the past three years, employees have received a 12-cent increase in wages as a result of the escalator clause and a 5-cent-an-hour wage increase in each of the past two years from the operation of the contract's so-called annual improvement feature. The current wage rates in the plant include the increases generated from the escalator clause and the annual improvement factor.

The Pigget plant, built five years ago, started with a modest-size labor force, but during the past three years, the southern plant expanded sharply, now employing 1,500 production and maintenance workers. Union efforts to organize the southern plant have so far been unsuccessful. The union lost a NLRB election last year by 300 votes. Of the 1,500 employees, 1,300 cast ballots, with 800 voting against the union and 500 voting for it. The average wage in the Pigget plant is $8.10 per hour.

During the last eight months, 300 employees at the Ft. Wayne plant have been laid off. It is no secret that one reason for this has been the increase of output in the Pigget plant. Another reason for the layoffs was due to a large decrease in sales at the Ft. Wayne plant. In Pigget, essentially the same products are made as in Ft. Wayne.

In general, relations between the management and the union have been satisfactory. There have, of course, been the usual disagreements, but all in all, relations have been quite harmonious. Last month, however, there was a "wildcat strike." This was the first wildcat since the union came into the picture. It occurred in the oil-pump department. The alleged cause of the strike was the discharge of a union steward on the grounds that she shoved a foreman after discussing a grievance with him. The union disclaimed all responsibility for the strike, and its officers stated that they did all they could to get the employees back to work. However, the employees in the oil-pump department picketed the plant, and the incident, which lasted two days, shut down all production in the plant for the two days. The no-strike clause in the contract states:

> There will be no strikes, slowdowns, or other interruption of production because of labor disputes during the contract period. Employees who engage in such prohibited activity are subject to discharge.

The company threatened to sue the union for damages under the Taft-Hartley law but finally decided not to go to court after the employees returned to work. No employee was disciplined because of the strike; however, at present, the steward remains discharged. The union has demanded that the company return her to her job. Under the contract, the company has the right to discharge for just cause. The steward, Josephine Ruiz, a relative of the Indiana secretary of labor, is sixty-three years old and has been involved in the hierarchy of the union since her employment with the company at the age of eighteen.

The existing contract contains a standard grievance procedure. It provides for arbitration for all disputes arising under the contract, except production standards. Management maintains it has the unilateral right to establish all standards. During the last contractual period (three years), employees protesting "unreasonably" high production standards filed 275 written grievances. As required by the contract, the company negotiated the production standard grievance, but the union did not have the right to appeal to arbitration or to strike over the issue. In three cases sparked by the production standard grievances, the company reduced standards. In all other cases, the company denied the grievances. The management-rights clause states that the company retains all rights except as limited by express provisions of the labor agreement.

Provided in the contract is a series of fringe benefits: eight paid holidays, a very good hospitalization and surgical benefits insurance plan, and a vacation plan in which employees receive one week's vacation for one year of service and two weeks' vacation for five or more years of service. The total costs of all these fringe benefits amount to $2.50 per hour.

The medical plan has been in existence for quite some time, and some employees believe it is obsolete and not fully up-to-date. Basically, the company decided to self-insure the program based upon the premiums provided. Last year, the plan paid for all expenses this way, and the company had to spend an additional $2,483,000 not covered by the premium. The plan provides for coverage of plan participant expenses on an 80-20 basis once a deductible has been met. The deductible per year is $2,000.00 per family. The present charge is $353.00 per employee per month, and all employees are plan participants. There is, however, no coverage presently provided for members of the Arkansas plant. Some employees have complained to the human-relations department that this plan is unfair as it rewards an employee for having a family and children. Additionally, many employees contend the program does not consider significant others in the household and thus discriminates against the unmarried.

The current contract does not require that employees retire when eligible for pension. The company maintains, however, that any further accrual for retirement ceases upon the age of sixty-five. At present, the retirement plan is a defined plan providing workers with a monthly pension at the age of sixty-five of $36 for each year of service to the company. That figure, of course, is coupled with their Social Security payment, giving them their total retirement income per month. The company plan is reduced by 5 percent of the normal retirement rate should the employee retire before age 65.

With respect to the seniority clause, it provides for promotion based on length of service and ability. That is, seniority governs when the senior employee has qualifications reasonably equal to those of junior employees who bid on a job. During the contract period, employees who protested against the company's filling jobs with junior service employees filed twenty-one grievances. The company's position in these grievances has consistently been that the junior employees have far more ability than do senior employees. Five grievances went to arbitration, the company winning four and the union winning one. Promotions are bid on a departmental basis.

The seniority area of the existing contract provides for plantwide application of seniority credits for layoffs and recalls. During the recent period in which layoffs occurred, the company, as required by the contract, laid off many junior employees. This was based on the plantwide seniority system. Foremen, however, have complained to upper management that in many cases, the junior laid-off employees are more efficient than the senior employees who had to be retained because of the plantwide system.

Also, the current contract provides that an employee whose job is eliminated or whose job is preempted by a more senior employee may bump any junior employee in the plant, provided he/she has the qualification to fill the job. During layoff periods, the company became aware that this situation caused a great deal of expense because of an unreasonable amount of job displacement. Since the current contract does not contain a temporary layoff clause, a displaced employee may exercise his/her bumping rights. He or she can exercise these rights based on their plantwide seniority, no matter the duration of the layoff. Foremen have complained to the management that employees should be laid off without regard to seniority when the layoff is for a short period of time.

The existing contract also provides "super seniority" for stewards and other union officials. This provision protects the stewards and union officials only from layoffs. Sixty stewards are in the plant. Last year, stewards spent, on average, ten hours each per week on grievance work, for which the company paid them. There are no limitations on steward grievance work. Foremen have complained that some stewards are "goofing off," using "union business" as a pretext to not work. All stewards deny this. In fact, the stewards claim that it is the unreasonable attitude of foremen that provokes grievances and complaints. The stewards believe there cannot be a true measure of their time on the basis of the number of written grievances filed (a total of 205 filed last year). They contend a good share of their time is spent discussing grievances, on an oral basis, with the employees and supervisors. There is no record to show how many of these oral discussions ended problems without written grievances being filed.

Last year, because the government unexpectedly ordered more product, the plant worked Saturday and Sunday overtime for two weekends. Under the existing contract, the company has the right to require overtime. About 200 employees refused to work overtime. Ultimately, because the company threatened to fire them for refusal, they relented and worked the overtime hours. These 200 employees have been raising a lot of trouble in the union about this overtime affair. Pursuant to the contract, the company has the right to select the employees to work overtime; there is no provision for seniority.

Another sidelight to the overtime issue is that some employees have claimed that foremen are not fair in the distribution of overtime hours. These employees contend supervisors give their personal friends the opportunity to earn the extra money. They believe this to be a violation of their seniority rights and discrimination against the other employees.

For many years, by custom, each skilled tradesman has worked only within his/her trade. The five maintenance trades at the company are A&P mechanics, mechanics, carpenters, tool-and-die workers, and electricians. Five months ago, the company required a mechanic to do a job normally performed by an electrician. The employee and union filed a grievance, and the case went to arbitration. The arbitrator sustained the position of the union on the basis of the "past-practice" principle. The company, still using out-of-classification employees to finish jobs, contends the arbitration decision is only for normal practices. With the large number of layoffs, that decision has been vitiated.

Some maintenance people have been affected by the current layoff. Twenty-five maintenance personnel have been furloughed to date. They charge that the company has been subcontracting skilled work that could be done by them. Last year, for example, the company subcontracted electrical work while three electricians were on layoff. The subcontract job lasted six days. Under current contract language, there is no restriction on the company's right to subcontract.

The present contract, as with most industry-standard agreements, was negotiated for a three-year period. Both sides have indicated that in the future, they may want to move away from this long-term arrangement. However, there is no assurance this attitude indicates the parities' sincere position or if it is merely an expression of a possible bargaining position.

With respect to the current layoffs, the facts show that of the 300 employees laid off, 75 have exhausted their benefits under the Indiana Unemployment Compensation Act. The present contract does not provide for a supplementary unemployment-benefit program.

Automation has been a problem in the company for several years. About 250 workers have been permanently separated because of automation. Union and management

meetings over the past several years have proved fruitless. Discussions have centered on the rate of automation, income for displaced employees, and training of employees for jobs created by automation. All indications are that the next wave of automation will encompass and cost about 400 to 500 additional bargaining-unit jobs. The 250 employees who have been permanently separated are in addition to the 300 employees who are currently on layoff because of the southern situation and the drop in sales.

There has been considerable controversy over the problem of temporary transfers. Under the existing contract, the company may not transfer an employee to a job not in his/her job classification.

There are also problems regarding other work rules. These now include a fifteen-minute rest period every four hours, a stipulation that supervisors may not perform bargaining-unit work under any circumstances, paid lunch periods of twenty-minute duration, and paid wash-up time of ten minutes prior to quitting time. The company contends that these "work rules" are costing an exorbitant amounts of money and are obsolete and antithetical to the best working performance. Whenever these issues have been brought up in the past, the union has refused any change.

Company records show that 60 percent of the workers have seniority up to ten years, 30 percent between ten and twenty years, and 10 percent more than twenty years. The average age of the employees in the plant is thirty-nine. About 5 percent are over sixty-five years of age. About 20 percent of the bargaining unit is female, and 15 percent are minority employees, mostly Hispanic. Some African American employees have complained that they have not been given equal opportunity to get better jobs. They have threatened to file complaints against both the company and the union under Title VII of the Civil Rights Act and also under Taft-Hartley provisions. They have retained an attorney for this purpose. Likewise, several Hispanic employees believe management has an inherent bias against females. As with the African American employees, many Hispanic employees have contacted the Equal Employment Opportunity Commission for redress. As of this date, no activity has been forthcoming from either the EEOC or the Indiana State Commission on Human Rights.

Some problems that plagued negotiations throughout the past decade seem to remain a major concern for the union. Additional issues include areas such as rising cost of health insurance, family care, health and safety concerns, the present state of the economy, and the rising fuel costs. Also, in recent years, the company has been employing the services of both psychological and medical providers to become involved in hiring aspects of the company selection process. More and more, the company is looking into psychological testing before hiring. Many employees are upset with this criterion as some of their immediate family members have been refused employment. From a medical standpoint, it has been rumored that the company intends to use gene identification to determine future physical aspects of employment candidates and make employment decisions based on the genome time clock.

Spitfire Aviation Manufacturing Corporation
Balance Sheet
Fiscal Year of 20xx

ASSETS

Current assets

Cash	1,150,000
Accounts receivable	1,000,000
Notes receivable	500,000
Inventories at cost	400,000
Securities held	22,500,000
Total current assets	25,550,000

Fixed assets

Land	3,229,170
Buildings and improvements	8,856,000
Equipment and vehicles	1,200,000
Furniture and fixtures	4,999,000
Less: Accumulated depreciation	(409,000)
Total fixed assets	17,875,170

Other assets

Raw materials	10,150,000
Goodwill	2,000,000
Research and development	4,761,000
Other intangible assets	3,000,000
Total other assets	19,911,000

Total Assets	$63,336,170

LIABILITIES

Current liabilities

Accounts payable			699,750
Accrued interest @ 6.9%			572,700
Accrued taxes			194,284
Note payable			830,000
Accrued salaries (one month)			10,339,902
	IND	LTR	
Skilled workers	568,697	317,000	
Unskilled workers	5,559,680	1,588.645	
Shift differential	9,880	n/a	
Admin/office	1,531,000	765,000	
Pension fund/benefits			724,534
Total current liabilities			13,361,170

Long-term liabilities

Notes payable	7,470,000
Total long-term liabilities	7,470,000

STOCKHOLDERS' EQUITY

Preferred stock, cumulative @ 10.0% (par $1.00) held by president and three corporate vice presidents	10,000,000
Common stock (par $1.00)	5,500,000
Contributions to equity	22,505,000
Retained earnings (previous years)	2,920,000
Retained earnings (current year)	1,580,000
Total stockholders' equity	42,505,000
Total Liabilities and Stockholders' Equity	$63,336,170

Audited and agreed to by XYZ Accounting

Spitfire Aviation Manufacturing Corporation
Income Statement
Fiscal Year of 20xx

REVENUES

Gross Sales		211,879,100
Less:		
Returns and allowances	4,802,700	
Sales discounts	2,500,000	7,302,700
Net sales		204,576,400

COST OF GOODS SOLD

Beginning inventory, Jan. 1		750,000
Merchandise purchases	14,000,000	
Freight	400,000	14,400,000
Cost of goods for sale		15,150,000
Less: Ending inventory, Dec. 31		(400,000)
Cost of goods sold		14,750,000
Gross profit (Gross margin)		189,826,400

OPERATING EXPENSES

Selling expenses		
Labor costs, Ft. Wayne (includes $5,000,000 overtime costs)	86,224,200	
Labor costs, Pigget	25,272,000	
Advertising	2,000,000	
Supplies	5,000,000	
Other expenses	122,000	
Total selling expenses		118,618,200

GENERAL EXPENSES

Admin/office salaries (IND)	20,693,800	
Admin/office salaries (LTR)	13,585,400	
Depreciation	2,500,000	
Taxes	17,067,700	

	FT. WAYNE	PIGGET
FICA	8,228,158	2,865,682
SUTA	1,075,831	374,400
FUTA	547,788	187,300
WCMP	3,226,728	561,900

Insurance	2,483,000	
Rent	2,800,000	
Light, heat, power	120,000	
Miscellaneous expenses	41,000	
Total general expenses		59,290,900

TOTAL OPERATING EXPENSES	178,909,100
Net profit (income) from operation	10,917,300
Other expenses	317,300
Net income before taxes	10,600,000
Less: income tax expense	2,700,000
NET INCOME (LOSS) AFTER TAXES	7,900,000

Audited and agreed to by XYZ Accounting

Net Income Distribution and Related Facts

Recent stock price on New York Stock Exchange	3.00
Earning per share	1.436
Total dividend payout, common	4,925,000
Dividend payout per share, common	.8950
Yield per share common	.2983
Yield per share preferred	.1000
Retained earnings per share common	.2872
Improvement per share common	.0719
Preferred dividends per earnings	.0181
Net income	7,900,000
Total dividend payout	5,925,000
Earnings retained	1,580,000
Improvement	395,000

6. Unfair Labor Practices

1. The term *unfair labor practice* is found:

   a. In both the RLA and NLRA

   b. Only in the RLA

   c. Only in the NLRA

   d. None of the above

2. Is it important for airline management and union personnel to be aware of NLRB rulings on the subject of unfair labor practices? Why?

3. Is it important for aerospace manufacturing management and union personnel to be aware of NLRB rulings on the subject of unfair labor practices? Why?

4. What did America West Airlines do during a union certification election that the NMB found to be a violation of the RLA's prohibition against interfering with, influencing, or coercing employees in the election process?

5. What did the NMB order as a remedy in question 4?

6. Which oversight agency more closely scrutinizes actions on the part of the company in a certification election for unfair labor practices: the NLRB or NMB?

7. True or False. Some kinds of conduct by an aerospace manufacturer that would constitute an unfair labor practice would be permissible for an airline.

8. True or False. The potential consequences of the company committing an unfair labor practice are more serious in the aerospace manufacturing industry than in the airline industry.

9. What did Horizon Airlines do in collective bargaining negotiations with the company's flight attendants that caused the company legal difficulties? What did it cost the company?

10. How many airlines have been fined and how many airline officers have been jailed for committing unfair labor practices in the course of a union-organizing effort?

11. What do the authors mean when they say, when discussing NLRB prosecution of unfair labor practices, "the actions taken by the NLRB are remedial, not punitive"?

12. Are NLRB decisions in unfair labor practice cases subject to judicial review?

13. An employee of a major aerospace manufacturer is called to the company's personnel office. There, the director of personnel calls the employee into his or her office and asks the employee directly, "Are you in favor of the International Association of Machinists and Aerospace Workers' effort to unionize your shop?" Is this legal? Explain.

14. An employee of a major airline is asked in the company's lunchroom by a coworker, "How do you feel about the IAMAW wanting to represent us?" The coworker is anti-union and is feeding the information gained to management without the knowledge of his/her coworkers or the union. Is this legal? Explain.

15. A major aerospace manufacturer has plants in Phoenix, Arizona, and Nogales, Mexico. The IAMAW is seeking certification to represent the aircraft sheet-metal workers in the Phoenix plant. The manufacturer could consolidate the operations to Nogales.

a. Is it legal for the company to put the word out that if the union wins, the company will close the Phoenix plant and move the work to Nogales?

b. Is it legal for the company to close the plant and move the work to Nogales if the union wins certification? Why?

Online Assignment

For an airline, aerospace, or other company or agency that you or your instructor selects, locate an appropriate board decision in a case involving a union's claim of an unfair labor practice on the part of the company or agency and:

a. Describe the acts of the company alleged to constitute an unfair labor practice.

b. Give the company's argument why the action should not be considered an unfair labor practice.

c. Give the board's decision.

d. Give the URLs of online sources used.

Supplemental Readings

*National Mediation Board Rulings
in Certification Elections*

**Laker Airways Ltd., 8 NMB no. 79
Findings upon Investigation; Order
Case nos. R-5131 and R-5132
February 24, 1981**

**In the Matter of the Application of the
INTERNATIONAL BROTHERHOOD
OF TEAMSTERS
alleging representation disputes pursuant to
Section 2, Ninth, of the Railway Labor Act
involving employees of
LAKER AIRWAYS LTD.**

On August 21, 1980, the International Brotherhood of Teamsters (IBT) filed applications pursuant to Section 2, Ninth, of the Railway Labor Act, 45 U.S.C. §152, Ninth, alleging the existence of representation disputes among personnel described as "Office Clerical Employees" and "Passenger Service Employees," employed by Laker Airways Ltd. (Laker). Said applications were docketed as NMB Case Nos. R-5131 and R-5132, respectively.

At the time the applications were received, these employees were not represented by any individual or organization.

Investigation disclosed that disputes existed among the subject employees, and by order of the Board, secret ballot elections were conducted. Ballots were mailed on December 19, 1980. Tabulation of the ballots was originally scheduled for January 23, 1981.

On January 5, 1981, the IBT protested certain conduct on the part of Laker, and requested that the election be cancelled and that certain other remedial actions be taken. Specifically, IBT alleged that Laker officials had collected employees' ballots, made promises of benefit or threats of reprisal, and had otherwise interfered with the election. On January 16, 1981, the IBT submitted an additional Statement of Position, and on January 19, 1981, the IBT submitted an affidavit in support of its Statement.

On January 19, 1981, the Board ordered that ballots in both elections be impounded pending further investigation, and ordered that Laker file a response to the IBT Statement of Position. In addition, Laker was ordered to turn in any ballots collected, as well as a list of employees who turned in ballots. 8 NMB no. 65.

On January 22, 1981, Laker informed the Board that, while it had collected ballots, all such ballots had been destroyed, and that no list was maintained. On February 3, 1981, Laker submitted a Statement of Position and fifteen affidavits of carrier officials.

During the period of January 5, 1981, to the present time, Chief Hearing Officer David M. Cohen and Hearing Officer Roland Watkins conducted an investigation on behalf of the Board. Mr. Watkins interviewed a number of employees and other witnesses with respect to the IBT's allegations.

Based upon the investigation, the Statements of Position, and the affidavits, the Board finds as follows:

ISSUE

The issue in these cases is whether Laker interfered with, influenced, or coerced its employees in their choice of a representative pursuant to Section 2, Ninth, of the Act.

CONTENTIONS

The IBT contends that Laker has violated the Act by carrying out a "comprehensive and coercive campaign to restrict employees' right to vote by collecting their ballots." In addition, the IBT asserts that Laker has "dramatically" increased wages and benefits during the course of the organizing campaign for the purpose of influencing the employees.

Laker characterizes the IBT Statement as "gross exaggerations and misrepresentations" and asserts that it acted in accordance with the Act. Laker additionally accuses IBT of improper actions.

FINDINGS OF LAW

Determination of the issue here involved is governed by Section 201, Title II, and Section 2, Title I, of the Railway Labor Act, as amended, 45 U.S.C. §181, 152. Accordingly, the board finds as follows:

I.

Section 201 of the Act, extends all of the provisions of Title I of the Act, except the provisions of Section 3, thereof, 45 U.S.C., §153, to "every common carrier engaged in interstate or foreign commerce . . . and every air pilot or other person who performs any work as an employee or subordinate official of such carrier, subject to its or their continuing authority to supervise and direct the manner or rendition of his service."

II.

Laker Airways Ltd. is a common carrier by air as defined in Title II, Section 201 of the Act, 45 U.S.C. §181.

III.

Section 2, Fourth, of the Act, U.S.C. §152, Fourth, gives employees subject to its provisions "… the right to organize and bargain collectively through representatives of their own choosing. The majority of any craft or class of employees shall have the right to determine who shall be the representative of the craft or class for the purposes of this Act." Section 2, Fourth, also allows employees the right to select representatives without carrier influence or interference. That particular subsection reads as follows:

> No carrier, its officers or agents, shall deny or in any way question the right of its employees to join, organize, or assist in organizing the labor organization of their choice, and *it shall be unlawful for any carrier to interfere in any way with the organization of its employees*, or to use the funds of the carrier in maintaining or assisting or contributing to any labor organization, labor representative, or other agency of collecting bargaining, or in performing any work therefor, or to influence or coerce employees in an effort to induce them to join or remain or not to join or remain members of any labor organization … (emphasis supplied).

IV.

Employee-carrier isolation with respect to an employees' choice of a collective bargaining representative is expressed in Section 2, General Purposes Clause. The subsection states that one of the purposes of the Railway Labor Act is "to provide for the complete independence of carriers and of employees in the matter of self organizations."

V.

Section 2, Ninth, of the Act, 45 U.S.C. §152, Ninth, requires the National Mediation Board to investigate disputes which arise among a carrier's employees over representation, and to certify the duly authorized representatives of such employees. In determining the choice of the majority of employees under this section, the Board is "authorized to take a secret ballot of the employees involved, or to utilize any other appropriate method of ascertaining the names of their duly designated and authorized representatives in such manner as shall insure the choice of representatives by the employees *without interference, influence, or coercion exercised by the Carrier*" (emphasis supplied).

FINDINGS OF FACT

I.

Laker is a British carrier operating low-fare air service between the United States and Great Britain. Initially a charter carrier, Laker now operates as a scheduled carrier between London and New York, Los Angeles, and Miami. Future service to Tampa is planned.

Laker employs approximately 300 persons in the United States in four locations: John F. Kennedy International Airport in New York, the Laker Travel Center in New York, Miami, and Los Angeles. Employment has increased rapidly since scheduled operations began in 1977.

II.

IBT alleges that Laker actively solicited employees to turn their ballots in to carrier officials; provided stamped, pre-addressed envelopes for this purpose; and kept a record at which employees turned in their ballots.

Laker admits that it told its employees that the most effective way to vote against representation, in view of the form of the ballot used by the Board, was to turn the ballot in to the carrier.

In a letter dated December 15, 1980, addressed to all United States employees, Charles Maxwell, Manager USA, and the carrier's highest official in this country stated:

> If you send back a ballot marked, "No union," or "Laker Airways," "Sir Freddie Laker," "Charles Maxwell," or the like, or if you deface the ballot or indicate you don't want any union to represent you, then your ballot will be marked "Void" and not counted. Casting a "void" ballot amounts to the same thing as not voting at all.
>
> This fact again makes it imperative for you not to vote at all if you don't want the Teamsters.
>
> I am aware that many employees have decided they want to have a "ballot-burning party" in order to keep ballots from being cast for the Teamsters. I am extremely gratified that this means so many of you believe we are on the right track here at Laker and that you want to keep any outsiders from

coming in and disrupting our work environment while they take your money to sustain the lifestyle and fat salaries of Teamster bosses.

On the other hand, I am concerned that some of you while agreeing in principle with the ballot-burners, would like to keep your opinions private and to refrain from publicly displaying your views. You could simply tear your ballot up and throw it away. That would be just as effective as going to a ballot-burning party.

However, you could also send your ballot anonymously to Mark Hammer. This would probably be the most effective thing to do with your ballot, and would provide a safe solution if you are uncomfortable with destroying an official ballot. If Mark had a majority of the ballots we'd know for sure the Teamsters couldn't possibly win. Therefore, each of you will receive with your paycheck this week a stamped envelope addressed to Mark. Your name will not be on the envelope. If you don't want to go to a ballot-burning party or to destroy your ballot, when you get your ballot you can just put it in the envelope and mail it to Mark.

In any event, no matter how you decide to dispose of your ballot, you must remember that for the reasons I have described the only sure way to keep the Teamsters out is NOT TO VOTE AT ALL. Unlike elections for public office, in an election like the upcoming one the important thing is that you DON'T VOTE.

Mark Hammer is Laker's personnel manager. Envelopes were, in fact, distributed to employees with their paychecks.

On December 22, 1980, Sir Freddie Laker, Chairman and Managing Director of Laker Airways, sent a letter to employees in which he stated:

I earnestly urge you to demonstrate your continued support by *NOT VOTING FOR THEM!* Please hand your ballot in to us or destroy it, but *DON'T SEND IT BACK* to the Government. We all have too much to lose!

Laker supervisors received a number of ballots from employees, which they then forwarded to Hammer. Including those returned in the envelopes and those turned in to supervisors, Laker officials gained possession of 135 of the 189

ballots mailed to Passenger Service Employees, and 38 of the 51 ballots mailed to Office Clerical Employees. Thus, prior to the count date, carrier officials were in actual possession of 73 percent of the ballots in the two cases.

In view of the fact that Laker supervisors actually received ballots from individual employees and in view of the Board's conclusions below, it is unnecessary to determine whether Laker kept a list of names of employees who turned in ballots, or actively solicited ballots through personal interviews with employees.

III.

IBT contends that Laker officials sent employees home to retrieve their ballots, with pay. Laker asserts that any employee who went home with pay for this purpose did so without its knowledge, but notes that in any event employees received a paid lunch hour.

In view of the Board's conclusions with respect to the other evidence in this case, it is unnecessary to determine whether employees were sent home to retrieve ballots.

IV.

IBT further alleges that a Laker supervisor contacted an employee at home to ask about his ballot.

Laker, in its affidavits, admits that a supervisor did ask an employee whether the employee had received this ballot, "as several employees had not received ballots and I wanted to be sure [the employee's] had reached him in his absence." The supervisor suggested that the employees either destroy the ballot or return it to the carrier.

V.

Wages, benefits, and working conditions have improved dramatically at Laker in 1980. Salaries increased by some 40 percent, including a 12½ percent increase just prior to the mailing of the ballots.

In December 1979, Laker announced a policy of automatic increases in wages every time the consumer price index (CPI) rose 5 percent, plus merit increases on an individual basis each June 1 and December 1.

The December 1, 1980, increase was composed of 5 percent for the CPI and 7½ percent for "merit." The merit increase for that month, unlike earlier merit increases, was given to all employees across-the-board. The carrier concedes that this represented a conscious change in policy on the part of Laker.

VI.

Laker alleges or implies that the IBT harassed supervisors, broke into its offices on several occasions, and stole lists of employee names and addresses and employee performance evaluations. These allegations are irrelevant to the issue presented, and no evidence of any kind has been presented to link the IBT to the break-ins and thefts.

Laker further asserted that it collected ballots because of a fear that the IBT or its supporters would get hold of and cast ballots from employees who did not wish to vote. In spite of a request by Mr. Watkins for evidence of any such activity, Laker produced nothing to support this fear. Following Mr. Watkins' request, counsel for Laker filed a Freedom of Information Act (FOIA) request for the names of employees who had requested duplicate ballots "to determine whether fraudulent requests for duplicate ballots have been made..." This request was denied in order to preserve the confidentiality of the employees' representation desires.

DISCUSSION
I.

The Railway Labor Act gives employees of carriers the right to organize and select a representative without interference, influence, or coercion by the carrier.

The Board has the duty under Section 2, Ninth, of the Act, when ascertaining who shall represent employees in any craft or class for the purposes of the Act, to "insure" that the method used is such as to guarantee to the employees the opportunity to make such choice free of interference, influence, or coercion by the carrier. Whether the Board uses the device of a secret ballot or any other means to determine the desire of the employees as to who should represent them, the Board must conduct such proceedings in an atmosphere free of any interference or other conduct by the carrier that would tend to interfere with, influence, or coerce the employees in their choice.

The terms "interference," "influence," and "coercion" were defined by the Supreme Court shortly after the Act became law. In *Texas and New Orleans R. Co. v. Bro. of Railway and Steamship Clerks*, 281 U.S. 548 (1930), the court stated:

> It is thus apparent that Congress, in the legislation of 1926, while elaborating a plan for amicable adjustments and voluntary arbitration of disputes between common carriers and their employees, thought it necessary to impose, and did impose, certain definite obligations enforceable by judicial proceedings. The question before us is whether a legal obligation of this sort is also to be found in the provisions of subdivision third of Section 2 of the act providing that "Representatives, for the purposes of this Act, shall be designated by the respective parties ... without interference influence, or coercion exercised by either party over the self-organization or designation of representatives by the other."
>
> It is at once to be observed that Congress was not content with the general declaration of the duty of carriers and employees to make every reasonable effort to enter into and maintain agreements concerning rates of pay, rules, and working conditions, and to settle disputes with all expedition in conference between authorized representatives, but added this distinct prohibition against coercive measures. This addition can not be treated as superfluous or insignificant, or as intended to be without effect. While an affirmative declaration of duty contained in a legislative enactment may be of imperfect obligation because not enforceable in terms; a definite statutory prohibition of conduct which would thwart the declared purpose of the legislation cannot be disregarded. The intent of Congress is clear with respect to the sort of conduct that is prohibited. "Interference" with freedom of action and "coercion" refer to well-understood concepts of the law. The meaning if the word "influence" in this clause may be gathered from the context. Noscitur a sociis. The use of the word is not to be taken as interdicting the normal relations and innocent communications which are a part of all friendly intercourse, albeit between employer and employee. *"Influence" in this context plainly means pressure, the use of the authority or power of either party to induce action by the other in derogation of what the statute calls "self-organization." The phrase covers the abuse of relation or opportunity so as to corrupt or override the will, and it is no more difficult to appraise conduct of this sort of connection with the selection of representatives for the purpose of this Act than in relation to well-known applications of the law with respect to fraud, duress and undue influence.* If Congress intended that the prohibition, as thus construed, should be enforced, the Courts would encounter no difficulty in fulfilling its purpose, as the present suit demonstrates.

In reaching a conclusion as to the intent of Congress, the importance of the prohibition in its relation to the plan devised by the Act must have appropriate consideration. *Freedom of choice in the selection of representatives on each side of the dispute is the essential foundation of the statutory scheme.* All the proceedings looking to amicable adjustments and to agreements for arbitration of disputes, the entire policy of the Act, must depend for success on the un-coerced action of each party through its own representatives to the end that agreements satisfactory to both may be reached and the peace essential to the uninterrupted service of the instrumentalities of interstate commerce may be maintained. There is no impairment of the voluntary character of arrangements for the adjustment of disputes in the imposition of a legal obligation not to interfere with the free choice of those who are to make such adjustments. On the contrary, it is of the essence of a voluntary scheme, if it is to accomplish its purpose, that this liberty should be safeguarded. The definite prohibition which Congress inserted in the Act can not therefore be over-ridden in the view that Congress intended it to be ignored. As the prohibition was appropriate to the aim of Congress, and is capable of enforcement the conclusion must be that enforcement was contemplated.

Congress was not required to ignore this right of the employees but could safeguard it and seek to make their appropriate collective action an instrument of peace rather than of strife. Such collective action would be a mockery if representation were made futile by interferences with freedom of choice. Thus the prohibition by Congress of interference with the selection of representatives for the purpose of negotiation and conference between employers and employees, instead of being an invasion of the constitutional right of either, was based on the recognition of the rights of both. . . . The Railway Labor Act of 1926 does not interfere with the normal exercise of the right of the carrier to select its employees or to discharge them. The statute is not aimed at this right of the employers but at the interference with the right of employees to have representatives of their own choosing. *As the carriers subject to the Act have no constitutional right to interfere with the freedom of the employees in making their selections,* they cannot complain of the statute

on constitutional grounds. [Citations omitted, emphasis added].

The weaknesses of the 1926 Act led to the enactment in 1934, of certain amendments, including Section 2, Third, Fourth, and Ninth. In *Virginia Ry Co. v. System Federation no. 40,* 300 U.S. 515 (1937), the Supreme Court discussed the impact of these amendments on the right of self-organization.

The prohibition against such interference was continued and made more explicit by the amendment of 1934. [The carrier] does not challenge that part of the decree which enjoins any interference by it with the free choice of representatives by its employees. . . . That contention is not open to it in view of our decision in the [*Texas and N.O. Ry. v.*] Railway Clerks case, supra, and of the unambiguous language of §2, Third, and Fourth, of the Act as amended.

Cases since then have limited the scope of judicial review of the Board's actions under Section 2, Ninth, of the Act. *Switchmen's Union of North America v. NMB,* 320 U.S. 297 (1934). At the same time, the right and power of the Board to insure free representation elections has been affirmed.

Thus, in *Aircraft Mechanics Fraternal Assn. v. United Airlines,* 406 F. Supp. 492 (ND Cal. 1976), the court held that a complaint of interference was properly a matter for the Board, not the Federal courts. In addition, the Court noted that a finding of illegal influence by the board is binding on the courts. id. at fn. 11. *See also, Texidor v. Ceresa,* 590 F. 2d 357 (1st Cir. 1978).

Thus, the problem before the Board is to determine whether or not there was conduct on the part of the Carrier in this proceeding that prevented the employees from participating in a representation election free from interference, influence, coercion. The test in any case of alleged interference in a Board election is whether the laboratory conditions which the Board seeks to promote have been contaminated. *Zantop International Airlines,* 6 NMB no. 1247 (1979). The essential facts to such a determination were established by the parties' statements and affidavits, and are not in dispute.

II.

We turn now to a discussion of the specific actions of Laker and its officials.

A.

In all mail ballot elections conducted by the Board, ballots are sent to the home address of the employees using address labels supplied by the carrier. Employees are free to vote in the privacy of their own homes, without being subject to pressure from carrier or union officials. No one except employees of the National Mediation Board knows who voted in the election. No one, including the Board's employees, knows how the voters who do cast ballots actually marked their ballots. To vote for representation the employee simply marks the ballot and returns the properly attested envelope with the ballot enclosed to the Board. To vote against representation, the employee need only refrain from voting.

Laker admits that it actively solicited employees to turn in their ballots to the carrier. Stamped envelopes were provided with employees' paychecks for this purpose. Supervisors collected ballots from individuals.

Laker asserts that these actions were necessary to prevent IBT officials and supporters from collecting and returning ballots of nonsupporters, which ballots would be marked in favor of the IBT. It asserts that this Board would not cooperate to prevent this fraud because it would not check each signature on the attest portion of the return envelope.

The rationale given by Laker to support its conduct is patently transparent. No proof has been forthcoming which indicates even the threat of tampering by the union, in spite of a request by a Board representative for evidence of any election fraud. Instead, the carrier has created the specter of fraud and forgery out of whole cloth.

The Board mails ballots to employees' homes in order to avoid the problems envisioned by Laker. Given this safeguard, it is no business of the carrier or the organization whether or how any employee votes or does not vote. Nothing submitted by Laker indicates that employees were subject to undue influence from the union which would amount to election fraud. Had any evidence been produced, the Board would have undertaken an appropriate investigation, including a comparison of signatures.

Employees can not exercise their right to self-organization in an atmosphere where their employer seeks to control the outcome through the pressure evident in this case. Even employees who would otherwise simply throw their ballots in the trash feel compelled to turn them in as an act of "loyalty." The coercive effect of the carrier's actions is heightened when the FOIA request for names of employees requesting duplicate ballots is considered.

Furthermore, the actions of a supervisor in calling an employee at home to be sure he had received a ballot, because of the supervisor's concern that some employees had not received ballots, indicates that the carrier was keeping a close watch on the employees. If the supervisor knew who had not received ballots, the Board must conclude that she had that knowledge because she was keeping track of that information. See, e.g. *General Shoe Corp.*, 77 NLRB 124 (1948).

Given the procedure used in Board election requiring that the majority of eligible employees cast valid ballots for representation in order for there to be a certification, soliciting employees to turn in their ballots to the carrier is analogous to polling employees about their views. The National Labor Relations Board has developed a test for the lawfulness of polling which is helpful in considering Laker's conduct. The NLRB held, in *Struksnes Construction Co.,* 165 NLRB 1062 (1967), that:

> Absent unusual circumstances, the polling of employees by an employer will violate Section 8(a)(1) of the Act unless the following safe guards are observed: (1) the purpose of the poll is to determine the truth of a union's claim of majority, (2) this purpose is communicated to the employees, (3) assurances against reprisal are given, (4) the employees are polled by secret ballot, and (5) the employer has not engaged in unfair labor practices or otherwise created a coercive atmosphere.

The NLRB adopted this test in order to balance employer-employee interests. However, the Board went on to hold that:

> … a poll taken while a petition for a Board election is pending does not, in our view, serve any legitimate interest of the employer that would not be better served by the forthcoming Board election. In accordance with long-established Board policy, therefore, such polls will continue to violate the Act.

The NLRB's reasoning applies with even greater force when an election is actually under way and employees are deciding whether they wish to be represented. In the circumstances of the cases before us, nothing justified any form of polling. See also *NLRB v. I. M. Machinery Corp.*, 410 F. 2d 587 (5th Cir. 1969), fn. 3.

The Board holds that it is a *per se* violation of the Railway Labor Act for any carrier or its officials to solicit employees to turn their ballots in to the carrier. It is, furthermore, a *per se* violation to provide mailing envelopes for this purpose, and this violation is compounded when such envelopes are distributed with paychecks. It is a violation of the Act, under the circumstances present here, to keep track of which employees do or do not have ballots, and to thereby give the impression of surveillance. It is a *per se* violation to poll employees during a representation election conducted by this Board. Finally, it is a *per se* violation for a supervisor to personally receive a ballot from an employee under any circumstances, and without regard to the "voluntariness" with which it is turned over.

B.

In December 1980, Laker granted all employees a 5 percent cost of living increase and a 7½ percent "merit increase." While the cost of living increase was consistent with a year-old carrier policy, the merit increase was a radical departure from past policy. Instead of giving individual merit increases based upon employee evaluations, Laker made a conscious decision to give all employees a significant, across-the-board increase. Since counsel for Laker was in almost daily contact with the Board, Laker must be deemed to have known that a craft or class determination and finding of a dispute were imminent. In addition, counsel for Laker knew that ballots would likely be mailed in December 1980.

Under the circumstances, the Board concludes that the timing, amount, and nature of the merit increase were deliberately set to influence employees and to convey the idea that a union was unnecessary.

The offer of benefits to influence the outcome of an organizing campaign is a violation of the Railway Labor Act. As the court held in *Union of Professional Airmen v. Alaska Aeronautical Industries*, 95 LRRM 2868 (D. Ak. 1977):

> The court further finds that the offer to the employees of increased benefits during their organizational process may well interfere with their union efforts. While the benefits were not mandatory *it is the mere offer* which tends to undermine their activity. Accordingly, these activities on the part of [the carrier] also appear to be in violation of the Railway Labor Act, supra, and must cease. (Emphasis supplied.)

If the mere offer of benefits during an organizational campaign violates the Act, a fortiori, the granting of benefits almost contemporaneous with an election violates the Act.

This holding is consistent with the longest-established precedents of the National Labor Relations Board and the Supreme Court. In *NLRB v. Exchange Parts Co.*, 375 U.S. 405 (1964), the Court found the employer guilty of an unfair labor practice where it granted a permanent, unconditional wage increase in order to affect the outcome of the representation election, even though the employer was not charged with any other unfair labor practices. The court held:

> We think the Court of Appeals was mistaken in concluding that the conferral of employee benefits while a representation election is pending, for the purposes of inducing employees to vote against the union, does not "interfere with" the protected right to organize.
>
> . . . We have no doubt that [the National Labor Relations Act] prohibits not only intrusive threats and promises but also conduct immediately favorable to employee which is undertaken with the express purpose of impinging upon their freedom of choice for or against unionization and is reasonably calculated to have that effect.
>
> The danger inherent in well-timed increases in benefits is the suggestion of a fist inside the velvet glove. Employees are not likely to miss the inference that the source of benefits now conferred is also the source from which future benefits must flow and which may dry up if it is not obliged. The danger may be diminished if as in this case the benefits are conferred permanently and unconditionally. But the absence of conditions or threats pertaining to the particular benefits conferred would be of controlling significance only if it could be presumed that no question of additional benefits or renegotiation of existing benefits would arise in the future; and, of course, no such presumption is tenable. . . . The beneficence of an employer is likely to be ephemeral if prompted by a threat of unionization which is subsequently removed. Insulating the right of collective organization from calculated good will of this sort deprives employees of little that has lasting value.

See, also, *NLRB v. Crown Can Co.*, 138 F. 2d 263 (8th Cir. 1943); cert. denied 321 U.S. 769 (1944).

III.

Having determined that Laker has violated the Act in at least six ways, the question of an appropriate remedy must be resolved.

A.

The Board is not unmindful of Laker's constitutional right to communicate its views to its employees. However, this right is not without limit, and even conduct which is otherwise lawful may justify remedial action when it interferes with a representation election. *General Shoe Corp.*, supra.

The federal government has successfully prosecuted, under the criminal provisions of the Act, a carrier and its officials for, inter alia, soliciting the employees to turn in their ballots. Although the convictions were reversed on a legal technicality, *U.S. v. Winston*, 558 F. 2d 105 (2nd Cir. 1977), the case illustrates the serious nature of this type of conduct.

The Board views Laker's admitted conduct as among the most egregious violations of employee rights in memory. Rarely has a carrier waged such a deliberate campaign designed to override employee free exercise of the rights guaranteed by the Act. Extraordinary remedies are required to overcome Laker's violations and to restore conditions which will permit a free election.

B.

It is obvious that the original elections must be set aside. Since Laker collected almost three-quarters of the ballots mailed by the Board, counting those ballots which were returned would be futile. New elections must be conducted in an atmosphere free of unlawful conduct.

In addition, steps must be taken to provide both the employees and the carrier with an incentive to comply with democratic procedures. The new election must therefore encourage maximum employee participation, and provide complete safeguarding of ballots and polling procedures.

The Board has traditionally required that a majority of eligible voters cast valid ballots in order for a representative to be certified. However, it is clear that such a procedure is not required by the Act. For example, in 1935 the Board stated:

... the Board interpreted [Section 2, Fourth of the Act] as requiring a majority of all those eligible rather than a majority of the votes only. The interpretation was made, however, not on the basis of legal opinion and precedents, but on what seemed to the Board best from an administration point of view. Where, however, the parties to a dispute agreed among themselves that they would be bound by a majority of the votes cast, the Board took the position that it would certify on this basis, on the ground that the Board's duties

in these cases are to settle disputes among employees, and when an agreement is reached the dispute as to that matter is settled.

First Annual Report of the National Mediation Board (Fiscal Year 1935), at 19.

The Board then noted, id. at 20, that a court challenge had been made to the voting procedure it had adopted. When that challenge reached the Supreme Court, the Court held that a union need not receive the votes of a majority of those eligible in order to be certified. *Virginia Ry Co., supra.* The Court reasoned that those who do not participate are presumed to assent to the expressed will of those who do, and that "[t]here is the added danger that the absence of eligible voters may be due less to their indifference than to coercion by their employer." id. Later decisions involving the National Labor Relations Board held that less than a majority of eligibles could elect a representative where the organization certified received a majority of the votes cast. See, *NLRB v. Standard Lime & Stone Co.*, 149 F. 2d 435 (4th Cir. 1945); *cert. den.* 326 U.S. 723 (1945).

In 1947, in response to challenges to the Board's requirement that a majority of those eligible cast valid ballots, the Board sought the opinion of the Attorney General as to whether it had the power to certify a union where less than a majority of eligibles voted. The Attorney General replied:

... it is my opinion that the National Mediation Board has the power to certify a representative which receives a majority of the votes cast at an election despite the fact that less than a majority of those eligible to vote participated in the election. While the National Mediation Board has this power, it need not exercise it automatically upon finding that a majority of those participating were in favor of a particular representative. *Op. Atty. Gen.* (September 9, 1947).

The Board continued its prior practices, which were upheld in *Radio Officers Union v. NMB*, 181 F. 2d 801 (D.C. Cir. 1950), relying in part on the Attorney General's opinion in order to foster the stability in labor-management relations which the Act contemplates.

In *BRAC v. Assn. for the Benefit of Non-Contract Employees*. 380 U.S. 650 (1965), the Supreme Court upheld the form of the Board's ballot and the majority rule as being within the Board's discretion, noting that a failure to participate was treated as a vote against representation, under the Board's procedures in effect at that time.

Mail ballot elections have been favored because the voting population is generally a mobile one in the railroad and airline industries. In the instant cases, however, the employees are permanently based in only three cities, so that a ballot box election is feasible.

Under the circumstances of the present case, the Board finds that its usual election procedures will be unable to determine the true desires of Laker employees. This is because the factors normally existing in representation cases which support those procedures have been upset here by employer action. Therefore, exercising our discretion in representation matters. the Board concludes that a ballot box election is necessary and that the following ballot should be used:

Finally, to vitiate the clear violations of the law by Laker and to insure that there will no longer be incentives in cases such as this one for the employer to interfere with the free choice of its employees, the desires of the majority of those *actually casting valid ballots* will determine the outcome of the elections, whether or not a majority of those eligible participate in the elections. The action we take here should not be considered a precedent for the usual election situation, but is limited to situations where there is gross interference with a Board conducted election.

C.

Finally, employees must be reassured of the Board's determination to conduct a free election, and they must be fully informed of their rights under the Act and of the nature of the violations leading to the new elections. Copies of these "Findings Upon Investigation; Order" will be provided to all eligible employees. In addition, the carrier will be required to post notices assuring employees of their rights. The Notice is provided as an appendix to this decision.

D.

The remedies ordered in these cases are broad and, to some extent, innovative. However, like the NLRB, this Board has a statutory mandate to protect the right to self-organization. As the Court of Appeals stated in *Teamsters Local 115 v. NLRB*, Nos. 79-1619 and 79-2018, (D.C. Cir. 1981):

> The [National Labor Relations] Board has long struggled to accommodate the interests of employers and employees while assuring free choice of bargaining representatives. When one side or the other destroys the balance and creates a climate inimical to an un-

trammeled selection process, Congress intended the Board to exercise broad discretion in fashioning a remedy. The remedies chosen may or may not be sufficient to the task, but the Board is entitled to try all reasonable measures. The boundaries within which the Board may reasonably exercise its discretion will vary with the severity of the conduct and the needs that conduct creates. Quoted at *BNA Daily Labor Reporter*, February 6, 1981, at E-7.

This Board need not consider what other action may be required if the new elections are tainted. We trust they will be conducted under the democratic conditions required by the Act.

CONCLUSION

The Board finds that Laker has violated the right of its employees to self-organization free of interference, influence, or coercion.

It is Hereby Ordered That:

1. The prior elections in Case Nos. R-5131 and R-5132 are set aside.

2. Ballot Box elections are hereby authorized using a cut-off date of September 14, 1980. No follow-up mail ballot will be used.

3. The form of the ballot will provide "Do you desire to be represented by International Brotherhood of Teamsters, Airline Division?" with boxes marked "Yes" and "No." No write-in space will be provided. The majority of valid ballots actually cast will determine the outcome of the elections.

4. A copy of these Findings Upon Investigation; Order will be mailed to each eligible employee.

5. The carrier will immediately post the Notice attached hereto, and the Notice of Election, when issued, on each employee bulletin board. These materials will be posted until the next business day after the election.

By direction of the NATIONAL MEDIATION BOARD.

Rowland K Quinn Jr.

Executive Secretary

Copies furnished to:

Dennis A. Lalli, Esq.
Epstein Becker Borsody & Green, P.C.

Ronald M. Green, Esq.
Epstein Becker Borsody & Green, P.C.

Sir Freddie Laker, Chairman and Managing Director
Laker Airways Ltd.

Mr. Charles Maxwell, U.S. General Manager
Laker Airways Ltd.

Mr. Mark Hammer, Director of Personnel
Laker Airways Ltd.

Wilma B. Liebman, Esq.
International Brotherhood of Teamsters

Roland Wilder, Esq.
International Brotherhood of Teamsters

Mr. Norman Greene, Director National Airline Division
International Brotherhood of Teamsters

Copies furnished to:

Mr. William Genoese, Assistant Director
Teamsters Local Union no. 732

Mr. Alex Calder
Teamsters Local Union no. 732

All eligible employees in
Case Nos. R-5131 and R-5132
RKQ/dca

NOTICE TO ALL EMPLOYEES

PURSUANT TO FINDINGS UPON INVESTIGATION AND ORDER OF THE NATIONAL MEDIATION BOARD AND IN ORDER TO EFFECTUATE THE POLICIES OF THE RAILWAY LABOR ACT, AS AMENDED, WE HEREBY NOTIFY OUR EMPLOYEES THAT:

After an investigation conducted by the National Mediation Board in which we had the opportunity to present statements and evidence, the National Mediation Board found that the Carrier's conduct, taken as a whole, improperly interfered with employees' choice of representative under Section 2, Ninth, of the Act. It is unlawful for a carrier to interfere with the organization of its employees.

Section 2, Fourth of the Act, 45 U.S.C. §152, allows employees the right to select representatives without carrier influence or interference. That particular subsection reads as follows:

> No carrier, its officers or agents, shall deny or in any way question the right of its employee to join, organize, or assist in organizing the labor organization of their choice, and it shall be unlawful for any carrier to interfere in any way with the organization of its employees, or to use the funds of the carrier in maintaining or assisting or contributing to any labor organization, labor representative, or other agency of collective bargaining, *or in performing any work therefor, or to influence or coerce employees in an effort to induce them to join or remain or not to join or remain members of any labor organization. . . .*

Employee-carrier isolation with respect to an employee's choice of his collective bargaining representative is expressed in Section 2, General Purposes Clause of the Railway Labor Act. The subsection states that one of the purposes of the Railway Labor Act is "to provide for the complete independence of carriers and of employees in the matter of self organization."

Since the Board has found that the Carrier improperly interfered with the employees' choice of representation under the Railway Labor Act and has ordered re-run elections in NMB Case no. R-5131 (Office Clerical Employees) and NMB Case no. R-5132 (Passenger Service Employees) using a ballot box election:

> WE WILL NOT influence, interfere or coerce employees in any manner in an effort to induce them to participate or refrain from participating in the upcoming elections. All of our employees are free to express their desire to be represented by a labor organization or remain unrepresented.

> Laker Airways Ltd.

This notice must remain posted until the first business day following the elections, and must not be altered, defaced, or covered by any other material.

If any employees have any question concerning this notice or compliance with its provisions, they may communicate directly with the National Mediation Board, 1425 K Street, N.W., Washington, DC 20572, Telephone 202-623-6920.

Key Airlines, 16 NMB no. 88
Findings upon Investigation; Order to Show Cause
Case nos. R-5850, R-5855, and R-5869
April 19, 1989

In the Matter of the Application of the
INTERNATIONAL BROTHERHOOD OF
TEAMSTERS–AIRLINE DIVISION
alleging representation dispute pursuant to
Section 2, Ninth, of the Railway Labor Act
involving employees of
KEY AIRLINES

On December 9, 1988, the Board received an application filed by the International Brotherhood of Teamsters–Airline Division (IBT) pursuant to 45 U.S.C. §152, Ninth, alleging a representation dispute among Flight Attendants of Key Airlines Inc. (Key). The application was docketed as NMB Case no. R-5850. Subsequently on December 22, 1988, the Board received a representation application from the IBT for Flight Deck Crew Members at Key. This application was then amended to pertain to Pilots and Co-Pilots and Flight Engineers and these cases were respectively docketed as NMB Case Nos. R-5855 and R-5869.

At the time these IBT applications were filed, these employees were not represented by any organization or individual.

Mediator Joseph E. Anderson was assigned to investigate the case and during the investigation the IBT submitted evidence of carrier interference. A written response to the charges was filed with the Board by Key. Mediator Anderson and Hearing Officer David J. Strom were subsequently directed to examine the interference charges through interviews with certain Key employees as well as members of management.

ISSUE

The issue before the Board is whether Key violated the Act by interfering, influencing, or coercing employees in their choice of a representative.

CONTENTIONS

The IBT alleges that Key has engaged in "a pervasive pattern of interference, influence, or coercion" which has "tainted the laboratory conditions for a fair election." IBT further contends that "this conduct is deliberate, well planned, and orchestrated by high management officials" and that a Laker

ballot procedure is necessary to remedy the adverse effects of such carrier interference.

Key "denies the Teamsters' allegation of carrier interference and requests that they be summarily dismissed."

The specific IBT allegations and carrier responses are described below:

The IBT claims that the Carrier "has sought to make examples of one flight attendant and one pilot, both active and visible union adherents." The pilot was discharged by Key assertedly because he was discussing the benefits of unionization with two new flight attendants. The flight attendant was removed from flying the line and transferred from her duty station in Las Vegas, Nevada, to a clerical assignment in Herndon, Virginia. It is alleged that the purpose of this transfer and change of assignment was to "isolate an active union supporter from fellow flight attendants during this election period" and to make an example of her "to intimidate others to refrain from union activities."

The Carrier admits that the pilot was discharged as a result of his conversation with certain flight attendants but asserts that the pilot was "discharged for disparaging the Carrier while on duty in violation of Carrier policy and for unprofessional conduct." Key claims that its decision to remove the flight attendant from flying the line and to reassign her to a different duty station "was based solely on objective business considerations."

The Organization alleges that Key has conducted numerous one-on-one and group meetings with the flight attendants, pilots, and flight engineers. Key management is accused of having questioned certain employees about their own and other employees' "union sentiments or activities"; threatened that if the flight attendants unionize Key will merge with World Airways, its sister subsidiary, and that such merger would result in a loss of jobs for Key's flight attendants; threatened that if the flight attendants vote to unionize when the company starts its DC-10 operations, flight attendant work will be contracted out; and solicited and discussed employee grievances with flight attendants, flight engineers, and pilots.

Key claims that it did not conduct one-on-one meetings with employees concerning the union but rather "discussed the union situation with employees in voluntary, non-coercive settings." Key acknowledges that it "has discussed with employees the possibility of a merger of World Airways and Key, including the feasibility and efficiency of maintaining two carriers in the event of Teamsters representation at both carriers." Key maintains that these statements are "predictions based on objective facts" and are "unrelated to any retaliation for support of representation." With regard to the subcontracting of flight attendant DC-10 work, the Carrier states, "the flight attendants have been told that subcontracting of DC-10 flight attendant duties was an option being considered because of the complications related to the shifting of bases necessary in the first year of operations." Concerning the charge of solicitation of grievances, Key asserts that it has "discussed grievances with employees without promising any resolution thereof."

IBT also alleges that a pay raise, granted to pilots and flight engineers, was withheld from the flight attendants in order to discourage unionization and to send a message that flight attendants would have had a raise had they not filed a representation application. IBT further claims that Key has engaged in numerous acts of unlawful surveillance in a calculated effort to discourage organizing activity.

The Carrier responds that once it "had knowledge of the [flight attendants'] application, it might have been unlawful to grant a pay raise which had not previously been decided upon." Key distinguishes the raises granted to the pilots and flight engineers on the basis that "the new pay scale for flight deck crew members was restructured and finalized prior to the time the Company learned that an application [for these individuals] had been filed. . . ."

Concerning the IBT's contention of improper surveillance of employee organizing activities, the Carrier "denies that it has engaged in any form of unlawful surveillance of the employee's union activities."

On March 27, 1989, after the Organization's unsuccessful election results in R-5855 and R-5869 involving pilots and co-pilots and flight engineers, respectively, were known, the IBT renewed its earlier request for Laker balloting procedures in these cases. The Organization contends that in addition to the prior evidence submitted to the Board on carrier interference, "the result of the elections demonstrates that the carrier effectively undermined the union's organizing campaign."

Key is opposed to re-run elections in R-5855 and R-5869 because it believes the record does not support a finding of carrier interference.

FINDINGS OF LAW

Determination of the issues in this case is governed by the Railway Labor Act, as amended, 45 U.S.C. §151, et seq. Accordingly, the Board finds as follows:

I.

Section 201 of the Act, extends all of the provisions of Title I of the Act, except the provisions of Section 3, thereof, 45 U.S.C. §153, to "every common carrier engaged in interstate or foreign commerce . . . and every air pilot or other person who performs any work as an employee or subordinate official of such carrier, subject to its or their continuing authority to supervise and direct the manner of rendition of his service."

II.

Key is a common carrier by air as defined in 45 U.S.C. §181 of the Act.

III.

IBT is a labor organization and representative as provided by 45 U.S.C. §151, Sixth, and §152, Ninth of the Act.

IV.

Employee-carrier isolation with respect to an employee's choice of collective bargaining representative is expressed in Section 2, General Purposes Clause. The subsection states that one of the purposes of the Railway Labor Act is "to provide for the complete independence of carriers and of employees in the matter of self-organization."

V.

45 U.S.C. §152, Third, provides:

Representatives . . . shall be designated . . . *without interference, influence, or coercion* (emphasis added).

VI.

45 U.S.C. §152, Fourth, gives employees subject to its provisions "the right to organize and bargain collectively through representatives of their own choosing. The majority of any craft or class of employees shall have the right to determine who shall be the representative of the craft or class for the purposes of this chapter." This section also provides as follows:

No carrier, its officers or agents, shall deny or in any way question the right of its employees to join, organize, or assist in organizing the labor organization of their choice, and *it shall be unlawful for any carrier to interfere in any way with the organization of its employees . . . or to influence or coerce employees in an effort to induce them to join or remain or not to join or remain members of any labor organization. . . .* (emphasis added).

VII.

45 U.S.C. §152, Ninth, provides that the Board has the duty to investigate representation disputes and shall designate who may participate as eligible voters in the event an election is required. In determining the choice of the majority of employees, the Board is "authorized to take a secret ballot of the employees involved or to utilize any other appropriate method of ascertaining the names of their duly designated and authorized representatives by the employees *without interference, influence, or coercion exercised by the carrier*" (emphasis added).

FINDINGS OF FACT
I.

Key Airlines and World Airways (World) are subsidiaries of World Corp., and all three companies are based in Herndon, Virginia. Key's prior home office was in Las Vegas, Nevada, which to this date remains a major base of operations. The other primary base of Key's operations is Philadelphia, Pennsylvania.

Thomas Kolfenbach, who has been a Key employee since early 1986, is the Vice President and General Manager. His affidavit submitted to the Board states that "my responsibilities include primary authority for conduct of the Carrier's campaign resisting the Teamsters' organizing efforts."

II.

The IBT's organizing effort at Key commenced in May or June of 1988 when the union began holding employee meetings and distributing authorization cards to the Carrier's personnel.

III.

In July of 1988 Key responded to the IBT organizing drive by distributing anti-union literature and holding employee meetings. A letter from Mr. Kolfenbach dated July 13, 1988, and addressed to "Fellow Key Employees" states in part:

> We had previously planned employee meetings over the next several weeks. During these meetings we will have more to say about the subject of unionization.

One meeting took place on or about July 28, 1988, and was attended by approximately fifteen flight attendants as well as several cockpit crew members. Other smaller meetings, which were primarily attended by flight attendants,

took place at various times over the course of the summer.

The meetings, which were convened by senior management officials, were held for the express purpose of discouraging Key's employees from organizing. Among the subjects discussed by the Carrier at the meetings was the possible merger of Key with its sister subsidiary World Airways should Key's employees vote for IBT representation. In the event of such merger, Key has indicated at several of the meetings that its employees may well be adversely affected by the merger of seniority lists, as there are presently a number of senior World employees on furlough. It should be noted that the IBT represents flight deck crew members and flight attendants at World.

Additionally, in a letter from Mr. Kolfenbach dated July 21, 1988, to all Key flight crew members, the carrier makes the following statements:

> In closing, I would ask each of you to carefully consider whether or not you want to be a partner with an organization that has such a sordid reputation as the Teamsters. Ask yourself the following questions: Why do the Teamsters have an interest in you? Is it because they want you to grow within the organization? Do they want to see you retain your job? (Several hundred people are currently on furlough at World.) Do they want to see you upgraded? . . . Is it really a fair deal for you or do they want to help the unemployed crew members at World Airways at your expense?

Another subject discussed by the Carrier during these meetings was the possible subcontracting of DC-10 flight attendant duties when that new service commenced. At the time these statements were made, the Carrier indicated that the final decision was pending. Subsequently, on March 1, 1989, the Carrier decided to allow its flight attendants to bid on the DC-10 work.

IV.

Since December of 1988 and through January, February, and into March of 1989 Key has repeatedly sent senior management personnel, including its Vice President, to meet with employees during their layover. Approximately eight such meetings took place. These meetings were typically conducted in informal settings and the subjects discussed have included the potential merger with World Airways and the sub-contracting of DC-10 flight attendant work should Key's flight attendants vote to unionize. The express purpose of the meetings, which were a result of the IBT organizing drive, was to discourage unionization. In addition, Key has continued to communicate with its flight deck crew employees by letters including one dated February 22, 1989, which contain sharp criticism of the "Teamsters." The Board notes the conspicuous involvement of Key's highest officials including the Vice President and General Manager in these activities.

V.

The Carrier denies that any one-on-one employee meetings have taken place. However, the IBT has submitted evidence to the contrary.

VI.

On December 21, 1988, Key called an employee meeting in Herndon, Virginia, which was attended by roughly 30 flight attendants, flight engineers, and pilots. At the meeting Key's General Manager and Vice President, Tom Kolfenbach, stated that pay raises would be given to all flight deck crew members, except the flight attendants.[1] Mr. Kolfenbach announced that the flight attendants would not receive pay raises because of the pending IBT representation application and because such raises could constitute unlawful interference. In explaining why the flight attendants would not be granted a raise, Mr. Kolfenbach singled out and pointed to flight attendant Mary Cook and suggested that the employees ask her as she was an avid union supporter. Mr. Kolfenbach admits to making such statements.

On December 22, 1988, one day later, Key convened a similar meeting at its Las Vegas, Nevada, base. With the exception of the flight engineers, this was the first pay raise granted by Key in well over two years, and the raise was not part of a regularly scheduled program of salary increases.

VII.

On December 16, 1988, flight attendant Mary Cook, who has been employed with Key for six years, was reassigned from her Las Vegas base to Herndon, Virginia, to perform certain office "projects." At the time the assignment was made, the Carrier knew that Mary Cook was "one of the leading union adherents." Key states that Mary was chosen because of her experience with the company. This assignment consisted of such tasks as "revision of flight attendant recurrent training examinations, creation of policies for morale enhancement

and motivational slogans, revision of weight and grooming programs . . . and proofreading of the revised flight attendant manual." Mary Cook was not pleased with the transfer and, according to the Carrier "from the time she arrived in Herndon, Cook began complaining about her assignment, and was unproductive and uncooperative." Despite the fact that in the Carrier's own words Mary Cook did not seem to be working out at this assignment, Key acknowledges to making "numerous subsequent attempts to have Cook . . . complete her assignment" in Herndon.

Before the assignment was completed, Mary Cook was put on medical leave and returned to Las Vegas, Nevada. As of the present time, she remains on medical leave. It is not clear whether the tasks assigned to Mary Cook in Herndon have subsequently been completed by another individual.

VIII.

Tony Russell, a pilot with twenty years' experience, has served as a co-pilot at Key for eighteen months. In mid-1988, Mr. Russell was recommended for an upgrade to Captain by the Chief Pilot and other Captains who had flown with him. Without prior warning and on the day the NMB mediator conducted his field investigation of the instant case, January 12, 1989, Mr. Russell was discharged.

The Carrier states that Russell was fired because on January 8, 1989, he engaged in a discussion with two new flight attendants which "upset the flight attendants and left them with a negative overall impression of the Carrier." The IBT has submitted evidence which indicates that Mr. Russell and the flight attendants were discussing how the union could be helpful to establishing such practices as duty time limits. No members of the public were present when this conversation took place.

Mr. Russell had no prior disciplinary record with Key Airlines and appears to have been held in high regard by his colleagues. There is no evidence in the record that any Key employee other than Russell has been discharged for a similar infraction. A reinstatement action, which alleges that Mr. Russell was improperly discharged for organizing activities, has been filed in Federal court.

IX.

On February 13, 1989, the Organization requested that the Board proceed and conduct elections in the pilot and co-pilot and the flight engineers crafts or classes (R-5855 and R-5869), notwithstanding the pending charges of carrier interference. This request was made "without prejudice to our right to raise the *Laker* arguments at the conclusion of the elections, should that be necessary." On March 23, 1989, the ballots were counted in R-5855 and R-5869 with the following results:

Number of Employees Voting (R-5855)

	No. of Employees		
	IBT	ALPA	Eligible
Pilots and Co-pilots	9	1	39

Number of Employees Voting (R-5869)

	No. of Employees	
	IBT	Eligible
Flight Engineers	8	22

Subsequently, on March 27, 1989, the Organization filed a letter with the Board which stated in relevant part:

> The results of the elections demonstrate that the carrier effectively undermined the Union's organizing campaigns.
>
> Accordingly, the Union hereby requests that the Board conclude its investigation of the carrier's interference, invalidate those elections, whose results were tainted by carrier misconduct, and order new elections utilizing *Laker* balloting procedures.

In support of its request for re-run elections by *Laker* ballot, the IBT's letter of March 27, 1989, incorporated by reference its earlier allegations, with supporting documentation, of carrier interference.

DISCUSSION
I.

These cases are disturbingly similar to a prior Board action concerning this Carrier involving charges of improper carrier interference. Just three years ago in *Key Airlines*, 13 NMB 153 (1986), the Board found that Key had violated the pilots and co-pilots and flight engineers' freedom of choice of a representative when, among other things, two individuals involved in union activities were summarily forced to resign, and employees were polled on their support for the union. As a remedy for carrier interference in the prior case, the Board conducted elections by *Laker* ballot, but the organization was unsuccessful in garnering sufficient votes for certification.

The Board's consideration of all the facts and circumstances present here in view of the applicable legal standards strongly supports the conclusion that Key has again engaged in a carefully designed and calculated campaign to interfere with, influence, and coerce its employees in their choice of a representative.

II.

The employees' right to organize and select a representative without interference, influence, or coercion is expressly provided in at least three provisions of the Railway Labor Act—Section 2, Third, Fourth, and Ninth, as well as the General Purposes Clause, Section 151a(3). In the context of a representation dispute and pursuant to Section 2, Ninth, of the Act, the Board is specially empowered with the authority for assuring that employees are provided the opportunity to choose a representative free from the taint of carrier interference. See *Mid-Pacific Airlines*, 13 NMB 178 (1986); *Key Airlines*, 13 NMB 153 (1986); and *Laker Airways Ltd.* 8 NMB 236 (1981).

The test used by the Board in evaluating instances of alleged carrier interference is whether the "laboratory conditions" which the Board seeks to promote in representation elections have been contaminated. See *Metroflight Inc.*, 13 NMB 284 (1986); *Key Airlines*, supra; *Mid-Pacific Airlines*, supra; *Laker Airways Ltd.*, supra; and *Zantop International Airlines*, 6 NMB 834 (1979). Where the Board finds interference in the employees' freedom of choice, the NMB has devised remedies to purge the taint and ensure a fair election. In the past, the Board has used the Laker ballot to remedy such infractions. However, the Board's remedial powers are not limited to such ballot procedures. See *Norfolk & Portsmouth Belt Line Railroad*, 16 NMB 162 (1989). See generally *Metroflight*, supra; *Key Airlines*, supra: *Rio Airways*, 11 NMB 75 (1983); *Mercury Services*, 9 NMB 312 (1982); and *Laker Airways Ltd,* supra. The Board is mindful that in an appropriate case reliance on authorization cards alone could result in certification. See *NLRB v. Gissell Packaging Co.*, 395 US 575 (1969).

From this vantage point the Board turns to the case at hand.

III.

With respect to the discharge of Tony Russell and the reassignment of Mary Cook, the Board does not find the Carrier's explanation credible. Key states that the reason for terminating Tony Russell was that he expressed negative opinions about the company to other employees. These statements occurred in the context of a union organizing drive. Tony Russell had a solid employment record and no history of prior disciplinary action with the company. He received the maximum punishment possible, discharge, for an alleged violation of Carrier policy for which no other employee has ever been similarly disciplined. As in the prior *Key* case, the termination occurred in the midst of the Board's field investigation, just before formal NMB election procedures were to commence and at a crucial juncture in the employees' organizing campaign. The effect was to send a threatening message to all Key employees concerning the possible consequences of voicing support for a union.

Only a few days after the IBT's representation application was filed, Mary Cook was reassigned from one of Key's major bases of operation, Las Vegas, Nevada, to an office job in Herndon, Virginia. Cook's transfer had the effect of severely limiting her exposure to other flight attendants. The carrier admits that it knew Mary Cook was an "avid union supporter" and even singled her out as such at a company meeting on December 21, 1988. While Key has gone to elaborate lengths to economically justify her reassignment, the Board finds that the Carrier intended to isolate this union supporter from her co-workers and thus interfere with its employees' organizing efforts.

IV.

The Carrier's explanation that it was denying a pay raise to the flight attendants because it did not want to engage in improper interference during an election campaign but was granting such a raise to pilots and flight engineers who had not yet filed an application, is under these circumstances implausible. The raises were not part of a regularly scheduled increase. Just as the offer of benefits during an organizing campaign may constitute improper interference, so may the denial of benefits. In the flight attendant situation, the impact of the Carrier's actions was to place the blame on the union for the denial of the pay increase. The pay increase for the pilots, co-pilots, and flight engineers, one day before the representation application for these individuals was filed, was a calculated attempt to improperly undermine the union's organizing drive and curry the employees' favor. The key distinction in each case is that a representation application for the flight attendants had already been filed, whereas the petition for the pilots and flight engineers had not yet been filed. Thus, the denial of the wage increase to

the flight attendants could naturally be expected to be seen as a penalty for showing union support; whereas the granting of wage increases to the pilots and flight engineers could be expected to be seen as a benefit for not filing and a threat against filing.

The evidence is clear that Key was aware of the IBT's organizing drive since at least early July of 1988, well before the wage increases were given on December 21, 1988. From that date onward until the conclusion of the election, laboratory conditions must be maintained.

In *NLRB v. Exchange Parts Co.*, 375 US 405 at 409 (1964), the United States Supreme Court explained the impact of such a grant of benefits:

> The danger inherent in well-timed increases and benefits is the suggestion of a fist inside a velvet glove. The employees are not likely to miss the inference that the source of benefits now conferred is also the source from which future benefits must flow and which may dry up if it is not obliged.

Thus, Key's handling of the pay raises amount to improper interference in the employees' representation drive.

V.

The Board is deeply troubled by Key's repeated statements concerning the possible merger with World Airways and the sub-contracting of flight attendant work should Key's employees vote to unionize. Implicit in these statements is the thinly veiled threat that the future job security of Key Airlines' employees would be at stake should they vote to be represented. While the carrier maintains that such statements "are based upon objective facts related to economic efficiencies," the Board finds otherwise. Indeed, these communications reasonably tended to convey the impression that a vote for unionization by Key's employees could lead to the loss of jobs by Key personnel.

VI.

The Board finds that Key's conduct here amount to egregious interference and that the NMB's usual election procedures will be ineffective for determining the true representation desires of Key's employees. This is the second time in three years that Key has engaged in improper interference, and, indeed, Key has here repeated many of the same coercive acts taken in the prior case. The effects of the Carrier's interference on a work-force as small as Key's are certain to have pervaded the entire complement of flight crew employees. Based on the foregoing determinations of carrier interference, the Board finds that re-run elections are necessary for NMB Case nos. R-5855 and R5869 involving pilots and co-pilots and flight engineers, respectively, and special election procedures are required in all three crafts or classes in order to protect the rights of the employees to exercise their franchise rights independent of carrier interference.

The Board notes that the *Laker* ballot procedure has not proved to be an effective remedy for cases where there is serious and repeated carrier interference such as this. That is because in those situations the *Laker* ballot does not restore to the voters the desired "laboratory conditions." While the *Laker* ballot may still be an appropriate remedy in certain instances of carrier interference, it has not been effective in egregious cases. The Board's remedial authority in this area is expressly provided in Section 2, Ninth of the Act which states that in investigating representation disputes the Board "shall be authorized to take a secret ballot of the employees involved, or to utilize *any other appropriate method . . . as shall insure the choice of representatives by the employees without interference, influence or coercion exercised by the Carrier*" (emphasis added).

Therefore, further remedial steps beyond the *Laker* ballot may be necessary to help provide a climate where the employees can freely express their representational desires. Towards this end, the Board hereby issues an order to show cause why it should not utilize a ballot procedure in which the IBT–Airline Division will be certified unless a majority of the eligible voters return votes opposing IBT representation. No space for write-in votes would be provided. This is the first time such a ballot procedure will be utilized, and in the interest of soliciting the participants' views, the Board is issuing a show cause order. Responses to the show cause order should be limited solely to the question of the Board's proposed ballot procedure and not to the aforementioned findings of carrier interference.

The Board will further require that the Carrier post, and each flight attendant, flight engineer, and pilot and co-pilot receive a notice which states that the NMB has found that Key has engaged in improper carrier interference. Such notice will state that the employees have a right to organize free of carrier interference and that Key will not interfere with such rights. The notice is intended to inform the employees of their rights under the Act, of the Board's determination

to conduct a free election, and of the nature of the Carrier's violations. Under Section 2, Tenth of the Act, conduct described herein may be the subject of criminal prosecution. Accordingly, the Board, as it has traditionally, weighs its responsibilities with respect to those who have prosecutorial authority.

CONCLUSION

The Board finds that Key has violated the rights of its employees to self-organization free of interference, influence, or coercion.

It is Hereby Ordered That:

1. An all-mail ballot election is authorized for the craft or class of flight attendants using a cut-off date of December 28, 1988. Re-run elections for the flight engineers and pilots and co-pilots are authorized as well using the same cut-off date.

2. The participants respond within ten calendar days of this decision to show cause why the Board should not use a ballot which will provide "Are you opposed to representation by the International Brotherhood of Teamsters–Airline Division?" with a box for the employee to so vote if he or she chooses. An employee that desires representation by the IBT need not return a ballot. No write-in space would be provided. Unless a majority of the eligible employees vote *against representation* by the IBT, that organization would be certified. Responses to the show cause order must be limited to the form of the ballot and not to the merits of the Board's findings of carrier interference.

3. The Carrier will provide the Board with a set of gummed, alphabetized address labels for all eligible flight attendants, flight engineers, and pilots and co-pilots within three business days of receipt of this decision.

4. The designated Carrier official shall sign and return the attached notice by pre-paid express mail to the NMB within three business days of its receipt. Copies of the notice and Findings Upon Investigation will be mailed to each eligible flight attendant, flight engineer, and pilot and co-pilot with their ballot.

5. The Carrier will immediately sign and post the attached notice as well as the Notice of Election, when issued, on each employee bulletin board. These materials will be posted until the next business day after the election.

By direction of the National Mediation Board.

Charles R. Barnes
Executive Director

—Attachment—

Copies to:
Mr. Clifford E. Farnham
Mr. William F. Genoese
Mr. Marvin L. Griswold
Mr. Ray Benning
Bruce Friedman, Esq.
Wilma Liebman, Esq.
Mr. Thomas Kolfenbach

NOTICE TO ALL EMPLOYEES

Pursuant to Findings Upon Investigation and Order of the National Mediation Board and in Order to Effectuate the Policies of the Railway Labor Act, As Amended, We Hereby Notify Our Employees That:

After an investigation conducted by the National Mediation Board in which we had the opportunity to present statements and evidence, the National Mediation Board found that the Carrier's conduct, taken as a whole, improperly interfered with employees' choice of representative under Section 2, Ninth, of the Act. It is unlawful for a carrier to interfere with the organization of its employees.

Section 2, Fourth of the Act, 45 U.S.C. §152, allows employees the right to select representatives without carrier influence or interference. That particular subsection reads as follows:

No carrier, its officers, or agents shall deny or in any way question the right of its employees to join, organize, or assist in organizing the labor organization of their choice, and it shall be unlawful for any carrier to interfere in any way with the organization of its employees, or to use the funds of the carrier in maintaining or assisting or contributing to any labor organization, labor representative, *or other agency of collective bargaining, or in performing any work therefor, or to influence or coerce employees in an effort to induce them to join or remain or not to join or remain members of any labor organization. . . .*

Section 2, General Purposes Clause of the Railway Labor Act, states that one of the purposes of the Railway Labor Act is "to provide for the complete independence of carriers and of employees in the matter of self organizations."

WE WILL NOT influence, interfere or coerce employees in any manner in an effort to induce them to participate or refrain from participating in the upcoming elections.

All of our employees are free to express their desire to be represented by a labor organization or remain unrepresented.

Key Airlines Inc.
Thomas Kolfenbach
Vice President/Manager

This notice must remain posted until the first business day following the elections and must not be altered, defaced, or covered by any other material.

If any employees have any question concerning this notice or compliance with its provisions, they may communicate directly with the National Mediation Board, 1425 K Street, N.W., Washington, DC 20572, Telephone 202-523-5920.

America West Airlines Inc., 16 NMB no. 38
Findings upon Investigation—
Authorization of Election
Case no. R-5817
January 5, 1989

In the Matter of the Application of the
ASSOCIATION OF FLIGHT ATTENDANTS
alleging a representation dispute pursuant to Section 2, Ninth, of the Railway Labor Act, as amended involving employees of
AMERICA WEST AIRLINES INC.

On September 9, 1988, the Association of Flight Attendants (AFA) filed an application pursuant to the Railway Labor Act as amended, 45 U.S.C. §152, Ninth, alleging a representation dispute among "Flight Attendants (Customer Service Representatives)," employees of America West Airlines Inc. This application was docketed as NMB Case no. R-5817.

At the time the application was filed, these employees were unrepresented.

The Board assigned Mediator John B. Willits to the case. The cut-off date for purposes of eligibility was established as of September 30, 1988. During the investigation, the carrier raised the issue of the appropriate craft or class of the employees in question.

The carrier filed a position statement on September 21, 1988, and a "Motion for Hearing and Determination of Customer Service Representative Craft or Class" on September 28, 1988. AFA filed a response on October 3, 1988.

America West filed a reply brief on October 14, 1988, to which AFA replied on October 31, 1988. The carrier filed a final brief on November 16, 1988.

ISSUES

There are several issues before the Board in this case. The primary question is whether there is a distinct craft or class of Flight Attendants on America West or whether the individuals AFA seeks to represent are part of a larger craft or class of "Fully Cross-Utilized Customer Service Representatives." A second issue is whether the carrier has interfered with the employees' freedom to select a representative. A third issue is whether the use of a preponderance check is appropriate in this case to determine eligibility. Additionally, AFA questions the eligibility of trainees and the use of recurrent training time in a preponderance check. A final procedural question is whether a hearing should be held in order to resolve these issues.

CONTENTIONS

AFA maintains that there is a distinguishable group of employees on America West who spend a majority of their time performing flight attendant functions. In support of its contention, the organization cites the Board's previous craft or class determination involving this carrier, in which the Board found appropriate a craft or class of Flight Attendants.

AFA also takes the position that trainees are not eligible voters and that recurrent training time should not be counted in the NMB's preponderance check. Further, the organization alleges that the carrier has interfered with the employees' freedom of choice by manipulating the September bid awards, which would affect voter eligibility. AFA proposes as a remedy a ninety-day preponderance check.

The carrier takes the position that due to extensive cross-utilization and cross-training, there is no identifiable craft or class of Flight Attendants. America West contends that the more appropriate craft or class is "Fully Cross-Utilized Customer Service Representatives" (CSRs). According to the carrier, these individuals regularly perform in-flight functions, passenger service functions, and fleet service functions. It is the carrier's position that the Board's prior determination is not binding, both because the Board makes its decisions on a case-by-case basis and because "the facts have changed considerably in the intervening two years."

America West contends further that a preponderance check should not be applied and that trainees should be included in the craft or class. If the Board does use preponderance, America West urges that all recurrent training days be counted. Finally, the carrier claims that AFA's allegations of interference are unsupported by evidence and that the carrier has not engaged in any activity which interferes with the employees' freedom of choice.

FINDINGS OF LAW

Determination of the issues in these cases is governed by the Railway Labor Act, as amended, 45 U.S.C. §151, *et seq.* Accordingly, the Board finds as follows:

I.

America West Airlines Inc. is a common carrier by air as defined in 45 U.S.C. §181 of the Act.

II.

AFA is a labor organization and representative as provided by 45 U.S.C. §151, Sixth, and §152, Ninth, of the Act.

III.

45 U.S.C. §152, Fourth, gives employees subject to its provisions "the right to organize and bargain collectively through representatives of their own choosing. The majority of any craft or class of employees shall have the right to determine who shall be the representative of the craft or class for the purposes of this chapter."

IV.

45 U.S.C. §152, Ninth, provides that the Board has the duty to investigate representation disputes and shall designate who may participate as eligible voters in the event an election is required.

FINDINGS OF FACT
I.

America West Airlines is a national air carrier operating from the dual hubs of Phoenix, Arizona, and Las Vegas, Nevada. The airline currently serves 46 cities in the U.S. and Canada. According to the carrier, "all employees who are in the portion of the work force which deals directly, or indirectly, with customers . . . are designated as [CSRs]." CSRs are divided into three categories: Fully Cross-Utilized, Cross-Utilized, and Non-Cross-Utilized. There are approximately 1,700 Fully Cross-Utilized CSRs, virtually all of whom are stationed in Phoenix, Arizona.

II.

According to the carrier, Fully Cross-Utilized CSRs perform the following functions: ramp, ticket counter and gate, reservations and in-flight services. All Fully Cross-Utilized CSRs are paid at the *same* rate, receive the same benefits, and are subject to the same terms and conditions of employment. These individuals are all FAA-certified and are all subject to an annual recurrent training program. Fully Cross-Utilized CSRs are part of a separate supervisory structure, CSR Resources.

III.

Job assignments for Fully Cross-Utilized CSRs are made through a bidding process. The bid schedule, which contains several hundred bid lines, includes ramp, reservations, in-flight, and ticket counter and gate assignments. According to the carrier, in some instances, "job assignments are entirely in one area (i.e. 100% in-flight or 100% reservations). Most commonly, the bid lines involve a combination of duties." Since bids of the most senior Fully Cross-Utilized CSRs are given preference, the senior employees generally receive the schedules they bid. Job assignments may be traded under certain circumstances, and adjustments may be made due to illness or vacations. If a CSR is outbid by a more senior CSR and has not bid alternative lines, that CSR will not receive any bid line.

According to AFA, "bid period after bid period, senior CSRs perform the duties of a flight attendant...," due to a "CSR-wide preference for flight attendant time."

IV.

There are approximately 1,300 Cross-Utilized CSRs who are stationed at locations other than Phoenix. These individuals perform ticket counter and gate duties (including reservations duties), and ramp functions. They are neither trained to perform in-flight functions nor are they FAA-certified. Cross-Utilized CSRs are on a different pay scale than Fully Cross-Utilized CSRs and are not under the CSR Resources supervisory structure.

V.

In addition to the Fully Cross-Utilized CSRs, in Phoenix there are approximately 1,600 Non-Cross-Utilized CSRs who either perform exclusively ramp functions or exclusively reservations functions. Neither in-flight-trained nor FAA-certified, these individuals are on a different pay scale

than Fully Cross-Utilized CSRs and are part of a different supervisory structure.

VI.

The carrier provides a recurrent training program for Fully Cross-Utilized CSRs. This training encompasses all of the functions performed by the Fully Cross-Utilized CSRs. According to the carrier, the four days include training for all CSR functions.

VII.

The training program for newly-hired CSRs at America West involves both classroom training and on-the-job training. While undergoing the on-the-job portion of the training programs, trainee CSRs are paid at the same rate of pay as regular Fully Cross-Utilized CSRs, receive the same benefits and are subject to the same supervisory structure and carrier policies. However, trainees are not paid during the time they undergo classroom training which accounts for approximately 50% of the training time. According to the carrier, "of the 53 trainee CSRs in question, approximately 50 were already employed by the carrier in other capacities. All trainees who successfully complete their training are guaranteed a position at America West."

VIII.

A comparison of the bid periods in July, August, and September reveals no significant discrepancy in either the number of CSRs performing in-flight functions or bid awards to junior CSRs versus senior CSRs in each month. However, according to the carrier, an error in the October 15–October 31 bid period resulted in the creation of additional awards and a limited opportunity for re-bidding. The Board did not use bid periods beyond September 30, 1988, in making its determination of potential eligible voters.

DISCUSSION
I.

Two years ago the Board found there was an identifiable craft or class of Flight Attendants on America West. *America West Airlines*, 13 NMB 259 and 346 (1986). The Board's determination was based upon the limited amount of information provided by the carrier. In the present case, the carrier has provided the Board with more information including bid assignment and actual work schedules for the Fully

Cross-Utilized CSRs. Further, the carrier has provided the Board with information regarding both the trainee program and the recurrent training program. The carrier and AFA have submitted several briefs in support of their respective positions.

II.
A.

The National Mediation Board makes its craft or class determination on a system-wide basis. *Simmon Airlines*, 15 NMB 124 (1988).

In determining the appropriate craft or class on a particular carrier, the Board examines a number of factors. These factors include functional integration, work classifications, terms and conditions of employment and work-related community of interest. *USAir*, 15 NMB 369 (1988), *British Airways Inc.*, 10 NMB 174 (1983), *Air Canada*, 6 NMB 1216 (1979). The factor of work-related community of interest is particularly important. *USAir,* supra, *Airborne Express Inc.*, 9 NMB 118 (1981).

The carrier argues that the "Fully Cross-Utilized" CSRs constitute an appropriate craft or class. The carrier asserts that Fully Cross-Utilized CSRs share a work-related community of interest, and maintains that if the Board should find otherwise, the carrier's business would suffer significantly.

The Board has been presented with similar arguments on several previous occasions. In *USAir,* supra, the carrier asserted that its "Customer Service Agents" performed both fleet service and passenger service functions on a regular basis. USAir maintained that if the Board found a separate Fleet Service craft or class, the carrier would lose the flexibility necessary for the airline to function efficiently.

The Board found, based upon its investigation, that a separate Fleet Service craft or class did exist on USAir. One of the factors in the Board's decision was that there was a group of individuals who regularly performed Fleet Service functions.

America West argues that it is unique among air carriers in that certain of its employees are part of a non-traditional cross-utilized craft or class. The investigation establishes that a significant number of individuals bid and work as flight attendants 100% of their time. For example, during the month of September, at least 580 Fully Cross-Utilized CSRs worked 100% of their time as flight attendants. In addition, several hundred individuals work as flight attendants a preponderance of their time. Few CSRs work an equal percentage of their time in two or more functions.

Further, although the carrier argues that seniority is not a basis to determine a craft or class, both the carrier and the organization agree that the more senior CSRs are more likely to regularly bid for, and regularly be awarded, flight attendant duties. The craft or class determination in this case, however, is based not upon seniority, but on the fact that there is an identifiable craft or class of flight attendants who share a work-related community of interest.

B.

Section 5.3.13 of the Board's Representation Manual provides, in part:

> On many carriers, employees may hold seniority rights or work regularly in more than one craft or class and work back and forth between these crafts and classes.
>
> Additionally, when the [mediator] finds that employees not considered eligible by virtue of their assignment on the cut-off date, do work a preponderance of their time in the craft or class involved, a preponderance check may be used.

The investigation in this case reveals that there is an identifiable group of individuals who work a preponderance of their time in flight attendant functions.

III.

AFA takes the position that a 90-day preponderance period should be used to remedy the carrier's interference. In support of its allegation of carrier interference, AFA has submitted affidavits from two senior CSRs who maintain that they were not awarded in-flight bid lines in September, and one individual who maintains that the "Crew Scheduling Department" stated that "the September bid lines were not designed to utilize the entire work force" and that therefore, America West was short 80 lines. AFA alleges that as a result "when the bids were awarded, the eighty most junior CSRs held preponderantly in-flight lines." In response, the carrier has submitted company records and states that the two senior CSRs were either outbid by more senior CSRs or had bid improperly. Further, the carrier has submitted evidence that there were no irregularities in the September bidding periods but admits there were errors in October. However, since the cut-off date is September 30, 1988, the October bid awards were not taken into consideration by the Board.

The Board finds insufficient evidence of carrier interference to warrant any remedial action. Nevertheless, the

Board finds that a 90-day preponderance period, which includes all those CSRs working in in-flight functions on the cut-off date, as well as those CSRs who worked a preponderance of the 90 days as flight attendants, is the most effective method of ensuring that as few individuals as possible are inadvertently disenfranchised. The 90-day preponderance check is one option provided under Section 5.3 13 of the Board's Representation Manual, *supra*.

IV.

Although the carrier has argued that preponderance should not be used to determine eligibility, America West urges the Board to consider all the "recurrent training days" if preponderance is used. AFA requests that the Board use none of the days. The record reveals that the training for the Fully Cross-Utilized CSRs includes FAA required flight attendant training as well as training for non–flight attendant functions: However, it is virtually impossible to segregate the time allotted to training for flight attendant and non–flight attendant functions based upon the nature of the training program. CSRs who receive recurrent training are compensated as if they actually work those days, and this training is mandatory. The Board finds, therefore, that recurrent training will be counted towards preponderance.

V.

In several recent decisions, the Board has considered the question of whether flight attendant trainees are eligible. In *Simmons Airlines*, 15 NMB 228 (1988) the Board stated its policy on this subject:

> For the Board to find trainees eligible, the Board must be presented with evidence that the individuals in question have performed line functions in the craft or class as of the cut-off date. Factors such as accrual of seniority and receiving pay and benefits are not determinative of employee status absent substantive evidence of performance of line work in the craft or class.

See also *Westair Commuter Airlines*, 15 NMB 213 (1988), *Midway Airlines*, 15 NMB 26 (1987) and *Horizon Air*, 14 NMB 406 (1987).

Until individuals training for in-flight functions have successfully completed their IOE, they have not performed line functions and therefore are not eligible. The 50 individuals whom the carrier alleges have been employed in other functions are not eligible to participate in an election among

the craft or class of Flight Attendants unless they have performed work as Flight Attendants as of the cut-off date.

The Board finds that only those individuals who had completed their IOE and performed line functions as Flight Attendants as of September 30, 1988, will be eligible.

CONCLUSION

The Board finds that there is an identifiable craft or class on America West consisting of individuals who regularly and preponderantly perform flight attendant functions. Therefore, the Board finds a dispute to exist among the craft or class of Flight Attendants on America West and authorizes an all-mail ballot election using a cut-off date of September 30, 1988. The count will take place in Washington, DC. The list of eligible voters shall include all individuals working as flight attendants on the cut-off date, as well as those who worked a preponderance of their time during the 90-day period ending September 30 on in-flight functions. Recurrent training time will be counted. Trainees are not eligible to vote. The Board further finds that there is insufficient evidence that the carrier has interfered with the employees' freedom of choice. Finally, the Board denies the carrier's request for a hearing, based upon the sufficiency of the record and the absence of unique facts and issues.

By direction of the National Mediation Board.

Charles R. Barnes
Executive Director

Copies to:
Michael J. Conway
Martin J. Whalen
Susan Bianchi-Sand
Deborah Greenfield, Esq.
David J. Hamilton, Esq.
John B. Willits

America West Airlines Inc., 16 NMB no. 62
February 15, 1989

Deborah Greenfield, Esq.
Edward J. Gilmartin, Esq.
Association of Flight Attendants
1625 Massachusetts Avenue, N.W.
Washington, DC 20036

Mr. Martin J. Whalen
Senior Vice President

Administration and General Counsel
America West Airlines
4000 E. Sky Harbor Boulevard
Phoenix, AZ 85034

Re: NMB Case no. R-5817
         America West Airlines

Gentlemen and Ms. Greenfield:
This will address the January 30, 1989, objections and challenges to the list of eligible voters filed by the Association of Flight Attendants (AFA). The individuals whom AFA alleges are eligible have been sent "challenged" ballots. The carrier submitted evidence and argument in response on February 7, 1989. Final submissions were received on February 13, 1989.

I.

A.

AFA asserts that five individuals on medical leave during the 90-day preponderance period used to determine eligibility in this case are eligible to vote. The carrier maintains that these individuals are ineligible. The organization contends that Martha Jones was on maternity leave from the craft or class of Flight Attendants between April and September of 1988. According to the carrier, however, Ms. Jones was working as a secretary from June 4 through June 29, 1988, although prior to that time she was working as a fully cross-utilized Customer Service Representative (CSR).

AFA also contends that Barbara Foster, Linda Summers, and Mitzi Loretz were on maternity leave, and that Valerie Paulson was not working in the craft or class due to an "on the job injury" from July 29, 1988, to October 22, 1988.

According to the carrier's records, Barbara Foster went on leave from September 15, 1988. However, she worked as a CSR from July 1, 1988, to September 15, 1988, but did not work a preponderance of that time performing flight attendant functions. The carrier's records also indicate that Mitzi Loretz was not on leave at all but in fact worked "passenger service duty" through August 27, 1988, when she was assigned "to a desk position." Finally, the carrier states that Valerie Paulson worked as a CSR from July 1 through July 28, 1988, but did not work a preponderance of that time as a flight attendant.

The carrier states that its records indicate that Linda Summers worked as a flight attendant prior to taking leave commencing June 3, 1988.

B.

AFA also asserts that Scott Fallentine was on medical leave from June 13, 1988, to July 15, 1988, and restricted to ground duties from July 21, 1988, to August 30, 1988. The organization further contends that Theresa Rivera was "forced to work reservations in July and August 1988 due to illness."

In response, the carrier states that Mr. Fallentine last worked as a flight attendant on May 10, 1988, was on leave through July 19, 1988, and performed "ground assignment" functions through September 11, 1988. The carrier also states that Theresa Rivera last worked as a flight attendant on April 28, 1988, "was assigned to the reservations functions because her right to bid was revoked for disciplinary reasons" from May 26, 1988, through August 26, 1988, and continued to perform reservations functions through September 11, 1988.

C.

Section 5.306 of the Board's Representation Manual provides, in part:

> An employee on authorized leave of absence . . . from the craft or class in dispute, who is neither working in another craft or class [nor] working for the carrier in an official capacity . . . will be considered eligible . . .

In determining whether an individual on leave is eligible, the Board frequently examines whether or not that individual was working in the craft or class involved in the representation dispute prior to taking leave. However, in this case eligibility in the craft or class was determined using a 90-day preponderance period, from the beginning of July 1988 to the end of September 1988. Individuals either working in the craft or class as of September 30, 1988, the cut-off date, or who worked a preponderance of their time as flight attendants during the 90-day period, were found eligible, pursuant to Section 5.313 of the Board's representation Manual, *America West Airlines Inc.*, 16 NMB 135 (1989).

As eligibility to vote in this case was determined by preponderance of days worked in the craft or class, the Board must have substantive evidence that the individuals in question worked preponderantly in the craft or class of flight attendants or worked their last day in the craft or class prior to taking leave in order to find these individuals eligible. Therefore, the Board finds that none of the individuals discussed above is eligible, with the exception of Linda Summers, who is eligible.

II.

AFA challenges the eligibility of six other individuals on the basis that they are "supervisory" In support of this allegation, AFA cites Section 5.312 of the Board's Representation Manual, which provides, in part:

If an individual is determined not to be an employee-subordinate official, the individual shall be considered ineligible. The Board representative shall consider, in the investigation, whether the involved individual has the authority to discharge and/or discipline employees or to effectively recommend the same; the extent of supervisory authority; the ability to authorize and grant overtime; the authority to transfer and/establish assignments; the authority and the extent to which carrier funds may be committed; whether the authority exercised is circumscribed by operating the policy manuals; the placement of the individual in the organizational hierarchy of the carrier; and, any other relevant factors regarding the individual's duties and responsibilities.

AFA has not provided the board with substantive evidence in support of its contentions regarding these six individuals. The carrier responds that Kay Rzonga is an inflight supervisor, Sabrina Anderson a CSR trainer, Richard Canfield a gate supervisor, John White a Customer Service Supervisor, Brent Boyd a pilot scheduler, and Kimberly Romine a "supervisor" in CSR resources.

According to information provided by the carrier, an Inflight Supervisor on America West "works closely with Inflight CSRs onboard . . . flights ensuring quality/consistency of . . . Inflight procedures and adherence to [FAA] Regulations." Responsibilities include: conducting inflight evaluations; observing CSRs with reported problems and counseling or recommending corrective action; monitoring inflight CSR appearance; maintaining inflight CSR activity records; and reviewing passenger feedback and following through with "appropriate action." Inflight Supervisors report to the Staff Manager, Inflight Line Operations.

CSR Trainers on America West perform various functions. CSRs who work in inflight service training are "responsible for the classroom and hands-on training segments of Inflight Service for all cross-utilized CSR trainers. . . ."

CSR Resource Supervisors supervise fully cross-utilized CSRs. Responsibilities include: providing support and assistance to CSRs including career counseling, and authorization of pay increases/anniversary awards; administration of company guidelines, including "ensuring that the availability, appearance and job performance standards established by the company are maintained and accurately reflected in CSR performance records." CSR Resource Supervisors also "interface with CSRs in sensitive matters relating to leaves of absences, transfers, promotions, resignations, and terminations."

The evidence presented, when viewed in light of Board policy, establishes that none of the individuals in question possess the authority of carrier officials. However, the record also establishes that only the position of In-Flight Supervisor falls within the craft or class of Flight Attendants. Therefore, Kay Rzonga is eligible, but Sabrina Anderson, Richard Canfield, John White, Brent Boyd, and Kimberly Romine are ineligible. Further, Suzanne Nilges, who transferred to Supervisor, CSR Resources, in July, is also ineligible.

On February 10, 1989, the carrier took the position that all In-Flight Service Supervisors (and CSR Resource Supervisors) should be considered eligible. The list of eligible voters in this case is comprised of individuals working as Flight Attendants on September 30, 1988, and those individuals who worked as Flight Attendants a preponderance of the time during the 90-day period in question. Therefore, as there is no substantive evidence that any of the twelve other In-Flight Supervisors alleged by the carrier to be eligible met either criterion used in this case, none of those individuals is eligible.

III.

AFA maintains that six individuals are ineligible because they have resigned. According to the Carrier, however, only two of the six have resigned. Of the other four, two are on medical leave, one is an active CSR, and one is a CSR trainer.

The Board finds that Jodi Mizell and Michelle Ducusin are ineligible as they are no longer employed by the carrier. Deanna McFarland, who is a CSR trainer, is ineligible because she is not working in the craft or class of Flight Attendants. John Shurr, as an active member of the craft or class, is eligible. Janet Yarner and April Ballard are on authorized medical leave. Both individuals previously had been determined to be eligible in the craft or class of Flight Attendants; therefore, they are eligible voters.

IV.

AFA contends that Virginia Gulden, Guy Muhammed, and Nancy Merkle are ineligible because they no longer work in the craft or class. The carrier's records confirm this contention. These individuals are, therefore, ineligible.

v.

Finally, AFA asserts that two individuals, Elizabeth Robinson and Dorothy Gaber, worked a preponderance of the period in question as flight attendants. As America West's records confirm this, these individuals are eligible voters. The ballot count will take place as scheduled at 10:00 A.M., Wednesday, February 15, 1989. No further challenges to the list of eligible voters will be considered prior to the count without substantive evidence in support.

By direction of the National Mediation Board.

Charles R. Barnes
Executive Director

America West Airlines Inc., 17 NMB no. 24
Findings upon Investigation—Order
Case no. R-5817
January 12, 1990

In the Matter of the Application of the
ASSOCIATION OF FLIGHT ATTENDANTS
Alleging a Representation Dispute
Pursuant to Section 2, Ninth, of the Railway Labor Act,
As Amended Involving Employees of
AMERICA WEST AIRLINES INC.

On September 9, 1988, the Association of Flight Attendants (AFA) filed an application pursuant to the Railway Labor Act, as amended, 45 U.S.C. §152, Ninth, alleging a representation dispute among "Flight Attendants (Customer Service Representatives) (CSRs)," employees of America West Airlines Inc. This application was docketed as NMB Case no. R-5817.

At the time the application was filed, these employees were unrepresented. The Board assigned Mediator John Willits to investigate.

During the investigation, an issue arose concerning the appropriate craft or class of the employees covered by AFA's application. The carrier took the position that all of its fully cross-utilized CSR's constituted an appropriate craft or class. AFA maintained that there was an identifiable group of CSRs who preponderantly worked as Flight Attendants.

On January 5, 1989, in 16 NMB 135, the Board determined that the appropriate craft or class was that of Flight Attendants. The Board also found a dispute to exist and authorized an all mail ballot election using a cut-off date

of September 30, 1988. The eligible electorate consisted of CSRs who worked a preponderance of their time as flight attendants during the 90 days prior to the cut-off date, and those who worked as flight attendants on the cut-off date. Ballots were mailed on January 17, 1989, and the count was scheduled for February 15, 1989.

On February 13, 1989, AFA filed a "Motion for Board Determination of Carrier Interference." The organization requested that the Board defer resolution of its Motion pending the count of ballots.

The results of the ballot count conducted on February 15, 1989, were as follows: 1,193 eligible voters; 301 votes for AFA; 10 "void" ballots; and 2 votes for IBT. The votes ruled "void" were those cast for the carrier's CSR Panel.

On March 2, 1989, the carrier filed a Response to AFA's Motion. AFA filed a Reply to the carrier's Response on March 17, 1989. Both AFA and America West filed affidavits or declarations and exhibits in support of their arguments. On June 5, 1989, AFA requested that the Board use a "Key" ballot as a remedy for carrier interference. The carrier filed a position statement opposing a "Key" ballot on June 15, 1989.

ISSUES

The issue before the Board is whether the laboratory conditions which the Board is required to ensure in representation elections were tainted by the carrier's actions and if so, what remedy shall be applied.

The final issue is whether votes cast for the CSR Panel discussed infra should have been ruled void.

CONTENTIONS

AFA contends that the carrier's actions at various points during the organizational campaign and election have tainted the laboratory conditions necessary for a fair election. The organization alleges that the carrier "illegally conferred benefits" on eligible voters, and provided funds to assist in an anti-AFA campaign; that carrier officials used mandatory work-rule meetings as a forum to discuss the election; that during these meetings carrier officials "used threats, distortions, and untruths about AFA to discourage CSRs from voting"; that despite the fact that CSRs were prohibited from wearing AFA insignia, America West supervisors were encouraged to wear anti-AFA insignia.

Additionally, the organization maintains that the carrier circulated anti-union propaganda designed to influence employees in their choice of representative, which contained "false" statements and "deliberate mischaracterization of the Board's statutory duties." AFA's final contention is that the carrier failed to post the Board's official notices of election.

The carrier denies AFA's allegations. Specifically, the carrier asserts that the "conferred benefits" had been planned and announced well before AFA filed its application; that carrier officials did not make any statements during the work rule meetings that constituted "threats, promises, or misrepresentations" and that the carrier's campaign literature "merely" stated the carrier's opinion; that its policies prohibit the wearing of insignia on company uniforms; that the board's election notices were posted; and that it did not provide funds "to support an anti-AFA labor organization."

FINDINGS OF LAW

Determination of the issues in this case is governed by the Railway Labor Act, as amended, 45 U.S.C. §151, et seq. Accordingly, the board finds as follows:

I.

America West Airlines Inc. is a common carrier by air as defined in 45 U.S.C. §181 of the Act.

II.

AFA is a labor organization and representative as provided by 45 U.S.C. §151, Sixth and §152, Ninth, of the Act.

III.

45 U.S.C. §152, Third, provides:

> Representatives . . . shall be designated . . . *without interference, influence, or coercion. . . .* (emphasis added)

IV.

45 U.S.C. §152, Fourth, gives employees subject to its provisions ". . . the right to organize and bargain collectively through representatives of their own choosing. The majority of any craft or class of employees shall have the right to determine who shall be the representative of the craft or class for the purposes of this chapter." This section also provides as follows:

> No carrier, its officers or agents, shall deny or in any way question the right of its employees to join, organize, or assist in organizing the labor organization of their choice, and *it shall be unlawful for any carrier to inter-*

fere in any way with their organization of its employees . . . or to influence or coerce employees in an effort to induce them to join or remain or not to join or remain members of any labor organization . . . (emphasis added).

V.

45 U.S.C. §152, Ninth, provides that the Board has the duty to investigate representation disputes and shall designate who may participate as eligible voters in the event an election is required. In determining the choice of the majority of employees, the Board is "authorized to take a secret ballot of the employees involved, or to utilize any other appropriate method of ascertaining the names of their duly designated and authorized representatives by the employees *without interference influence, or coercion exercised by the carrier*" (emphasis added).

FINDINGS OF FACT

I.

America West, headquartered in Phoenix, Arizona, commenced operations in 1983. The carrier employs approximately 9,000 people. The Chairman of the Board and Chief Executive Officer is Edward R. Beauvais. Michael J. Conway is the President and Chief Operating Officer. The Senior Vice-President and General Counsel is Martin J. Whalen, and the Senior Vice-President of Customer Services is Thomas P. Burns.

II.

AFA filed its application in this case on September 9, 1988. However; according to AFA, the organization's campaign commenced in February 1988. As stated previously, ballots were mailed in January 1989, and the ballot count took place on February 15, 1989.

III.

America West's CSR Panel consists of six CSRs and one "designated manager." Thomas Burns is the official under whom the Panel operates. According to documents submitted by the carrier, the objectives and functions of the Panel are:

> To provide an ongoing and effective method of communication between America West [CSRs] and management. To facilitate the development, refinement and application of the CSR job function. The Panel

will . . . review and present to management various matters on suggestions such as, but not limited to compensation, scheduling and cross-utilization. . . .

The term of office for each panel member is one year. While Panel members are elected by the CSRs, the carrier has established several eligibility requirements which must be met to qualify for election. The carrier reserves the right, in joint agreement with the Panel members, to remove from the ballot "any individual significantly deficient in meeting the determined criteria." The final decision is made by management and management continues to evaluate the performance of Panel members after election.

The Panel functions partially as a grievance resolution body. The Panel periodically issues a newsletter, the "Panel Channel," which provides information about its activities and other matters.

IV.

In July of 1988, the CSR Panel announced in the "Panel Channel" that the panel would develop work rules for the CSRs similar to those previously developed for the pilots and implemented on July 1, 1988. In August of 1988, America West's management authorized the CSR panel to proceed with the formulation of new work rules. Work rule meetings were held in September with Beauvais, Conway, and Burns as "guest speakers" at these meetings.

The work rules were approved on December 1, 1988, and were scheduled to be implemented March 1, 1989. The work rules included monetary and scheduling benefits, with "increased compensation for layover time [to] be effective January 1, 1989." According to Thomas Burns, that date was selected because the carrier planned to implement a new per diem rate for the pilots on that same date, and "company practice has always been to provide new benefits both to pilots and to the fully cross-utilized CSRs."

V.

On December 23, 1988, the new work rules were announced. Sixty-two work rule training classes were conducted in January and February of 1989. Each class was attended by 30 or more CSRs. Beauvais, Conway, and Burns attended and spoke at several of these sessions. CSRs were required to attend these meetings. Each CSR bid for the meeting they wished to attend, and each CSR was paid time and a half to attend these meetings.

AFA has submitted affidavits from several CSRs who attended these meetings. Each CSR states that the sessions were approximately four hours in duration. Each CSR states further that the first three hours of each session was devoted to the work rules and the CSR bidding system. The fourth hour of each of these sessions was led by a carrier official.

A.

According to AFA's affiants, America West President Michael J. Conway spoke at several of these meetings. CSRs who attended these meetings allege that Conway made a number of remarks concerning the election and AFA. Conway purportedly said that if AFA were certified, the carrier's Employee Assistance Program would be eliminated. Other comments attributed to Conway include statements that: profit-sharing would be eliminated if AFA won the election; CSR benefits would probably not be as good if AFA was certified; AFA was misleading the CSRs about the possibility of USAir expanding in Phoenix; AFA's radio campaign was causing the carrier to lose business; the carrier's child care program may be at risk if AFA were elected; and CSRs should not vote for the union since it wasn't necessary.

B.

America West Chairman Edward Beauvais also spoke at several work rule meetings. Remarks attributed to Beauvais include: CSRs should throw away their ballots because if AFA won the election it would be detrimental to the carrier; other union carriers were not happy with their flight attendant unions; if AFA won the election, CSRs would start with a "clean slate" with respect to pay and benefits; the benefits now enjoyed by the CSRs would be in jeopardy if AFA won; if AFA won the election, it would ruin America West; and AFA was not necessary for the CSRs.

C.

On January 19, 1989, Senior Vice-President of Customer Services Thomas Burns spoke at a work rule meeting. According to an affidavit submitted by AFA, Burns told the CSRs that America West did not need a union. Burns also allegedly stated that despite AFA's failure to reach an agreement on Midway Airlines, the flight attendants had to pay dues. When a CSR told Burns that his statement about the Midway flight attendants was incorrect, Burns purportedly acknowledged that he may have been wrong. Finally, AFA's affiant contends that Burns said the CSRs would lose everything they had if AFA were certified.

VI.

The carrier has submitted Declarations regarding the work rule meetings (and other matters) from Conway, Beauvais, and Burns.

Conway and Beauvais state that they attended several work rule meetings during which they expressed opinions regarding the election. According to Conway and Beauvais, they never made any statements that CSRs would lose benefits if AFA were elected. They state further that they never suggested that the carrier would not negotiate in good faith with AFA.

Beauvais' declaration states that he did say that AFA's campaign flyer comparing salaries at America West with salaries on other carriers "was inaccurate, because the flyer failed to include the annual longevity bonus which America West CSRs receive." Burns also denies the remarks attributed to him.

VII.

The Declaration submitted by Burns provides details about America West's CSR work rules, profit-sharing plan, and 401(k) plan.

According to the carrier, the 401(k) plan, which covers all employees, had been under development for over a year prior to it being announced in April of 1988. On June 15, 1988, the carrier announced that the 401(k) plan would be implemented on January 1, 1989. The plan was, in fact, implemented on that date.

VIII.

America West has had a profit-sharing plan since the carrier commenced its operations. Profit-sharing checks were distributed in April of 1985 at a party at which Beauvais and Conway were present. According to the carrier, no checks were distributed in 1986 and 1987, because the carrier had not made a profit.

On July 28, 1988, America West announced that if the carrier were profitable for an entire year, its employees would receive profit-sharing checks. The carrier made a profit in 1988 and profit-sharing checks were distributed at a party held on January 27, 1989, in the middle of the election period. Beauvais and Conway were present at this party.

IX.

AFA has submitted an affidavit from an individual who viewed a videotape "purportedly produced" by CSRs who did not support AFA. AFA's affiant watched this tape at the CSR Resources Department in Phoenix. The CSR asserts that the tape was labeled "Live Shoot—1/20/89—Produced by AWA Corporate Communications/Audio-Visual Department" According to the CSR, the "tape was a prolonged anti-union/AFA tirade." The tape featured several CSRs discussing the election, unions, and AFA in particular. The individual who viewed the tape states, "it was my impression that these CSRs were provided ... some Company assistance in the production of this video tape."

According to Burns, during the campaign, "a group of CSRs approached America West and requested permission to create a video tape concerning the election." Burns states that the carrier allowed the CSRs to use company equipment in making the tape.

X.

On January 25, 1989, an America West CSR was in the main terminal in Las Vegas, Nevada, when he was noticed by Michael Conway. The CSR asserts that Conway, who was standing with a group of people, called out, "I heard from D.C. and they received one ballot and it was yours." According to the CSR, several passengers witnessed this incident.

In response, Conway states that he had conversed with the CSR a few weeks earlier on a flight concerning the election. Conway maintains that the CSR was comfortable in expressing his views as to "why AFA should be elected." Conway states that when he saw the CSR in Las Vegas a few weeks later, he made the remark as a joke in reference to the prior conversation.

There is no evidence that any other CSRs were present during the Las Vegas incident.

XI.

In an affidavit submitted in support of AFA's contentions, an individual states that there did not seem to be any official Notices of Election posted on America West property during the election period.

While investigating another case on the property in January 1989, Mediator Willits inquired of America West's Senior Vice-President of Administration and General Counsel Martin J. Whalen as to whether the carrier had posted the Board's Notices of election. Whalen submitted a letter to Mediator Willits on January 30, 1989, stating that Notices were posted on January 9, 1989. Attached to Whalen's letter were copies of letters from two members of Whalen's staff who stated that the Notices were posted at various locations on the property.

XII.

According to another CSR who has submitted an affidavit, on or about January 17, 1989, the CSR was asked by an America West supervisor, Thomas Marcellino, to attend a meeting of carrier managers. The CSR asserts that Whalen, who was at the meeting, stated that he did not know how AFA had obtained a master list of employees, but that there would be an investigation and "retribution."

Whalen contends that the CSR in question attended the meeting because the CSR requested to speak to America West's managers. Whalen denies that there was any discussion of employee lists or of retribution.

Thomas Marcellino has submitted a declaration in which he states that the CSR asked him if he could meet with carrier managers to discuss issues relating to CSRs. Marcellino further states that the CSR expressed his view to the managers and that "at no time did anyone at this meeting discuss an employee list or threaten retribution. . . ."

XIII.

During the election campaign, the carrier and the organization circulated literature and disseminated information regarding their views. Each has accused the other of providing false information to the electorate.

A.

On June 15, 1988, America West issued a letter to its Pilots and CSRs regarding an ALPA/AFA radio announcement. The letter, signed by Beauvais and Conway, characterized the radio ad which mentioned "rumors of merger or acquisition" as a "Scare Tactic of the highest order" and concluded that the "unions are in a desperate race against America West's return to profitability."

B.

In a letter dated October 7, 1988, Beauvais and Conway answered questions concerning AFA's campaign. One response dealt with the determination of who was eligible to vote in the election. Beauvais and Conway stated,

> The AFA . . . is attempting to limit the extension of the "voting right" by asking the government to conduct an election involving 947 Fully Cross-Utilized CSRs out of a total of 1,700.

C.

In another letter, Beauvais and Conway discussed payment of union dues by fully cross-utilized CSRs not eligible to participate in the election, and the situation at Midway Airlines.

> What exactly has taken place at Midway Airlines in the 12 months since the AFA was voted in by a narrow margin. Lawsuits have been filed, nothing positive has happened to the Midway Flight Attendants, and the situation there has gotten outright ugly. Why does the AFA believe things would be any different at America West?

D.

On January 13, 1989, Beauvais and Conway sent a letter to all Fully Cross-Utilized CSRs regarding the impending election. Included in this letter was the following:

> It is very important to keep in mind that all of the time and expense that has been devoted to the "Who Gets to Vote" issue could have been avoided if the AFA had petitioned the NMB to call an election involving all Fully Cross-Utilized CSRs. We certainly would not have objected to this approach, and the NMB would have sanctioned this, provided the AFA had a sufficient "showing of interest."

E.

In another letter from Beauvais and Conway, the Board's craft or class determination was discussed. The carrier officials re-stated their position that all Fully Cross-Utilized CSRs should be eligible to vote. Beauvais and Conway continued,

> It is quite clear to us that the AFA strategy to prevent a large number of Fully Cross-Utilized CSRs from voting stems from the fact that the AFA does not have the support of a majority of the 1,700 Fully Cross-Utilized CSRs at the Company. The AFA has stated they are only following the "rules" by soliciting ballots from those CSRs who worked more than 50% Inflight for a given period of time. *This is nonsense.* The AFA had conducted a *malicious and distorted* campaign over the past several months, relying heavily on AFA organizers who are employed by airlines who compete against us. Over the next few weeks, we intend to play

back to you documented statements made by the AFA which will support our assessment of their behavior (emphasis in original).

The letter concluded with . . . "if you receive a ballot and do not want to be unionized by the AFA, the only legal way to vote 'NO' is to destroy your ballot and not vote."

F.

On January 23, 1989, Beauvais and Conway issued another letter to the CSRs which contained statements about the progress of AFA's negotiations at Midway. Beauvais and Conway suggested that the CSRs ask themselves:

If the situation at Midway is any indication of what it would be like at America West, are you likely to benefit from sending at least $400 of your after tax earnings each year to AFA outsiders from Washington?

Is employee owned America West likely to be a better and stronger Company as a result of AFA outsiders attempting to manage your future for a fee of approximately $500,000 a year (1,200 CSR's x $34.00 per month x 12 months)?

Vote "NO" BY DESTROYING YOUR NMB BALLOT.

The carrier attached "The Midway Chronology" to this letter.

G.

The final piece of America West campaign literature, issued in January 1989, described the results of another election conducted by the NMB as follows:

[A]t USAir [t]he Teamsters union got 1854 votes . . . 12 less than a majority. The union would have lost the election . . . but then the NMB added 16 write-in ballots and decided that a majority of the employees wanted to be unionized. Next, the NMB decided that the Teamsters union got a majority of the votes for unionization. So now all 3,733 employees have been unionized even though the union didn't get a majority of the votes!

AFA is trying to make the same thing happen here. They know that they do not have the support of a majority of the CSRs . . . or even of the smaller group that they didn't argue to disenfranchise. . . .

VOTE FOR AMERICA WEST. DESTROY YOUR NMB BALLOT ON RECEIPT.

XIV.

AFA has submitted affidavits from CSRs who state that America West supervisors made them remove pro-AFA insignia from their apparel. These individuals allege further that certain supervisors wore anti-AFA insignia during this campaign.

The carrier has submitted sections of its policy manual which indicate that wearing of pins and buttons on uniforms is prohibited.

AFA has also submitted copies of photos showing signs urging CSRs to destroy their ballots which were posted around the outside of the CSR Panel Office.

DISCUSSION

I.

In cases involving allegations of carrier interference, the Board examines whether or not the laboratory conditions which the Board seeks to promote in representation elections have been tainted. *Metroflight Inc.,* 13 NMB 284 (1986), *Key Airlines,* 13 NMB 153 (1986), *Laker Airways Ltd.,* 8 NMB 236 (1981), *Zantop International Airlines,* 6 NMB 834 (1979). Although the issue of interference has been before the Board many times, the Board does not order remedial action in each case. In reaching its determination in this case, the Board has relied upon the evidence and arguments submitted by the organization and the carrier, as well upon the Board's own experience with cases of this nature.

The most recent case dealing with the question of carrier interference was *Key Airlines,* 16 NMB 296 (1989). In *Key,* the Board found that the carrier had violated its employees' right to freedom of choice in selecting a representative under the Act. This finding was based upon several acts of the carrier: discharge and re-assignment of leading union organizers; denial of a scheduled pay increase to one group of employees immediately after a representation application was filed, but the granting of a pay increase to another group of employees immediately prior to the filing of its application; holding meetings for the express purpose of discouraging organization; and threats to employees' job security should they vote for representation. The carrier issued letters criticizing the organization which included comments such as "[Do] you want to be a partner with an organization that has such a sordid reputation as the Teamsters?" and "Do they want to help the unemployed crew members at World Airways at your expense?" Significantly, the carrier had violated employee representation rights in a similar manner three years previously. As a remedy for this situation, the Board ordered a new election using a ballot procedure in which the organization would be certified unless a majority of eligible voters returned votes opposing union representation. No write-in space was provided.

The Board has found other election remedies appropriate depending on the extent of the carrier interference found. In *MidPacific Airlines*, 13 NMB 178 (1986), the Board held that the carrier had violated the Act by polling its employees and implying that the carrier's financial future rested on the employees' rejection of union representation. The Board ordered a "Laker" election as a remedy. A "Laker" election involves the use of a "Yes" or "No" ballot. No write-in space is provided, and the majority of votes cast will determine the outcome of the election. In *Zantop International Airlines, supra*, the Board found that the carrier had contaminated the "laboratory conditions" by misinforming its employees of the Board's voting procedures and by holding meetings with small groups of employees. The Board ordered a re-run election to offset the carrier interference. In *Allegheny Airlines Inc.*, 4 NMB 7 (1962), the Board found, that the carrier had sent the employees involved in the election a letter, the "obvious purpose" of which the Board found, was "to discredit the [union]." In addition, the Board found that the carrier had mis-represented the Board's ballot and voting procedures. The Board noted that,

> the carrier's *totality of conduct* in the course of this representation election prevented this Board from fulfilling its obligation under Section 2, Ninth, to insure the choice of representative by the employees without interference, influence, or coercion exercised by the carrier (emphasis added).

II.

America West has advanced a number of arguments in support of its position that its actions did not constitute interference with the election. The carrier attempts to justify the timing of the new work rules by citing both legal and factual factors. First, the carrier states that since the new work rules were scheduled well in advance of the election or the filing of AFA's application, to withhold these benefits would have been unlawful. Second, in response to AFA's contention that the carrier was well aware of AFA's organizational drive in the months prior to the filing of the application, the carrier asserts that "America West had had 'organizational

campaigns' . . . almost constantly since . . . 1983" and that most of them never proceeded beyond the stage of collection of authorization cards.

The carrier also asserts that the opinions expressed in the work rule meetings and in the campaign literature were protected by the First Amendment of the Constitution.

The Board is persuaded that the carrier did post the Notices of Election as required. Further, the Board finds that the 401(k) plan had been under development for a substantial period of time, well prior to AFA's campaign.

The evidence presented by the carrier and AFA as to the specific content of the discussions in the work rule meetings, and the meeting on January 13, 1989, was inconclusive. While numerous coercive comments were alleged by several different CSRs to have been made by senior carrier officials, those officials denied making the comments.

III.

The Board finds that the carrier has improperly interfered with, influenced, and coerced its flight attendants in their freedom of choice, by the "totality" of its conduct. First, the Board finds that the timing of both the announcement of the work rule changes, and the implementation of the increase in layover benefits on January 1, 1989, immediately prior to the balloting period, improperly influenced the employees' freedom of choice. The Carrier submitted no evidence which would indicate that these events were scheduled or occurred for reasons independent of the election. As the Board stated in its recent decision in *Key Airlines, supra*.

> from that date [the time from which the carrier was aware of the organizing drive] until the conclusion of the election laboratory conditions must be maintained.

The Board gave consideration to the decision of the United States Supreme Court in *NLRB v. Exchange Parts Co.*, 375 U.S. 405 (1964) in its decision.

Similarly, the Board finds that the timing of the profit-sharing party with Beauvais and Conway present, on January 27, 1989, during the balloting period and approximately two weeks before the ballot count, had the effect of improperly influencing the employees. As AFA has pointed out, the last profit-sharing party was held in April 1985. For the carrier to distribute these checks during the election period shows careless disregard of Act's requirements at best and a serious violation of those same provisions at worst.

In *Allegheny Airlines, supra,* the carrier claimed the First Amendment protected its actions, as America West does here. The Board stated in Allegheny, "[t]he privilege of free speech, . . . is not absolute. It must be evaluated in the context of the rights of others." As the Supreme Court said in *Texas & New Orleans Railroad v. Brotherhood of Railway and Steamship Clerks,* 281 U.S. 548 (1930),

The petitioners, the Railroad Company and its officers, contend that the provision confers merely an abstract right which was not intended to be enforced by legal proceedings; that, in so far as the statute undertakes to prevent either party from influencing the other in the selection of representatives, it is unconstitutional because it seeks to take away an inherent and inalienable right in violation of the Federal Constitution. . . .

The intent of Congress is clear with respect to the sort of conduct that is prohibited. "Interference" with freedom of action and "coercion" refer to well understood concepts of the law. The meaning of the word "influence" in this clause may be gathered from the context. Noscitur a sociis. The use of the word is not to be taken as interdicting the normal relations and innocent communications which are a part of all friendly intercourse, albeit between employer and employee. *"Influence" in this context plainly means pressure. the use of the authority or power of either party to induce action by the other in derogation of what the statute calls "self-organization." The phrase covers the abuse of relation or opportunity so as to corrupt or override the will, and it is no more difficult to appraise conduct of this sort in connection with the selection of representatives for the purpose of this Act than in relation to well-known applications of the law with respect to fraud, duress and undue influence.* If Congress intended that the prohibition, as thus construed, should be enforced, the Courts would encounter no difficulty in fulfilling its purpose, as the present suit demonstrates.

In reaching a conclusion as to the intent of Congress, the importance of the prohibition in its relation to the plan devised by the Act must have appropriate consideration. *Freedom of choice in the selection of representatives on each side of the dispute is the essential foundation of the statutory scheme.* All the proceedings looking to amicable adjustments and to agreements for arbitration of disputes, the entire policy of the Act, must depend for success on the un-coerced action of each party through its own representatives to the end that agreements satisfactory to both may be reached and the peace essential to the uninterrupted service of the instrumentalities of interstate commerce may be maintained. There is no impairment of the voluntary character of arrangements for the adjustment of disputes in the imposition of a legal obligation not to interfere with the free choice of those who are to make such adjustments. On the contrary, it is of essence of a voluntary scheme, if it is to accomplish its purpose, that this liberty should be safeguarded. The definite prohibition which congress inserted in the Act can not therefore be overridden in the view that Congress intended it to be ignored. As the prohibition was appropriate to the aim of Congress, and is capable of enforcing the conclusion must be that enforcement was contemplated.

Congress was not required to ignore this right of the employees but could safeguard it and seek to make their appropriate collective action an instrument of peace rather than of strife. Such collective action would be a mockery if representation were made futile by interferences with freedom of choice. Thus the prohibition by Congress of interference with the selection of representatives for the purpose of negotiation and conference between employers and employees, instead of being an invasion of the constitutional right of either, was based on the recognition of the rights of both. . . . The Railway Labor Act of 1926 does not interfere with the normal exercise of the right of the carrier to select its employees or to discharge them. *The statute is not aimed at this right of the employers but at the interference with the right of employees to have representatives of their own choosing. As the carriers subject to the Act have no constitutional right to interfere with the freedom of the employees in making their selections,* they cannot complain of the statute on constitutional grounds (citations omitted, emphasis added).

Viewing the carrier's conduct in its totality, including inter alia the timing of benefits, the presence of Beauvais and Conway at the profit-sharing party, as well as the timing of the party, the letters from Beauvais and Conway with their criticism of AFA—leads the Board to conclude that the laboratory conditions necessary for a fair election were contaminated.

CONCLUSION AND ORDER

AFA has requested as a remedy either a re-run election using a *Laker* ballot or a certification based upon authorization cards or a *Key* ballot. Based upon the circumstances in this case, the Board finds none of these remedies to be appropriate. The Board finds insufficient basis to use the remedy used in the *Key Airlines* case. That method, which involves the use of a presumptive "No" ballot was a remedy for Key's "serious and repeated interference." This was Key's second violation in three years and the carrier had taken adverse action against known union supporters. Further, the carrier's actions in this case do not compare to those of the carriers in either *Laker, supra* or *MidPacific, supra.*

The Board hereby authorizes a re-run election among Flight Attendants of America West Airlines. Further, a special "Notice to All Employees" (attached) will be distributed along with the ballot materials to each eligible voter in these elections.

The Board's craft or class determination in this case remains in effect and a mediator will be assigned to continue the investigation and make appropriate determinations that will, in fairness, enable the Board to carry out its responsibilities pursuant to Section 2, Ninth of the Act.

In view of the fact that a new election will be held, the Board makes no finding on whether votes for the CSR Panel in the first election were properly ruled "void." Finally,

> [t]his Board need not consider what other action may be required if the new election [is] tainted. We trust [it] will be conducted under the democratic conditions required by the Act.

Laker, supra, at 258.
By direction of the National Mediation Board.
　　Charles R. Barnes
　　Executive Director
copies:
Mr. Edward R. Beauvais
Mr. Michael J. Conway
Mr. Martin J. Whalen
Robert A. Siegel, Esq.
Tom A. Jerman, Esq.
Edward J. Gilmartin, Esq.
Ms. Susan Bianchi-Sand
Deborah Greenfield, Esq.

NOTICE TO ALL EMPLOYEES

Pursuant to Findings Upon Investigation and Order of the National Mediation Board and in Order to Effectuate the Policies of the Railway Labor Act, As Amended, All Employees Are Hereby Notified That:

After an investigation conducted by the National Mediation Board in which the Carrier and the Union had the opportunity to present statements and evidence, the National Mediation Board found that the Carrier's conduct, taken as a whole, improperly interfered with employees' choice of representative under Section 2, Ninth, of the Act. It is unlawful for a carrier to interfere with the organization of its employees.

Section 2, Fourth of the Act, 45 U.S.C. §152, allows employees the right to select representatives without carrier influence or interference That particular subsection reads as follows:

> No carrier, its officers or agents, shall deny or in any way question the right of its employees to join, organize, or assist in organizing the labor organization of their choice, and it shall be unlawful for any carrier to interfere in any way with the organization of its employees, or to use the funds of the carrier in maintaining or assisting or contributing to any labor organization, labor representative, or other agency of collective bargaining, or in performing any work therefor, *or to influence or coerce employees in an effort to induce them to join or remain or not to join or remain members of any organization* (emphasis added).

Section 2, General Purposes Clause of the Railway Labor Act, states that one of the purposes of the Railway Labor Act is "to provide for the complete independence of carriers and of employees in the matter of self organization."

All employees are free to express their desire to be represented by a labor organization or remain unrepresented. The Carrier is not permitted to influence, interfere, or coerce employees in any manner in an effort to induce them to participate or refrain from participating in the upcoming elections.

If any employees have any questions concerning this notice or compliance with its provisions, they may communicate directly with the National Mediation Board, 1425 K Street, N.W., Washington, DC 20572, Telephone 202-523-5920.

America West Airlines Inc., 17 NMB no. 63
June 6, 1990

Robert S. Siegel, Esq.
Tom A. Jerman, Esq.
O'Melveny & Myers
400 South Hope Street
Los Angeles, CA 90071-2899

Edward J. Gilmartin, Esq.
Deborah Greenfield, Esq.
Association of Flight Attendants
1625 Massachusetts Avenue, N.W.
Washington, DC 20036

Re: NMB Case no. R-5817
        America West Airlines

Ms. Greenfield and Gentlemen:
This determination will address the carrier's Motion for Reconsideration of the Board's decision in 17 NMB 79 (January 12, 1990), as well as the various documents filed by the Association of Flight Attendants (AFA) in support of the organization's request for a "Laker" election.[2] The Board will also address the question of appropriate cut-off date and other issues which were the subject of the numerous submissions filed by America West and AFA.

I.

In *America West Airlines*, 17 NMB 79, the Board found that the carrier had interfered with its employees' freedom of choice of a representative in an election involving the craft or class of Flight Attendants. The Board's finding of interference was based upon the "totality" of the carrier's conduct, including but not limited to, timing of the grant of certain benefits, and discussions at work rule meetings.

The Board held the election after receiving an application filed by AFA in September 1988. The election period was from January 17, 1989, to February 15, 1989.

Prior to the election, the Board had undertaken a lengthy and thorough investigation of several issues including the question of craft or class.

The Board, in its January 12, 1990, decision authorized a re-run election using standard ballot procedures to remedy the carrier's interference. The question of appropriate cut-off date was not resolved. Mediator Andrew J. Stites was assigned to investigate this issue, as well as other eligibility issues.

On January 26, 1990, the carrier filed a Motion for Reconsideration of the Board's January 12, 1990, decision. AFA filed a position statement in response on February 5, 1990. AFA also filed letters alleging continuing carrier interference on February 8, 1990, and February 15, 1990.

On February 21, 1990, the carrier filed a Motion for an Expedited Ruling on its earlier Motion for Reconsideration. The Board declined to issue an expedited ruling on February 22, 1990. On that same date, the carrier filed a Supplemental Memorandum in Support of its Motion for Reconsideration. The carrier filed a response to AFA's February 15, 1990, position statement on March 9, 1990.

AFA filed a letter on April 5, 1990, alleging that America West Customer Service Representative (CSR) Kevin Gillihan is an active AFA supporter who had been disciplined due to his union activities. Documents in support of AFA's allegations regarding Kevin Gillihan were filed on April 12, 1990. On that same date, AFA filed a position statement and affidavit regarding remarks made by America West Manager David Coulson. The carrier filed a position statement on April 23, 1990, and AFA filed additional submissions on April 27, 1990. The organization also submitted a videotape April 5, 1990, in support of its request for a "Laker" election. The carrier submitted a final response to AFA's allegations regarding Coulson and regarding the videotape on May 16, 1990.

The carrier and the organization also filed several position statements and other documents with Mediator Stites on the question of the cut-off date.

II.

A.

The carrier argues that the Board should reconsider several aspects of its January 12, 1990, decision. It is America West's position that the Board's findings of fact "preclude" a determination of interference and that the Board's decision is a violation of the First Amendment. America West also contends that the level of interference found by the Board was *de minimis*.

Should the Board decide to proceed with the re-run election, the carrier requests that the Board "clarify" its rules on carrier interference. The carrier also argues that the Notice to Employees which the Board has ordered appended to the ballots is not justified. In the alternative, the carrier proposes a revised version of the Notice. Finally, the carrier continues to insist that the Board conduct a hearing on the question of interference.

B.

In support of its Motion for Reconsideration, the carrier has submitted an affidavit from Raymond T. Nakano, Vice President and Controller for America West. Nakano states that it is the carrier's policy to distribute profit-sharing checks in the month following a profitable quarter.

On February 8 and 15, 1990, AFA filed letters with the Board regarding a profit-sharing party scheduled for February 23, 1990. (America West had informed the Board of this event in its Motion for Reconsideration.) The organization contended that the planned party was another example of the carrier's "illegal conduct" which required a "Laker" election as remedy.

C.

AFA takes issue with the carrier's Motion for Reconsideration on all points, and characterizes the carrier's request for Board "rules" on carrier conduct in representation elections as a request for an advisory opinion.

As support for its position that a "Laker" election should be used, AFA cites a videotape dated June 16, 1988, which features three carrier officials: Senior Vice President for Customer Service Thomas Burns; General Counsel Martin J. Whalen; and Senior Director of Human Resources Alan Koehler. The topic of discussion is unions. The three participants discuss the merits of joining unions. (At this time, AFA was collecting authorization cards, but had not yet filed its application.) Burns, Whalen, and Koehler also discuss seniority integration, Board election procedures, and AFA. AFA asserts that the most "disturbing statement" is that of Koehler, who, in essence, states that once employees vote for a union the union is there forever. AFA contends that this videotape is "still available for viewing at many [America West] locations. . . ." According to the carrier, the tape was available for viewing in CSR break room for approximately 60 days in the summer of 1988. The carrier asserts that all but one copy of the tape (which is still missing) were collected and that the carrier's records indicate that "the library copy of the . . . tape has never been viewed or checked out by anyone."

AFA also refers to a newsletter sent by Michael J. Conway, President of America West, dated January 18, 1990. According to the organization, Conway "distorts" Board rules and "mischaracterizes" the Board's January 12, 1990, decision. The organization contends that Conway's memorandum and the carrier's announcement of the February 23, 1990, profit-sharing party have "already . . . tainted" the laboratory conditions necessary for the re-run election.

AFA has submitted an affidavit from a CSR who attended a recurrent training class in February of 1990. According to the CSR, the carrier's Manager of CSR Administration, David Coulson, asked the CSRs a series of questions during the session, including, "Is the NMB a union?" The CSR states further that most of the CSRs indicated their belief that the "NMB is a union." The CSR states that Coulson's response was that the Board was a federal agency "but "traditionally its sympathy is with labor and it tends to side with labor."

In addition, the affiant states that Coulson referred to "Frequent Flier," a publication of CSRs who support AFA, as "filled with inaccuracies and distortions."

In its March 8, 1990, response to AFA's allegations, the carrier, as in the past, asserts that Conway's statements in the January 18, 1990, newsletter are protected by the First Amendment. The carrier also disputes AFA's assertion that any profit-sharing party violates the Railway Labor Act. America West re-states its position that the February 23, 1990, party was consistent with its past practice of holding such parties four to six weeks after the end of each profitable quarter. Finally, in response to AFA's position statement regarding David Coulson, the carrier asserts that Coulson's statements were true and that what Coulson actually said about the Board was that it "was created to protect the rights of employees and unions at a time when such protection was particularly needed."

D.

The final basis for AFA's request for a "Laker" election is the series of disciplinary actions involving America West employee Kevin Gillihan. The personnel actions in question took place between March 13, 1990, and April 5, 1990. AFA contends that these actions were taken against Gillihan because of his union activities. Gillihan has appeared on local television in Phoenix, and has been listed as an AFA supporter on "almost all the literature sent to the Company's CSRs." Therefore, the organization maintains that the carrier's actions constitute "egregious" violations of the Railway Labor Act, which must be rectified by a "Laker" ballot. In response, the carrier states that there was no anti-union motivation behind the actions taken against Gillihan. America West asserts that Gillihan was disciplined due to his engaging in various violations of company policy, which were detailed in the carrier's filings as discussed below.

III.

AFA urges the Board to use the cut-off date used in the last election, which was September 30, 1988. In support of this position, the organization cites previous Board interference cases where the original cut-off date was retained in the second election in order to restore the requisite laboratory conditions.

America West takes the position that the Board should use December 31, 1989, as the cut-off date. This date represents the last day of the last payroll period prior to the Board's January 12, 1990, decision. The basis for the carrier's position on this issue is that use of the original cut-off date would disenfranchise a substantial number of individuals. Despite the Board's express statement in 17 NMB 79 that it would not reconsider the craft or class issue, the carrier continues to argue that there is no Flight Attendant craft or class on America West. Instead, America West contends that the appropriate craft or class is all Fully Cross-Utilized Customer Service Representatives (CSR's). As of December 31, 1989, there were 2,307 such individuals employed by America West.

IV.

A.

The Board has carefully reviewed and considered the carrier's Motion for Reconsideration and finds no basis to reverse or alter its decision in 17 NMB 79. Absent new substantive evidence presented in support of such requests, the Board generally does not reverse its decisions upon request for reconsideration. *USAir Inc.*, 17 NMB 22, (1989), *Air Wisconsin*, 16 NMB 290 (1989), *USAir*, 16 NMB 194 (1989).

The Board remains unpersuaded that the timing of the January 26, 1989, profit-sharing party, which occurred in the middle of the balloting period, was not intended to influence the employees' decision regarding representation. The evidence submitted by the carrier in support of its request for re-consideration is insufficient to support a finding that

there was either an established historical pattern or that this was a regularly scheduled benefit at the time the January 26, 1989, party was held.

In addition, the Board finds that the carrier's First Amendment arguments have been previously presented, considered, and rejected by the Board.

As the Board stated in Laker, supra. at 253,

> [t]he Board is not unmindful of Laker's constitutional right to communicate its views to its employees. However, this right is not without limit, and even conduct which is otherwise lawful may justify remedial action when it interferes with a representation election. *General Shoe Corp., supra* (77 NLRB 124 (1948).

Although the carrier maintains that the Board did not find "egregious" violations of the Act, but only de minimis "interference which could not possibly have had an effect on the outcome of [the] election," such is not the case. Nowhere in the Board's decision did the Board refer to the carrier's conduct as "de minimis." While the level of interference found was insufficient, in the Board's view, to grant the relief requested by AFA ("Laker" election, "Key" election or certification based upon showing of interest), neither was the interference found so minimal as to warrant no relief at all.[3]

The Board also denies the carrier's request for clarification of "the rules for carrier conduct." It is the Board's policy to decline to issue advisory opinions on any subject. *Overseas National Airways*, 12 NMB 269 (1985). Further, the Board makes its representation decisions on a case-by-case basis. The Board's finding of whether carrier interference has occurred depends upon the particular facts and circumstances of each case. Certain conduct which is proscribed in all cases has been discussed by the Board in previous decisions.[4] Finally, the Board takes note of the decision of the United States Supreme Court in *NLRB v. Gissell Packing Co.*, 395 U.S. 575 (1969), where the Court stated,

> . . . an employer, who has control over [the employer-employee] relationship and therefore knows it best, cannot be heard to complain that he is without an adequate guide for his behavior.

The Board also declines to either rescind or revise the Notice to be attached to the ballots in the re-run election.[5] It is not true, as America West asserts, that the "notice was developed for, and has been used only in, cases involving . . . egregious misconduct." As a remedy for the interference found in *Laker, supra*, and *Key, supra*, the Board ordered the use of a Notice to the employees. Since it has been Board policy to require the Notice to be used in all cases where there has been a finding of interference and an order of remedial action. For example, in *Florida East Coast Railway Company*, 17 NMB 177 (1990), the Board found that the interference was not at the level of the interference found in *Laker* or *Key*. Nevertheless, the Board ordered a re-run election with the Notice in question to be attached to each employee's ballot.

B.

The Board also denies AFA's request for a "Laker" ballot. With the exception of the June 18, 1988, videotape, the organization has not presented any new evidence regarding the previous election which could persuade the Board to reconsider or alter the remedy ordered in 17 NMB 79.

The majority of AFA's allegations in support of the request for a "Laker" election deals with actions taken subsequent to the Board's January 12, 1990, decision. After a review of the arguments and evidence before it, the Board finds that there is insufficient basis to conclude that the laboratory conditions for the forthcoming election have been tainted.

C.

The carrier has presented evidence that it has held profit-sharing parties within four to six weeks of the end of a profitable quarter since the last election (for at least five quarters). The Board finds that the February 23, 1990, party, delayed due to a change in the carrier's payroll system, was consistent with past practice. The Board's finding that the timing of the January 26, 1989, profit-sharing party constituted carrier interference does not mean that the carrier may never hold a profit-sharing party. We merely find here that the timing of such actions as the granting of benefits must not be with a blind eye toward the Act's requirements for "laboratory conditions."

AFA argues that the carrier's newsletter of January 18, 1990, "Executive Report' is an example of "illegal conduct" In the newsletter, Conway states, *inter alia*:

In 1988, the NMB made a determination that based on the specific urging of the AFA, there is a "craft or class of flight attendants" at America West.

Despite our protests that nearly half of the affected employees were being disenfranchised by not being allowed to participate in the voting process, the NMB,

nevertheless, conducted an election among the group that the AFA and it considers to be "flight attendants."

The NMB's decision . . . does not find any threats, intimidation, or other egregious misconduct on the part of America West, but only quarrels with the timing of work rule changes, benefits and profit-sharing. Apparently, the AFA and NMB believe we should have delayed our pre-existing plans to implement improvements until after the election. . . . this makes no sense to us at all.

To say the least, we are extremely disappointed by the NMB's decision to hold another vote and we find the entire process leading up to their decision to be bizarre.

AFA maintains that the newsletter "distorts the Board's Rules," attacks the Board's integrity and "its very legitimacy as the agency charged with supervising representation elections . . ." and "mischaracterizes" the Board's January 12 decision.

The carrier argues that "[t]here is absolutely nothing in the "Executive Report" which is not either an accurate statement of fact or a clearly labeled statement of opinion." America West asserts further that while it "has vigorously disagreed with several of the Board's rulings in this case. . . . [it] has never attacked the integrity of the Board."

The Board finds that the newsletter of January 18, 1990, does not provide a basis for a "Laker" election.

D.

David Coulson has submitted an affidavit in response to AFA's allegations regarding the remarks he made during a recurrent training class held in February 1990. Coulson, who is the Manager of CSR Administration, states that it is his practice to give a written quiz at the beginning of each recurrent training session. According to Coulson,

[t]he purpose of this quiz is to demonstrate that the CSRs may have misconceptions [o]ne question that I have asked in the past is whether the [Board] is a union organization. . . . I have [o]n all occasions made it clear to the class that the Board is Federal government agency organized to protect the rights of employees for representation and not a union. . . .

As historical background, I have informed training classes that the NMB is an agency which was created in the early 1900s to ensure that all employees in the railroad and airline industries were allowed to freely engage in collective bargaining. I also informed the class that agencies like the NMB were created . . . in order to protect employees from abuses by employers which were occurring at the time.

Coulson states further that the statements he made in regard to the "Frequent Flier" newsletter were true. The carrier has attached copies of issues of this publication in support of its May 16, 1990, position statement.

The Board has carefully reviewed the arguments and evidence regarding the remarks made by Coulson during the recurrent training session, and finds insufficient basis for ordering a "Laker" ballot. The question remaining therefore is whether Kevin Gillihan was disciplined due to his union activities, which would constitute a serious violation of the Act.

E.

Gillihan has been employed by America West since June of 1986 and has preponderantly performed Flight Attendant functions for the past three years. Since July of 1988 Gillihan has been an active supporter of AFA's efforts to represent America West's Flight Attendants.

On March 13, 1990, Gillihan was issued a letter of "Formal Warning" and restricted from performing In-Flight functions for 90 days. This action was triggered by a complaint filed against Gillihan by another Flight Attendant who worked with him on a series of flights in February of 1990. The complaint alleged that Gillihan had violated FAA and company policies. (There is no evidence or even any allegation that the Flight Attendant who filed the complaint was motivated by anti-union animus.) Both Gillihan and another individual have submitted affidavits stating that a member of the review board which upheld the disciplinary action, Scott Ramsey, told them that the carrier did not like Gillihan's outspoken support of AFA. Ramsey has submitted an affidavit denying the remarks attributed to him.

A second incident took place on March 14, 1990. Gillihan reported for work to perform his ground assignment but could not perform his ground functions because he did not have his computer password. Given the option of obtaining his password personally from another area of the carrier and losing pay for part of the day, or losing pay for the whole day (going home) Gillihan chose the latter. A "letter of concern" was issued to Gillihan on March 15, 1990.

The third incident resulting in disciplinary action occurred on March 31, 1990. One of Gillihan's supervisors reported that Gillihan had left at least 45 minutes before the end of his shift. On April 5, 1990, Gillihan was issued a "Letter of Final Opportunity."

The carrier has submitted several documents and affidavits relating to Gillihan, including the original complaint filed against him, and pertinent pages of the Company Policy Manual. Also submitted were affidavits from several individuals involved in the three incidents, including Gillihan's supervisors.

F.

In *Transkentucky Transportation Railroad Inc.*, 8 NMB 495 (1981), the Board, in finding that the carrier had interfered with its employees' freedom of choice of a collective bargaining representative, noted the decision of the United States District Court for the Eastern District of Kentucky, *Hughes v. Transkentucky Transportation Railroad Inc.*, Civ. no. 8 1–40.

The court found that after its evaluation of the evidence, it could only conclude that individuals who had been terminated were terminated because of their union activity. The court stated, however that

> . . . this doesn't mean that there can't be any discharges.
> . . . This means only that nobody can be discharged for union activities.

This Board has reviewed the record before it regarding the disciplinary actions taken against Kevin Gillihan and finds insufficient evidence to conclude that Gillihan was disciplined due to his union activity.

Based upon the foregoing, the Board does not find a basis for using a "Laker" ballot in the forthcoming election.

V.

The cut-off date for purposes of eligibility in the prior election was September 30, 1988. The Board determined in 16 NMB 135 (1989) that the list of eligible voters included all individuals working as Flight Attendants as of September 30, 1988, and all those who worked a preponderance of the 90 days prior to September 30, 1988, as Flight Attendants. On the date of the count, there were 1,193 eligible voters.

As of December 31, 1989, there were 1,522 individuals who preponderantly performed Flight Attendant functions for America West. Of the 1,193 individuals eligible to vote in the last election, approximately 107 were no longer eligible as of December 31, 1989, with 1,086 of the 1,193 remaining potentially eligible. Application of the September 30, 1988, cut-off date would therefore result in the eligibility of over 71% of the employees in the craft or class of Flight Attendants. The Board finds no basis to revise its previous craft or class finding or to accept the carrier's argument that the 2,307 Fully Cross-Utilized CSRs should be eligible.

A recent Board determination involving the issue of changing the cut-off date was *USAir*, 17 NMB 117 (1990). There the Board stated,

> [o]nce the Board establishes a cut-off date for purposes of eligibility, it changes that date only in unusual circumstances.

The carrier has cited two Board decisions, in support of its position that the cut-off date should be changed, *USAir*, 10 NMB 495 (1983), and *Piedmont Airlines*, 9 NMB 41(1981). In each case the cut-off date was changed due to "unusual circumstances." The unusual circumstance in the *USAir* case was that there had been a 100% turnover in the craft or class. In *Piedmont* there had been a five-year delay between the original cut-off date and the election due to protracted litigation.

In *USAir*, 16 NMB 63 (1988), the Board retained the original cut-off date despite the addition of 197 individuals into the craft or class during the five-month period between the establishment of the cut-off date and the Board's authorization of election.

The Board's investigation of this issue reveals no "unusual circumstances" which would warrant changing the cut-off date. In addition, the Board finds neither substantial turnover nor lengthy delay, the only two bases found in the past for changing the cut-off date. Therefore, the list of eligible voters in the re-run election authorized on January 12, 1990, will consist of all employees eligible to vote in the last election, with the exception of those individuals no longer employed by the carrier or no longer working in the craft or class.

CONCLUSION

Upon reconsideration, the Board finds that neither America West nor AFA has provided sufficient basis for granting the various forms of relief requested. The election will proceed forthwith. Should the Board find that the laboratory conditions which are required for a fair election have been tainted, the Board will use any method within its discretion as a remedy. Finally, as the result of its investigation, the Board finds that the appropriate cut-off date is September 30, 1988.

By direction of the National Mediation Board.

William A. Gill Jr.
Executive Director
Copies to:
Mr. Martin J. Whalen
Senior Vice President
America West Airlines Inc.
4000 East Sky Harbor Boulevard
Phoenix, AZ 85034

Mr. Andrew J. Stites
Mediator

Sample Management Guide to Permissible Campaigning under the Railway Labor Act

AUTHORS' NOTE: This supplemental reading is an example of appropriate advice for senior management to disseminate to all managers when a union organizing effort is expected at the company.

The Railway Labor Act (RLA) makes it unlawful for any carrier, including its management and supervisors, to interfere with, coerce, or influence employees in the choice of a bargaining representative. *Influence* has been defined by the Supreme Court to mean "undue influence or pressure." These statutory prohibitions apply to verbal and written communications. All written material must be carefully reviewed for compliance before distribution and usage.

Management Control Permitted

Management may do the following:

1. Enforce company rules on solicitation and distribution, so long as even enforcement is followed at all times. The solicitation and distribution rules
   a. Must be applied in the same manner whether the activity involves unions or is totally unconnected with union organizational activity.
   b. Must be applied uniformly among competing unions.
   c. Must be applied in exactly the same way to employees who are engaging in anti-union activity.
2. Prevent its facilities, including mail, telephone, and company records, from being used for organizational purposes.
3. Take steps to safeguard information. Do not give anyone a list of employees' names, phone numbers, addresses, job descriptions, and the like. Anyone requesting such in-

formation, whether it is an employee of the company or not, should be referred to the personnel office. You should also inform the personnel office of the specifics of the incident.

4. Provide complete factual information about the union and unionization. Management may

a. Tell employees the facts about any misleading statements made by a union organizer or appearing in handbills or other literature distributed by union organizers.

b. Tell employees what benefits they have already received and how they compare favorably with organized employees.

c. Tell employees they will take on certain obligations if they are union members, that they will be controlled by the union constitution, bylaws, and resolutions whether they agree with them or not. Tell them they are subject to the union's leadership with respect to union matters and that union leadership is not necessarily confined to company employees but includes the union's national leadership.

d. Tell employees about the necessity of paying union dues and initiation fees if there is a union security agreement. Tell them how much these dues are currently and what increases have occurred. Tell them that under union security agreements, retention of their jobs can be conditioned on payment of union dues or equivalent service fees. Tell them they are subject to union assessments to pay, for example, strike benefits to employees of other carriers. Tell them they are subject to union-imposed fines if they cross picket lines contrary to union dictates.

e. Tell employees that if a union represents them, their conditions of employment will be established by the union, and they will lose their individual bargaining rights.

f. Emphasize that once a union is certified as the employees' representative, there is no procedure to return to unorganized status. It is a one-way street with no return.

g. Tell employees that even if they signed an authorization card, they are not obligated to vote in the election. Explain the voting procedure, and inform employees that if they do not want union representation, they should not vote at all. (But do not tell or direct employees not to vote.)

h. Stress the positive side of being unorganized. Tell the employees they are currently compensated based on individual ability.

i. Tell employees about the strike record of the union but do not excessively emphasize this fact to induce employees into believing that a strike is inevitable if a union is successful in organizing them.

j. Bring to the employees' attention any unfavorable *factual* publicity that the union or its representatives have received as a result of Senate committee hearings, court proceedings, newspaper reports of picket-line violence, corruption, theft, and the like.

k. Reassure employees, if the union has threatened that employees will be discharged unless they support it, that the union has no way of carrying out these threats, and that the company will not permit it.

5. Point out that if any union makes lavish promises to employees to obtain their votes, none of the promises can be fulfilled except by agreement of the company. In doing so, the company must be careful not to portray an image that the employees are wholly dependent on the company so as to convey the power and authority exercised over them by the company. This kind of communication is particularly sensitive.

6. Point out that federal law forbids a union or its agents from restraining or coercing employees in the exercise of their rights, including the right not to support a union.

In communicating with employees under the RLA, several cautions must be emphasized:

1. The tone of all communications should be moderate, certainly never making inflammatory statements to disparage or discredit the union.

2. Communications should be as factual as possible, avoiding inflammatory statements to disparage or discredit the union.

3. Minimize small group meetings, particularly in managers' or supervisors' offices. Most communications will be in writing. If large group meetings are held, a written record or outline should be used to guide the discussion. This outline should be approved by the personnel office before the meeting.

4. Do not explicitly tell employees not to vote. Rather, explain that if they do not wish union representation, they can express their wishes by not voting. Emphasize that the choice is theirs and that the company respects the rights of its employees to make that choice.

Management Conduct Not Permitted

During a union organizational campaign under the RLA, management is under the following restrictions:

1. Company representatives may not make any statement, whether by direct conversation, letter, bulletin-board posting, or speech, that contains either explicitly or implicitly a

promise of benefit or threat of reprisal. Nor may management attempt to influence employees by use of superior management position, pressure employees, or contribute funds to defeat unionization. Thus, for example, it is not permissible to:

    a. Promise or hint that employees will get a wage increase, a better job, or any other similar benefit if they vote against the union or if the union is defeated in an election.

    b. Threaten or hint that employees will receive a wage cut, a less-desirable job, or any other loss of benefit or privileges if the employee supports the union or if the union wins the election.

    c. Threaten or hint that employees will be discharged, demoted, laid off, or otherwise discriminated against if the union succeeds in organizing employees.

    d. State or hint that the company will close down its entire operations, move the work location, or drastically reduce operations if the union succeeds in organizing the employees.

    e. State or hint that the company will refuse to bargain with the union if the union is successful in organizing the employees.

    2. The company may not interrogate employees at any time, including during hiring, regarding their union sympathies or union activities.

    3. The company may not solicit or suggest that employees demand the return of their union-authorization cards or assist employees in attempts to secure the return of authorization cards.

    4. Company representatives may not call employees individually or in small groups into the private offices of management or supervisory personnel for the purposes of making statements in opposition to the union or unions involved. Company representatives may, however, discuss unionization in places where usual employee communication takes place (work areas, briefing rooms, and the like).

    5. The company may not permit employees to engage in anti-union activities or distribute anti-union literature on company time and premises while denying pro-union employees similar rights to engage in pro-union activities. This applies also when one or more unions are competing.

    6. The company may not keep union meetings under surveillance for *any* purpose or create the impression of surveillance.

    7. Management or supervisory personnel may not visit employees in their homes for the purpose of discussing matters relating to union organizational activities.

8. Management cannot

    a. Discharge, discipline, or lay off an employee because of legitimate activities on behalf of the union.

    b. Discriminate against employees actively supporting the union by intentionally assigning undesirable work to the union employees.

    c. Transfer employees prejudicially because of union affiliation.

    d. Engage in any partiality favoring nonunion employees over employees active on behalf of the union.

    e. Discipline or penalize employees actively supporting a union for an infraction that nonunion employees are permitted to commit without being likewise disciplined.

    f. Make any work assignment for the purpose of causing employees who have been active on behalf of the union to quit their jobs.

    g. Ask employees for an expression of thoughts about a union or its officials.

    h. Ask employees how they intend to vote or if they intend to vote.

    i. Give financial support or assistance to a union or its representatives or to employees who oppose unionization.

    j. Ask employees about the identity of the instigator or leader of employees favoring the union.

    k. Make any misrepresentations about the union.

Rules on Solicitation and Distribution

Company rules on solicitation and distribution are long-standing and appear in the company's *General Rules of Conduct* and in the union contracts. The *General Rules of Conduct* states:

> No employee shall make an unauthorized appearance on Company property nor shall he solicit funds or services, sell tickets, distribute petitions or literature for any purpose on Company property at any time without the prior consent of his supervisor.

The pertinent section of the contract states:

> There shall be no general distribution or posting by employees of advertising or political matter or of any kind of literature upon the Company's property. No employees covered by this agreement shall during working hours, engage in solicitation of membership for any union, collection of dues or other union activity not provided for in this agreement.

It has long been the company's policy to affect strict control over unauthorized persons and unauthorized conduct on company time and property. This is particularly important in light of the intensified concern in the industry over all aspects of airline security. Activity that compromises or even might lead to compromise of airline security or safety is critical. To be specific:

1. Management must apply the company's rules in a uniform and firm manner. Management cannot, of course, give consent to anti-union solicitation activity without also giving consent to pro-union solicitation activity. If one is not absolutely certain what is the proper course of action, contact the personnel office immediately.

2. Management personnel should refuse to permit outside solicitors or union organizers to talk to employees on company time or on company property, which includes all property controlled by the company, such as cafeterias, parking lots, ramp offices, and the like. Union organizers have the same right to enter such public facilities as ticket offices and terminal areas as does any member of the public. But they do not have the right to solicit membership, either verbally or through the distribution of literature, or to interfere with the conduct of company business. An off-duty employee who has entered company premises for the purpose of conducting solicitation activities should be required to leave. If solicitation activities are conducted in such instances in conjunction with company business, the off-duty employee should be instructed to complete his/her business expeditiously and then leave.

3. Working time is for work. Employees may not engage in union solicitation during working time. This rule against solicitation applies to the working time of the employee doing the solicitation and the employee being solicited. Employees may discuss nonwork matters, including unionization, on their own time on company premises (lunch and break periods), so long as one employee does not unduly disturb or interfere with the rights of others.

4. Distribution of union literature, buttons, and the like may not be done on company time or premises.

5. Unions are not permitted to post on union or company bulletin boards notices or information that go beyond the specifics permitted in their contracts with the company. If such posting is made on union bulletin boards, contact the union official at the time of the posting and get him or her to remove it. If posting is made on company bulletin boards or if the union official refuses to remove such posting from a union bulletin board, management should remove such posting and forward it with an explanation to the personnel office.

6. Any contacts of the type described above should be reported to the personnel office immediately.

Materials Provided to Frontline Managers during Anti-union Campaign under NLRA

Management Statement to Employees concerning Labor Unions

In this plant, it is almost certain that one or more labor unions will try to gain additional members by aggressively soliciting you and conducting organizing activities over the months and years ahead. For this reason, it is appropriate that you understand management's position concerning unions. We are against a union coming into the plant because we sincerely believe that it would not be good for you or the business. You will not need a union to get fair treatment. It is our company-wide policy to provide fair treatment in pay, benefits, and working conditions for all employees alike—union or nonunion.

Signing a union card is a serious thing. Your signature is valuable because it may indicate to a union your desire to be represented. As with any agreement, before signing, understand the total particulars and what you are getting into. We feel strongly that it is in your best interest not to sign a union-authorization card. In any event, do not sign a card just to please someone else or get the union organizer to leave you alone.

At most of our plants, when the issue has been raised, employees have decided against having a union represent them. We think you will feel the same way. Our request is that you give us an opportunity to demonstrate to you that a union is not needed here.

Your plant management has pledged itself to high standards of treatment and respect for all employees. You can be certain that we will constantly seek to achieve and maintain this fairness of individual treatment for your best interests and long-term job security. As far as your complaints are concerned, we want you to feel free to express them to us. We know we are not perfect and that mistakes will be made. Through our problem-solving procedure, which can get your complaint all the way to the plant manager, we stand ready to investigate and, when warranted, adjust any decision that personally affects you and that you believe has not been handled fairly. It is a good thing to know that you have a complaint system available to you that even permits you to go around your supervisor to get an answer if you feel that he/she has not been fair.

Summing up, we ask that you not be persuaded that signing a union-authorization card is the thing to do and that you always carefully consider the many benefits of your job that are yours without the need to pay union dues and risk the loss of your pay through strikes, work stoppages, fines, and other costs of union membership.

Disadvantages of union representation from the company's point of view include:

1. Negative effects on customer service and satisfaction. A union is a third party that has no legal obligation to provide service. Naturally, its objectives will differ from those of the company. As a result, the union may

    a. Demand work rules that detract from the quality or quantity of service

    b. Demand special privileges, such as the right to conduct union business in the facility

    c. Call a strike and engage in picketing

These are only a few examples of how unionization could interfere with the service we provide.

2. Lack of managerial flexibility. The company now has the flexibility to adjust to meet changing company needs.

3. Wasted management time. With unionization, supervisors may spend a great deal of time dealing with petty union gripes and grievances. With a union, consultation with the union steward becomes standard procedure before changing duties, assignments, or schedules or before taking other actions affecting employment conditions. Time-wasting decisions and horse trading become a part of many management decisions.

4. Divided loyalty of employees. Unionization often means that management cannot get wholehearted cooperation and support from employees in solving problems.

5. Higher operating costs. Due to delays, time wasting, work-rule restrictions, grievances, arbitration, and the like, the cost of operating the company will go up. This rise in cost reduces the amount of money available for investing in new equipment, new programs, new facilities, and wages.

Disadvantages of union representation from the supervisor's point of view include:

1. Restrictions on the supervisor's freedom and authority. Union shop stewards will be constantly looking over your shoulder—second-guessing your decisions. Since the union can effectively override many supervisory decisions

by threatening arbitration, the individual supervisor loses prestige and authority.

2. Difficulties in dealing with employees. Unions often generate feelings of distrust toward supervisors. They may also create an uncooperative attitude among employees by telling them that they are untouchable. This attitude is especially prevalent among union delegates or stewards.

3. Time involved in handling petty grievances. Again, your time may be wasted in dealing with stewards over petty grievances.

4. Overemphasis on seniority. Many union contracts require that employment decisions be based solely on seniority, rather than on skill and ability.

5. Internal bickering. Unions often increase dissension, and a less-friendly, more formal work atmosphere results.

Disadvantages of union representation from the employee's point of view include:

1. High cost of union membership. Union representation has a hefty price tag. A few examples of the financial obligations employees will encounter with membership in the union are

    a. Union dues

    b. Initiation fees

    c. Special assessments

    d. General assessments

    e. Re-initiation fees

    f. Union fines

2. Loss of personal freedom. Because of union disciplinary rules and procedures (e.g., trials, fines, suspension, expulsion, and the like), employees will lose personal freedom.

3. Loss of individuality. Though employees will have the right to talk to management individually, the union will probably discourage this communication and insist that employees only use the union's formal grievance procedure. Under the labor law, the union has a right to be present at any supervisor-employee conference whether the employee likes it or not.

4. Incentives are limited. Merit increase and individual incentives for extra effort and skill are contrary to trade union philosophy.

5. Possibility of strikes. Despite these costs and disadvantages, employees have no guarantee that they will get more or better wages or benefits. In cases where the union is unable to achieve what it has promised at the bargaining table, unions sometimes draw employees into costly and unsuccessful strikes. While on strike, employees do not receive

wages, benefits, or unemployment compensation. They may even be *permanently* replaced in an economic strike.

Recognizing the Early Warning Signs of Union Activity

It is extremely important that supervisors react in a quick, positive, and aggressive manner following the first signs of union organizing. A delayed reaction is almost always damaging and often fatal to company efforts to remain union-free. But before the company can react to the attempted unionization of its employees, it must be aware of the attempt to organize. It is a tragic but all-too-common fact of labor relations that many employers are totally unaware of organizing until the union declares itself either in the form of a demand for recognition or a petition for an election filed with the NLRB. Should that happen; the company will have already lost the first battle in its fight to retain its freedom.

The key is to be aware of the early warning signs of union activity and how they can be recognized. The signs in the following list may or may not appear at the company, but if you recognize any of the activities in the list, you should report them immediately to the designated member of management who handles union-related concerns. You may have discovered important evidence of an attempted organization of employees if you notice

1. A change in the nature of employee complaints and an increase in their frequency
2. Employees forming into groups that include individuals who do not normally associate with each other
3. A large number of policy inquiries, particularly on pay, benefits, and discipline
4. Employees in work areas they do not normally visit
5. Avoidance of supervision, employees clamming up
6. Argumentative questions being asked in meetings
7. Exit-interview information indicating that people are attempting to escape an unpleasant environment
8. News items placed on bulletin boards about union settlements in local companies or other industries
9. Cartoons or graffiti that direct humorous hostility toward the organization, management, or supervision
10. A significant change in the rate of turnover, either upward or downward
11. A number of people applying for jobs who do not have relevant experience and appear to be willing to work in a job with lower status and pay than a job for which their record qualifies them

12. An unusual interest on the part of vendors and subcontractors in communicating with employees
13. Nonunion people beginning to meet and talk with known union members
14. Complaints beginning to be made by a delegation, rather than by single employees
15. Strangers appearing and lingering on the company premises or in work areas
16. Employees or strangers showing unusual curiosity about company affairs and policies
17. Employees adopting a new, technical vocabulary that includes such phrases as *protected activity, unfair labor practices,* and *demands for recognition*
18. Union-authorization cards, handbills, or leaflets appearing on the premises or in parking areas
19. Union representatives visiting or sending mail to employees at their homes
20. Any factor that is out of the ordinary and seems to be separating management from the workforce

Conditions that cause union organizing include

1. Lack of ability or care in screening applicants
2. Failure to remove misfits, preferably during introductory period
3. Expecting overqualified or higher-paid employees to do lower-qualified or lower-paid work
4. Lack of continuing courtesy, respect, and fair consideration from managers, supervisors, and others
5. Lack of effort to motivate employees
6. Failure to listen to and understand employees before making decisions or responses
7. Failure to persuade employees that wage and benefit terms are fair and competitive
8. Lack of attention to employee facilities—lavatories, eating areas, parking, and the like
9. Failure to give employees a sense of security and a feeling that they have a job that others want
10. Handing out nasty little surprises in work schedules, time-off allowances, work assignments, pay cuts, or other changes
11. Failure to truthfully communicate what employees need to know about the company and their jobs
12. Making or implying promises that are not kept
13. Making vague promises that are subject to misinterpretation by employees
14. Failure to persuade employees that criticism or discipline is for their benefit, not solely for company benefit

15. Having a "small" person for a boss, that is, a supervisor who sets a bad example, is snobbish, and/or has a little clique or favorites

16. Failure to respond to employee questions, problems, and complaints

17. Generally, absence of an effective employee-communication program

18. Absence of effective problem-solving procedures

19. Absence of an effective mechanism for monitoring employee complaints

20. Absence of an employee-evaluation procedure

21. Presence of supervisory favoritism

22. Absence of clear and consistent employee policies and procedures

23. Absence of fair, equal, and nondiscriminatory disciplinary procedures

The following steps are recommended for handling a demand for recognition:

1. If you are contacted in person by anyone purporting to represent your employees, follow the guidelines below:

   a. If the person is already in your presence or knows of your presence, do not refuse to talk with him or her. Get the person's business card.

   b. Get a witness, preferably another member of management or your administrative assistant.

   c. If the union representative claims that the union represents a majority of the employees, state that you do not believe it.

   d. Do not look at any list of employees.

   e. Do not look at any cards with names on them.

   f. Do not accept, touch, or examine in any way cards presented to you. If the cards are left on your desk, request that the union representative take the cards with him or her. If the representative refuses, have an employee place the cards in an envelope without looking at them, seal the envelope, and mail the cards back to the union.

   g. Do not discuss with the union representative any alleged complaints regarding employee grievances or other employee matters. State clearly, "I have no authority with respect to union matters. I will refer this to my superiors, who will be in touch with you immediately."

   h. Escort the union representative off the premises.

   i. Contact the designated management representative responsible for union-related matters and report what occurred.

   j. Record in writing what transpired and have your witnesses do the same.

2. If you are contacted by mail, use the following guidelines:

   a. Do not accept from a union any bulky, certified mail that might contain authorization cards.

   b. If, however, cards are received by mail, do not touch or examine them.

   c. Have your administrative assistant place the envelope containing the cards in another envelope, without looking at the cards, and mail them back to the union.

3. If you are contacted by mail with a letter requesting recognition from a union, forward it immediately to the designated management representative.

4. Immediately report any demands for recognition to the designated management representative. If he/she is personally unavailable, contact a previously designated alternate.

The following is reprinted with permission from the Economic Policy Institute: Kate Bronfenbrenner, *No Holds Barred: The Intensification of Employer Opposition to Organizing*, Briefing Paper 235 (Washington, DC: Economic Policy Institute, May 20, 2009).

EPI BRIEFING PAPER

ECONOMIC POLICY INSTITUTE • MAY 20, 2009 • BRIEFING PAPER #235

NO HOLDS BARRED
The Intensification of Employer Opposition to Organizing

BY
KATE BRONFENBRENNER
DIRECTOR OF LABOR EDUCATION RESEARCH
CORNELL SCHOOL OF INDUSTRIAL AND LABOR RELATIONS

Economic Policy Institute

AMERICAN RIGHTS AT WORK EDUCATION FUND

ECONOMIC POLICY INSTITUTE • 1333 H STREET, NW • SUITE 300, EAST TOWER • WASHINGTON, DC 20005 • 202.775.8810 • WWW.EPI.ORG

About the American Rights at Work Education Fund

The **American Rights at Work Education Fund** is an educational and outreach organization dedicated to promoting the freedom of workers to form unions and bargain collectively.

About the Economic Policy Institute

The **Economic Policy Institute** is a nonprofit, nonpartisan think tank that seeks to broaden the public debate about strategies to achieve a prosperous and fair economy. The Institute stresses real world analysis and a concern for the living standards of working people, and it makes its findings accessible to the general public, the media, and policy makers. EPI's books, studies, and popular education materials address important economic issues, analyze pressing problems facing the U.S. economy, and propose new policies.

ECONOMIC POLICY INSTITUTE • MAY 20, 2009 • BRIEFING PAPER #235

NO HOLDS BARRED
The Intensification of Employer Opposition to Organizing

BY KATE BRONFENBRENNER

Executive summary

This study is a comprehensive analysis of employer behavior in representation elections supervised by the National Labor Relations Board (NLRB). The data for this study originate from a thorough review of primary NLRB documents for a random sample of 1,004 NLRB certification elections that took place between January 1, 1999 and December 31, 2003 and from an in-depth survey of 562 campaigns conducted with that same sample. Employer behavior data from prior studies conducted over the last 20 years are used for purposes of comparison. The representativeness of the sample combined with the high response rate for both the survey (56%) and NLRB unfair labor practice (ULP) charge documents (98%) ensure that the findings provide unique and highly credible information. In combination, the results provide a detailed and well-documented portrait of the legal and illegal tactics used by employers in NLRB representational elections and of the ineffectiveness of current labor law policy to protect and enforce workers rights in the election process.

Highlights of the study regarding employer tactics in representational elections include:

- In the NLRB election process in which it is standard practice for workers to be subjected to threats, interrogation, harassment, surveillance, and retaliation for union activity. According to our updated findings,

www.epi.org

ECONOMIC POLICY INSTITUTE • 1333 H STREET, NW • SUITE 300, EAST TOWER • WASHINGTON, DC 20005 • 202.775.8810 • WWW.EPI.ORG employers threatened to close the plant in 57% of elections, discharged workers in 34%, and threatened to cut wages and benefits in 47% of elections. Workers were forced to attend anti-union one-on-one sessions with a supervisor at least weekly in two-thirds of elections. In 63% of elections employers used supervisor one-on-one meetings to interrogate workers about who they or other workers supported, and in 54% used such sessions to threaten workers.

- In combination, our survey and ULP findings reveal that employer opposition has intensified: the incidence of elections in which employers used 10 or more tactics more than doubled compared to the three earlier periods we studied, and the nature of campaigns has changed so that the focus is on more coercive and punitive tactics designed to intensely monitor and punish union activity.

- Many of these same tactics have been key elements of employer anti-union campaigns that we have studied for the last 20 years.[1] Although the use of management consultants, captive audience meetings, and supervisor one-on-ones has remained fairly constant, there has been an increase in more coercive and retaliatory tactics ("sticks") such as plant closing threats and actual plant closings, discharges, harassment and other discipline, surveillance, and alteration of benefits and conditions. At the same time, employers are less likely to offer "carrots," as we see a gradual decrease in tactics such as granting of unscheduled raises, positive personnel changes, promises of improvement, bribes and special favors, social events, and employee involvement programs.

- Unions filed unfair labor practice charges in 39% of the survey sample and 40% of the NLRB election sample. The survey and NLRB documents both show that the most aggressive employer anti-union behavior—that is, the highest percentage of allegations—were threats, discharges, interrogation, surveillance, and wages and benefits altered for union activity.

- The character of the process in the private sector is illuminated by survey data from the public-sector campaigns, which describe an atmosphere where workers organize relatively free from the kind of coercion, intimidation, and retaliation that so dominates in the private sector. Most of the states in our public-sector sample have card check certification as the primary means through which workers are organizing, where the employer is required to recognize the union if the majority of workers sign cards authorizing the union to represent them.

Highlights of the study regarding NLRB ULP charges include:

- Twenty-three percent of all ULP charges and 24% or more of serious charges—such as discharges for union activity, interrogation, and surveillance—were filed before the petition for an election was filed, and 16% were filed more than 30 days before the election petition was filed. These data confirm that employer campaigning, including the employer free speech provision, does not depend on a petition to kick into effect.

- Forty-five percent of ULP charges resulted in a "win" for the union: either the employer settled the charges or the NLRB or the courts issued a favorable decision.

- Thirty-seven percent of ULP charges result in the issuance of a complaint by the NLRB. Twenty-six percent are withdrawn by the union prior to the complaint being issued, and 23% are found to have no merit. Just under a third of all charges are resolved in whole or in part at the settlement level with 14% settling before the complaint is issued, with 18% settling after the complaint but before the Administrative Law Judge (ALJ) hearing process is complete. The content of the settlements is very similar except that settlements prior to merit determination are less likely to include reinstatement than those settled after the complaint.

- Employers tend to appeal most ALJ decisions, particularly Gissel bargaining orders and orders for second elections. This means that in the most egregious cases the employer is able to ensure that the case is delayed by three to five years, and in all the cases in our sample the worst penalty an employer had to pay was back pay, averaging a few thousand dollars per employee.

- Our findings and previous research suggest that unions are filing ULPs in fewer than half the elections for three main reasons: filing charges where the election is likely to be won could delay the election for months if not years; workers fear retaliation for filing charges, especially where the election is likely to be lost; and the weak remedies, lengthy delays, and the numerous rulings where ALJ recommendations for reinstatement, second elections, and bargaining orders have then been overturned, delayed, or never enforced, have diminished trust that the system will produce a remedy.

In 2007 there were only 1,510 representation elections and only 58,376 workers gained representation through the NLRB. Even for those who do win the election, 52% are still without a contract a year later, and 37% are still without a contract two years after an election. Yet researchers such as Freeman (2007) are showing that workers want unions now more than at any other time in the last three decades. Our findings suggest that the aspirations for representation are being thwarted by a coercive and punitive climate for organizing that goes unrestrained due to a fundamentally flawed regulatory regime that neither protects their rights nor provides any disincentives for employers to continue disregarding the law. Moreover, many of the employer tactics that create a punitive and coercive atmosphere are, in fact, legal. Unless serious labor law reform with real penalties is enacted, only a fraction of the workers who seek representation under the National Labor Relations Act will be successful. If recent trends continue, then there will no longer be a functioning legal mechanism to effectively protect the right of private-sector workers to organize and collectively bargain.

In a nation where union density stands at 12.4%, it is easy to forget that the majority of U.S. workers want unions. In fact, more workers would choose to be unionized if given the opportunity than at any time in the last 30 years. According to Richard Freeman (2007) the percent of the non-managerial workforce who say they would vote for a union has been steadily increasing from 30% in the early 1980s, to almost 40% in the mid-1990s, reaching 53% in 2005. Based on his estimates, if all workers who wanted a union were actually given the opportunity they desired, then as of 2005 union density would have been as high as 58% (BLS 2007; Freeman 2007). Yet, in 2009, the overwhelming majority of workers who want unions do not have them. The majority also believes that, due to employer opposition, they would be taking a great risk if they were to organize (Hart 2007). For these workers, the right to organize and bargain collectively—free from coercion, intimidation, and retaliation—is at best a promise indefinitely deferred.

Since the rise of the union-avoidance industry in the 1970s (Smith 2003), we have witnessed a significant increase in the intensity and aggressiveness with which private-sector employers have opposed organizing efforts in their firms. As companies have globalized and restructured, corporate anti-union strategies have become more sophisticated, through resorting to implied or real threats of ownership change, outsourcing, or contracting out in response to nearly every organizing campaign (Bronfenbrenner 1994; 2000; Compa 2004; Logan 2006).

The combination of deregulation, investor-centered trade and investment policies, and an underfunded and disempowered National Labor Relations Board (NLRB) appears to have emboldened employers to act with increasing disregard for the National Labor Relations Act (NLRA). Long-time "union free" companies such as Wal-Mart, Coverall North America, and Cintas have been able to accelerate their anti-union efforts on multiple fronts because of the dysfunction and ineffectiveness of our labor law regime (Ruckelshaus 2007; Compa 2004). As labor historian Nelson Lichtenstein (2008, 1,492) explains, between 1998 and 2003 unions filed 288 unfair labor practices against Wal-Mart alone:

These included forty-one charges claiming improper firings, forty-four instances in which Wal-Mart threatened employees if they joined a union, fifty-nine charges involving improper surveillance, and another fifty-nine asserting that Wal-Mart illegally interrogated its associates to determine their views on sensitive labor related issues. In all, ninety-four of these complaints were weighty enough to generate a formal NLRB complaint against the corporation.

What distinguishes the current organizing climate from previous decades of employer opposition to unions? The primary difference is that the most intense and aggressive anti-union campaign strategies, the kind previously found only at employers like Wal-Mart, are no longer reserved for a select coterie of extreme anti-union employers. In examining NLRB documents we discovered dozens of employers similar to Earthgrains—companies with a history of maintaining a stable collective bargaining relationship with the majority of their workforce—making a dramatic shift in how they respond to union organizing efforts. When faced with an organizing campaign in its London, Kentucky plant in the summer of 2000, Earthgrains unleashed a relentless campaign of threats, interrogations, surveillance, harassment, and intimidation against the union.[2] The charges against Earthgrains included videotaping workers as they spoke to union representatives; maintaining and showing to workers a list that supposedly revealed how other workers were going to vote; interrogating workers about whether they or their co-workers supported a union; threatening to fire workers for union activity; managers forcibly removing union literature from the hands of employees while they were on break; threatening to eliminate entire shifts, take away retirement plans, or gain-sharing benefits if the union won in the plant; telling the workers the union would go on strike as soon as the election was won; and promising improvements in benefits and a committee to resolve grievances if the union lost (Ahearn 2000).

The corporate anti-union strategy used in the Earthgrains campaign had an enormous emphasis on interrogation, surveillance, harassment, threats, and fear. Whereas these aggressive tactics have normally been associated with only the most extremely anti-union firms, the examples of Earthgrains and similar employers demonstrate that trend is changing. These trends show us that in today's organizing climate, even employers with no prior history of waging war against unions are increasingly running extremely aggressive anti-union campaigns with great success.

The changing behavior by companies such as Earthgrains raises several key questions critical to the labor policy debate currently before Congress. Has the nature and intensity of employer opposition changed over the last decade? Has the NLRB or the court system changed their interpretation or enforcement of the law in ways that might account for these changes in employer behavior? How does labor law need to be reformed in order to restore the promise embodied in Section 7 of the NLRA that workers have the right to organize and bargain first agreements?

For the past 20 years the primary focus of my research agenda has been to answer just these kinds of questions through a series of empirical studies examining the role of employer behavior and NLRB practice and policy in determining NLRB election certification of election outcomes. Combined, this research makes up the only extant national data on legal and illegal employer behavior during union election campaigns over time, controlling for election environment, company characteristics, union tactics, and bargaining unit demographics.[3] This report is the product of my most recent study, which set out both to update my earlier work and expand on it by doing a full Freedom of Information Act request (FOIA) from the NLRB for all unfair labor practice documents relating to the election sample.

Methodology and data

This study examines employer behavior in NLRB elections in the private sector as well as the process for filing charges of unfair labor practices to protect workers' rights to organize free from coercion, intimidation, and retaliation from employers.[4] It is based on a random sample of 1,004 NLRB campaigns taken from the full population of all certification elections in units with 50 or more eligible voters between January 1, 1999 and December 31, 2003 (BNA Plus 2000; 2002; 2004).[5] (Hereafter, this paper will refer to this broad set of 1,004 elections as the "NLRB

election sample.") Using in-depth surveys with the lead organizer conducted by mail, phone, or email, personal interviews, documentary evidence, and electronic databases, we compiled detailed data on election background, organizing environment, bargaining unit demographics, company and union characteristics and tactics, and election and first contract outcomes.

We believe that the methods we used have been proven to be the most effective means for collecting data on employer behavior in organizing campaigns (see Appendix). It would be preferable if scholars could interview workers in the aftermath of each organizing campaign and find out how the employer campaign had affected their vote. However, as indicated by the paucity of this kind of research on any scale, there are significant barriers to conducting such research. Most obvious is that the same climate of fear and intimidation that surrounds the certification election would influence how workers would respond to any survey. Workers would fear that the employer would figure out how they were answering the survey, just as they seemed able to determine which way workers intend to vote in elections. It would be extremely difficult to gain approval for such research from any university human subjects institutional review board because of the risks to the worker. The second problem is a matter of scale. Getting even modest funding for research on organizing is extremely difficult, but to conduct a study that would be representative of a broad enough cross-section of workers from different kinds of industries, unions, and employer campaigns would require an extremely large sample and a very labor intensive survey process, with the probability of a very small return rate. So instead, most research involves individual voter studies that poll unorganized workers about how they think employers would react to an organizing attempt.

Some critics have raised questions as to the reliability of union organizers as a data source. This question is answered by the consistency of our findings over time and by the fact that the organizer findings have been confirmed repeatedly by NLRB decisions and transcripts, primary campaign documents, first contracts, and newspaper reports. Also, it is simply not possible to use employers as an alternate source. As we have demonstrated in previous studies, the overwhelming majority of employers are engaging in at least one or more illegal behaviors (at minimum 75% of the employers in the current sample are alleged to have committed at least one illegal action). Not only would it be next to impossible to get employers to complete surveys in which they honestly reported on illegal activity, but that kind of question would not be permitted by university institutional review boards since it might put the subjects at risk of legal action. Our past survey research has shown that surveying lead organizers, combined with collecting supporting documentary evidence (such as employer and company campaign literature, newspaper articles, campaign videos, unfair labor practice documents, and on-line information about company strategy, ownership, and financial conditions) is a reliable method for answering these questions. We decided, however, that we would impose an even higher standard on the research data. Instead of sending out a one-time FOIA request to the NLRB based on whatever surveys were returned and accepting whatever documents we received, we made it a priority to get all available unfair labor practice documents for every case in our sample whether or not a survey was returned. This then would be the first comprehensive database examining the current practice of the NLRB in processing ULP charges, all the way from charge sheets through court decisions. Equally important, for those cases where we had both survey data and unfair labor practice data, we would be able to analyze the relationships between employer behavior, election outcomes, and the processing of ULP charges, and the implication of these relationships for the labor law reform debate.

Surveys were completed for 562 of the 1,004 cases in the sample, for a response rate of 56% (**Table 1**). We refer to these data as our "survey data" and the full sample of 1,004 cases as the "NLRB election sample." Furthermore, we were able to collect corporate ownership structure information—such as parent company name and base country; non-profit or for-profit status; whether the company is publicly or privately held; countries or regions of sites, operations, suppliers and customers; whether other units or sites are unionized—for all of the cases, and at least partial financial information for 75% of those in our sample. We also ran summary statistics across several key variables, such as union and industry, to ensure that the sample was representative of the population of all NLRB

certification elections in units of 50 or more voters that took place in 1999-2003 (BNA Plus 2003; 2004).

Unfair labor practice documents

We collected unfair labor practice documents from the NLRB for two purposes. First, we wanted to know whether the same trends we were finding in the most egregious behavior in the organizer surveys would reflect the most common allegations found in the ULP charges filed and upheld in whole or in part in settlements and NLRB dispositions. Second, we wanted to document NLRB practice and function in processing ULP charges in the current organizing climate, and the implications that their current methods and practices have for labor law reform.

Our goal in this process was to collect the full spectrum of ULP documents relating to each election in our sample. To do this, we first obtained data from the NLRB Case Activity Tracking System (CATS) to prepare a Freedom of Information Request for all legal documents relating to unfair labor practices tied to the elections in our sample. The request specifically included charge sheets, letters of withdrawal, no merit determinations, settlement agreements, complaints, Administrative Law Judge decisions, NLRB decisions, court decisions, and all other related documents for the elections in our sample. For those cases that had been closed because more than six years had passed, we requested and received the charge sheet and a letter from the NLRB outlining the disposition of the case.[7] Once surveys had been returned, we also sent an amended FOIA request that included all the cases in our survey sample where organizers reported a ULP charge had been filed but the ULP did not show up in the CATS database, either because of a change in the company name or a data-entry error in the database. We have gotten responses from every region of the NLRB, covering 99% of our original FOIA request sample and 98% of the amended request from the survey sample.[8]

Given the extent of the ULP documents received, it might seem that they, rather than organizer survey responses, should be used as the sole or preferred measure of illegal employer behavior. However, as previous research has shown (Bronfenbrenner 1997b; 2000; Compa 2004) while unfair labor practice prosecutions can help

TABLE 1

Summary data from NLRB election survey and unfair labor practice data collection

	All years	1999	2000	2001	2002	2003
Number of elections in total sample	1,004	248	218	198	174	165
Percent of total sample	100%	25%	22%	20%	17%	17%
Percent win rate in sample	45	41	45	43	47	48
Survey data						
Percent surveys returned	56%	50%	49%	64%	55%	67%
Percent by mail	39	48	39	43	33	32
Percent by phone	26	27	23	21	26	32
Percent by Web	33	22	38	34	38	33
Percent by fax	2	2	1	2	3	3
Percent win rate for returns	47	47	49	44	53	45
ULP data – full sample						
Percent of sample with ULP charges	40%	32%	44%	40%	43%	42%
Total response rate from FOIA (for all elections with ULP charges)	98	100	98	96	96	96
Percent full documents received	57	23	41	65	84	78
Percent partial documents received	21	34	33	13	11	13
Percent ULP charges confirmed but documents reported destroyed	14	39	12	7	0	0
Percent still awaiting NLRB response	5	5	10	9	4	4
Percent no records found	3	0	4	6	1	4
ULP data – sample with survey responses						
Percent of sample with ULP charges	39%	28%	41%	38%	47%	27%
Total response rate from FOIA (for all elections with ULP charges)	98	100	99	96	97	96
Percent full documents received	58	19	41	65	85	76
Percent partial documents received	21	38	33	17	7	15
Percent ULP charges confirmed but documents reported destroyed	11	36	12	6	0	0
Percent still awaiting NLRB response	7	6	10	6	7	4
Percent no records found	4	0	4	6	2	6

SOURCE: Bronfenbrenner's survey of NLRB elections 1999-2003; Bronfenbrenner's analysis of NLRB ULP documents, 1999-2003 NLRB election sample.

capture the nature and intensity of employer opposition to union activity, and while monitoring ULPs over time can help track changing patterns in employer behavior, ULPs are inadequate for measuring the totality of employer behavior.

First, unions are hesitant to file charges when there is a high probability that they are going to win the election because the employer can use the ULP charges to indefinitely delay or block the election. Even in the case of discharges for union activity (one of the most egregious

ULPs), unions often wait until after the election (as long as it is within the six-month filing period) to see if they are able to negotiate reinstatement before filing a charge. Given the long time that it takes to litigate a ULP case to conclusion, and the relatively weak relief available even for employees who ultimately win their cases, the statutory scheme does not provide strong incentives for workers to pursue such charges. As Lance Compa (2004, 68) explains:

> In practice, many discriminatory discharge cases are settled with a small back-pay payment and workers' agreement not to return to the workplace. At a modest cost and with whatever minor embarrassment comes with posting a notice, the employer is rid of the most active union supporters, and the organizing campaign is stymied.

Alternatively, in cases where the union lost the election badly, organizers reported to us that they had considerable difficulty getting workers to come forward and testify because they were afraid of retribution from the employer. Furthermore, workers are keenly aware that even in cases with egregious employer violations, the most likely penalty is a posting and a small amount of back pay, which could take more than two years from filing the charge to a final Board decision to collect (Organizer interviews

2008; Compa 2004). Therefore, the incentive to pursue such cases is limited.

And finally many union ULP victories are not captured in NLRB or court determinations but rather in informal settlements that occur after charges are filed but before the merit determination (the issuance of a formal complaint by the NLRB's general counsel) takes place, or after the election as part of the first contract process. Thus, with less than half of all illegal employer violations captured by ULPs, they are best used in combination with other measures to assess the totality of the changing nature of employer opposition.

The decline of organizing under the NLRB

In 1970, 276,353 workers organized through NLRB elections. There were a total of 7,733 elections that year. The win rate was 55%, and 49% of the eligible voters eventually gained union representation. Outside of several thousand railway and airlines employees who would have organized that year under the Railway Labor Act, and construction and entertainment industry workers who have rarely organized through the traditional NLRB process due to the short-term nature of their employment markets, those 276,353 workers represented close to the totality of the private-sector workforce organizing that year (Pavy 1994). The 1970s also saw the beginning

TABLE 2

NLRB representation elections, 1999-2007

Year	Number of elections	Percent win rate	Number of eligible voters	Number in elections won	Percent of voters in elections won
1999	3,108	52%	243,720	106,699	44%
2000	2,826	53	212,680	93,346	44
2001	2,361	54	193,321	68,718	36
2002	2,724	59	189,863	72,908	40
2003	2,351	58	150,047	77,427	52
2004	2,363	59	166,525	84,838	51
2005	2,137	61	125,305	64,502	52
2006	1,657	61	112,598	59,841	53
2007	1,510	61	101,709	58,376	57

SOURCE: BNA Plus 2003; 2008.

of the first big wave of organizing in the public sector. Although there are no official records of the total number of public-sector workers organized in the 1970s, we can assume that at least 50,000 to 100,000 new public-sector workers were added each year. Still, the majority of workers who organized into unions did so through the NLRB (Bronfenbrenner and Juravich 1995).

By 1987, when I conducted my first study of employer behavior, unions won only 1,610 elections out of 3,314 (49%), and the number of workers organized under the NLRB had plummeted to 81,453 (Pavy 1994). The NLRB as a means to organize was already in grave danger.

Twenty years later in 2007, the number of workers newly obtaining union representation through all possible mechanisms averaged somewhere between 600,000-800,000 workers a year.[9] At least 400,000 are public sector, 7,000-25,000 are under the Railway Labor Act depending on the year, and the rest are in the private sector. But as explained in **Table 2**, a diminishing portion, now less than 20%, of new workers organized in the private sector are using the means established for them by law to organize— the National Labor Relations Act.

In 2007, out of 101,709 workers who voted in NLRB elections, only 58,376 workers wound up with union representation. For years fewer and fewer workers have tried to use the NLRA, and fewer have been successful.[10] That is not to say that hundreds of thousands of workers, if not millions, are not trying to organize under the NLRB. To the contrary, many begin the NLRB process but eventually give up along the way because the odds are so stacked against them. Based on these findings and those discussed above, we conclude that the certification election process, as established by the Taft-Hartley Act and as it has been enforced by the NLRB and the courts, has failed to function as the legislation was originally intended. As mentioned earlier, opinion polling has consistently shown that the majority of private-sector workers want unions, but they do not see a safe and viable means to get representation (Freeman 2007; Hart 2005). Without reform, the NLRA no longer serves as a viable mechanism for workers to obtain union representation. Our findings explain why this is so.

Threats, interrogation, promises, surveillance, and retaliation for union activity

Over the last two decades there has been a gradual evolution in employer tactics during NLRB certification election campaigns. In the 1970s and 1980s, employers took the initiative, hiring consultants and pulling together many of the basic elements of the anti-union "tool-kit" that still make up the core of most employers' strategies today. But these tactics have not remained constant. Over time they have changed in both sophistication and intensity as employers adapted to changing economic, trade, and investment climates as well as changes in the political and regulatory environment. Similarly, as unions made strategic responses to these same changes, employers responded in kind with new initiatives to counter them.

Table 3 provides summary statistics on the full range of employer behavior data we collected in the NLRB survey. These findings capture the breadth and extent of employer opposition to organizing while also suggesting how employers continuously capitalize on the changing environment and use it to their advantage. We have grouped these tactics into the following categories: threats, interrogation, and surveillance; fear, coercion, and violence; retaliation and harassment; promises, bribes, and improvements; election interference; and public campaigns.

In combination, these numbers reveal a chilling pattern. First, they show that the overwhelming majority of employers—either under the direction of an outside management consultant or their own in-house counsel— are running aggressive campaigns of threats, interrogation, surveillance, harassment, coercion, and retaliation. Second, these tactics, both individually and in tandem, are part of a highly sophisticated, carefully crafted strategy that has withstood the test of time.

Under the free speech provisions of the NLRA, employers have control of the communication process, and as shown in Table 3, in today's organizing climate they take full advantage of that opportunity to communicate with their employees through a steady stream of letters, leaflets, emails, digital electronic media, individual one-on-one meetings with supervisors, and mandatory captive-audience

TABLE 3

Employer tactics in NLRB elections, 1999-2003

	Percent or mean of elections	Election win rate when employer tactic:	
		used	not used
Employer mounted a campaign against the union	96%	48%	72%
Hired management consultant	75%	43%	52%
Employer use of threats, interrogation, and surveillance			
Held captive audience meetings	89%	47%	73%
Number of meetings	10.4	-	-
More than 5 meetings	53%	47%	48%
Mailed anti-union letters	70%	46%	59%
Number of letters	6.5	-	-
More than 5 letters	28%	49%	45%
Distributed anti-union leaflets	74%	46%	59%
Number of leaflets	16.2	-	-
More than 5 leaflets	61%	46%	51%
Used E-mail communications	7%	49%	53%
Used anti-union DVDs/videos/Internet	41%	39%	57%
Held supervisor one-on-ones	77%	48%	56%
One-on-ones at least weekly	66%	48%	54%
Used them to interrogate workers	63%	49%	51%
Used them to threaten workers	54%	49%	50%
Used any type of surveillance	14%	58%	48%
Used electronic surveillance	11%	57%	49%
Attempted to infiltrate organizing committee	28%	44%	51%
Interrogated workers about union activity	64%	49%	52%
Threatened cuts in benefits or wages	47%	51%	48%
Threats of plant closing	57%	45%	53%
Actually closed plant after the election	15%	56%	44%
Threatened to file for bankruptcy	3%	63%	49%
Filed for bankruptcy	0%	50%	50%
Threatened to report workers to INS	7%	34%	51%
Actually referred workers to INS	1%	17%	50%
Made random document checks	3%	56%	49%
Fear, coercion, and violence			
Employer used events of 9/11 or national security	2%	57%	50%
Used guards, put up security fencing, or cameras	14%	50%	50%
Brought police into the workplace	21%	46%	51%
Police arrested workers on site	0%	0%	50%
Employer instigated violence and blamed union	7%	45%	50%
Retaliation and harassment			
Discharged union activists	34%	49%	50%
Number discharged	2.6	-	-
Workers not reinstated before election	29%	47%	72%

cont. on page 11

TABLE 3 (CONT.)

Employer tactics in NLRB elections, 1999-2003

	Percent or mean of elections	Election win rate when employer tactic:	
		used	not used
Other harassment and discipline of union activists	41%	55%	49%
Transferred pro-union activists out of the unit	5%	64%	49%
Laid off bargaining unit members	5%	50%	50%
Number laid off	32.6	-	-
Contracted out bargaining unit work	3%	71%	49%
Number of jobs contracted out	34.0	-	-
Alteration in benefits or working conditions	22%	49%	53%
Promises, bribes, and improvements			
Granted unscheduled raises	18%	49%	50%
Made positive personnel changes	27%	47%	51%
Made promises of improvement	46%	44%	54%
Used bribes and special favors	22%	47%	51%
Held company social events	16%	50%	50%
Established employee involvement program	15%	39%	50%
Upgraded health & safety conditions	7%	43%	50%
Promoted pro-union activists	11%	57%	49%
Election interference			
Solicitation/distribution rules	10%	43%	50%
Employer used NLRB-like front group	11%	54%	49%
Assisted anti-union committee	30%	41%	53%
Public campaign			
Ran media campaign	12%	43%	51%
Use free mass media	8%	35%	51%
Purchased time on paid media	3%	41%	50%
Involved community leaders/politicians	6%	46%	50%
Other tactics			
Distributed pay stubs with dues deducted	23%	42%	52%
Distributed union promise coupon books	22%	44%	51%
Held raffles relating to union dues	3%	32%	50%
Filed ULP charges against the union	3%	80%	49%
Filed election objections	8%	91%	46%
Intensity of employer campaign			
Number of tactics used	10.9	-	-
No tactics used	6%	72%	48%
Weak campaign (1-4 tactics)	10%	65%	35%
Moderate campaign (5-9 tactics)	30%	40%	52%
Aggressive campaign (10 or more tactics)	54%	45%	55%

SOURCE: Bronfenbrenner's survey of NLRB elections, 1999-2003.

meetings with top management during work time. Nearly 90% of employers use captive audience meetings, holding on average 10.4 meetings a year. Seventy-seven percent hold supervisory one-on-ones, and two-thirds hold them at least weekly throughout the campaign.

But this is nothing new. For years these tactics have been the primary means through which companies make their case against unions (Bronfenbrenner 2000; 2004). What stands out about these data is what they tell us about how the tactics are being used. These data provide additional insight into the critical role played by supervisor one-on-ones as the primary means through which employers deliver threats and engage in interrogation. As shown in Table 3, employers use supervisor one-on-ones to threaten workers for union activity in at least 54% of campaigns and to interrogate workers about their union activity and that of coworkers in at least 63% of campaigns. In addition to interrogation, 14% of employers use surveillance, primarily electronic (11%), and 28% of employers attempt to infiltrate the organizing committee in order to learn more about union supporters and activity.

Table 3 shows that these threats take many forms. Fifty-seven percent of employers make plant closing threats, and 47% threaten wage or benefit cuts. In 7% of all campaigns—but 50% of campaigns with a majority of undocumented workers and 41% with a majority of recent immigrants—employers make threats of referral to Immigration Customs and Enforcement (ICE).

We also confirmed new tactics involving fear, coercion, and violence that organizing directors say are increasingly common. They include such actions as bringing in security guards, putting up fencing, and putting in security cameras (14%), bringing in police to walk through the plant (21%), or instigating violence and trying to put the blame on the union (7%). However, despite the substantial number of police walkthroughs, none of the cases in our survey sample included any arrests, which makes the use of the police appear to be merely one more coercive strategy rather than reflecting any legitimate security concern.

In combination, these more aggressive coercive actions—threats of plant closure, referrals to ICE, benefit cuts, police walk-throughs, turning the workplace into an armed camp—send a clear message to workers: those who choose to move forward with the union do so at great personal risk. Employers send an even stronger message when they follow through on their threats with direct retaliation and harassment for union activity, such as when they actually refer workers to ICE (7% of all units with undocumented workers); discharge workers for union activity (34%); issue suspensions, written warnings, close supervision, and verbal abuse (41%); alter benefits or working conditions (22%); order layoffs (5%); contract out (3%); and transfer workers (5%). It is a message heard well beyond the workplaces where the organizing campaigns take place, discouraging not only the voters in that particular campaign, but holding back others from even attempting to get a campaign off the ground (Hart 2005).

In addition to punitive strategies, employers continue to use softer, less overtly coercive tactics such as promises of improvement (46%); bribes and special favors (22%); the use of social events (16%); or the use of employee involvement programs (15%). These tactics have commonly been the reward for supporting or cooperating with the employer campaign, and in the past they have been among the most effective employer strategies (Bronfenbrenner 1994; Rundle 1998). But it seems that in the current climate, such promises play a less central role because, as I have found in my research on global outsourcing, employers are willing and able to risk being more ruthless in their treatment of workers because they face fewer regulatory, economic, and social repercussions for doing so (Luce and Bronfenbrenner 2007; Bronfenbrenner 2000).

Employers also engage in tactics that directly interfere with the union campaign. The most common of these is assisting the establishment of an anti-union committee (30% of the campaigns). At least 10%[11] of employers illegally issue rules for union communications and distribution of union materials that are different from rules applied to other organizations and activities, while 11% have individuals who pose as agents of the NLRB spread misinformation among workers.

In this study's data, most of the more extreme employer tactics—supervisor one-on-ones at least weekly, police walk-throughs, plant closing threats, promises, bribes, or assisting the anti-union committee—are associated

---

TABLE 4

Changes in frequency and intensity of employer tactics over time

	Proportion of elections tactics employed in:			
	1986-87	1993-95	1998-99	1999-2003
Hired management consultant	72%	82%	76%	75%
Employer use of threats, interrogation, surveillance				
Held captive audience meetings	82%	93%	92%	89%
Average number of captive audience meetings	5.5	9.5	11.6	10.4
Mailed anti-union letters	80%	78%	70%	70%
Average number of letters	4.5	5.4	6.7	6.5
Used E-mail communications			6%	7%
Distributed anti-union leaflets	70%	81%	75%	74%
Average number of leaflets	6.0	10.8	13.3	16.2
Held supervisor one-on-ones	79%	82%	78%	77%
Used electronic surveillance		13%	6%	11%
Used anti-union DVDs/videos/Internet		63%	54%	41%
Threats of plant closing	29%	50%	52%	57%
Actually closed plant after the election	2%	4%	1%	15%
Threatened to report workers to INS/ICE		1%	7%	7%
Retaliation and harassment				
Discharged union activists	30%	32%	26%	34%
Workers not reinstated before election	18%	21%	23%	29%
Other harassment and discipline of union activists			9%	41%
Alteration in benefits or working conditions		27%	17%	22%
Promises, bribes, and improvements				
Granted unscheduled raises	30%	25%	20%	18%
Made positive personnel changes		38%	34%	27%
Made promises of improvement	56%	64%	48%	46%
Used bribes and special favors		42%	34%	22%
Held company social events	4%	28%	21%	16%
Established employee involvement program	7%	16%	17%	15%
Promoted pro-union activists	17%	16%	11%	11%
Other tactics				
Assisted anti-union committee	42%	45%	31%	30%
Ran media campaign	10%	9%	5%	12%
Intensity of employer campaign				
Number of tactics used by employer	5.0	8.2	7.2	10.9
No tactics	0%	3%	3%	6%
More than 5 tactics	38%	78%	63%	82%
More than 10 tactics	0%	26%	20%	49%

SOURCE: See Bronfenbrenner (1994) for the 1986-87 study, Bronfenbrenner (1997b) for the 1993-94 study, and Bronfenbrenner (2000) and Bronfenbrenner and Hickey (2004) for the 1998-99 study.

with union win rates several percentage points (between 5 to 7) lower than in campaigns where they are not used. Compared to my previous studies, this gap between the win rates when tactics are utilized and when they are not has been closing (except for the most extreme tactics). This difference is most likely explained by the fact that employers are now sophisticated enough in their opposition strategies that they can often discourage union formation even without having to use these most aggressive tactics, thus only resorting to them for campaigns in which they feel the union has a good chance of winning.

Changes in frequency and intensity of employer tactics over time

Table 4 presents data on the key tactics most commonly used by employers from our studies conducted over the last 20-plus years. These include data from this study as well as 1986-87 (Bronfenbrenner 1993), 1993-95 (Bronfenbrenner 1996), and 1998-99 (Bronfenbrenner 2000). Although on the whole we find the same list of tactics—a combination of threats, interrogation, promises, surveillance, and retaliation for union activity—that employers have used for the last two decades, we find in the last several years there has been certain shifting of focus, scale, and intensity in employer campaigns. Although the use of management consultants, captive-audience meetings, and supervisor one-on-ones has remained fairly constant, more recently we have seen an increase in more coercive and retaliatory tactics such as plant closing threats and actual plant closings, discharges, harassment and other discipline, surveillance, and alteration of benefits and conditions. At the same time employers are not bothering as much with promises of improvements, as we see a gradual decrease in tactics such as granting of unscheduled raises, positive personnel changes, bribes and special favors, social events, and employee involvement programs.

With the exception of plant closing threats (which nearly doubled by increasing from 29% in 1986-87 to 57% today) and discharged workers not being reinstated before the election (which gradually increased from 18% in 1986-87 to 29%), most of the increase in more coercive tactics occurred in the period since our last study. Discharges for union activity have increased from 26% to 34%, alterations in benefits or working conditions have

increased from 17% to 22%, and other harassment and discipline of union activists from 9% to 41%.[12]

In contrast, the decline for the softer tactics began in the late 1980s or early 1990s, continuing through the present. Most of these tactics, including the granting of unscheduled raises, promises of improvement, and social events, dropped 10 to 2 percentage points, but some, including bribes and special favors, decreased as much as 20 percentage points. It seems that most employers feel less need to bother with the carrot and instead are going straight for the stick.

Yet the employer behavior data tell a story that is more complex than simply a shift toward more coercive tactics. Our new findings also show a consistent pattern across the data, namely that threats, interrogation, surveillance, harassment, and retaliation were the most common tactics across all the campaigns surveyed.

As Administrative Law Judge (ALJ) Paul Bogas describes in his decision regarding Rugby Manufacturing, these patterns are not random. Rugby's anti-union campaign began after management was alerted to union activity and in response, "called its managers and supervisors together for a special Saturday meeting at which the attendees were instructed on techniques for discerning who was a union supporter."[13] Managers and supervisors were encouraged to casually broach the subject of unionization with their employees "in hopes that the employees would reciprocate by divulging their own sentiments" (Rugby 2002, 3). The results of these "conversations" were recorded on a chart detailing the contacts Rugby supervisors made with employees regarding the union.

Rugby "also engaged in frequent anti-union lobbying of individual employees" sometimes two or more times a day (Rugby 2002, 4). The engineering manager of the facility "gave daily anti-union speeches at the facility and stated that he was afraid the Respondent would close down if the employees unionized" (Rugby 2002, 4). Other managers and supervisors "warned employees that there could be negative repercussions if they discussed the Union among themselves" (Rugby 2002, 4). The consolidated complaints issued against Rugby included serious labor law violations such as "terminating two employees, laying off 16 employees, and refusing to recall 15 of the laid-off employees" because of union activity and to discourage further union activity, offering a promotion to the leading rank-and-file union activist (which he turned down), and "prohibiting employees from discussing union matters during company time, threatening employees regarding such discussions, maintaining a no-solicitation policy, and engaging in coercive interrogation" (Rugby 2002, 1). Given the intensity and aggressiveness of the employer campaign, it is not surprising that the Steelworkers lost the election 48 to 31 on November 30, 2000, just one month after they petitioned for the election.

The most important part of the Rugby story is not the most dramatic—the discharges and layoffs—but rather the full arc of the employer's plan, which in fact started not with the meeting with the supervisors, but as Bogas points out in his decision, with its aggressive union-free policy. This policy was clearly outlined in the employee handbook, and read out loud to all new employees upon hiring. It made it clear that unions would not be tolerated, laying the groundwork for the aggressive and intense effort that followed. But the model that Rugby and so many others of these campaigns adopt is one in which the priority task of frontline supervisors is to ascertain through whatever means possible the leanings of every worker and then use the more aggressive retaliatory tactics to sway those leaning toward unionization.

A case such as Rugby reminds us of the great deficiencies of the regulatory regime under which private-sector workers organize in this country. The United Steelworkers did file multiple unfair labor practices at Rugby for the discharges, interrogation, no solicitation policy, threats, layoffs, and denial of recall. It took a year to finally get a consolidated complaint, another year before the ALJ decision, and it was not until January 2003 (more than two years after the election) that the ALJ decision was finally enforced. The decision is what by NLRB standards would be considered "favorable" for the workers and the union. Rugby was found to have violated the NLRA on all charges except one of the discharges, and so was ordered to offer full reinstatement and a back pay award totaling more than $217,000 to be divided up among the 16 workers who lost their jobs (one discharged and the rest laid off and not recalled). In addition, Rugby had to post a notice in all its facilities stating it would cease and desist from all such violations from that point forward.[14]

However, in a case like this, where two years had gone by before the final NLRB decision, most laid-off workers had had to leave town to find employment and weren't coming back. Ultimately, only one of the 16 union activists was reinstated, and the union was unable to win a second election. In July 2007, six years after the workers first tried to organize at Rugby, they did win representation with a different union (NLRB Reports 2007), but 15 out of 16 workers who had been wrongfully terminated for leading the first organizing effort at Rugby, and had to move out of town to even find another job, never obtained union representation at Rugby.

The Rugby story comprises the key elements of our new survey findings. Employer campaigns have become more coercive, with an early emphasis on interrogation and surveillance to identify supporters, followed by threats and harassment to try to dissuade workers from supporting the unions, moving then to retaliation against employees who continue to move forward with the union campaign. Employers may still use promises, wage increases, social events, and other softer tactics, but with much less frequency and not as the focus of their campaigns.

Unfair labor practice findings

Unions filed unfair labor practice charges in 39% of the survey sample and 40% of the NLRB election sample (that was constructed by combining the CATS data and our FOIA request to the NLRB). For the surveys a total of 926 total allegations were filed in all ULP charges combined, while for the full NLRB sample the total number of allegations totaled 1,387.[15] The 39% ULP rate is higher than the 33% rate we found in our 2000 study, but that is not surprising given the increase in more egregious employer anti-union behavior (e.g., discharges and wage/benefit cuts), which can result in actual financial settlements rather than simply notice postings. Still, if we focus on the most common and serious employer anti-union tactics—threats, interrogation, surveillance, harassment, alteration of wages, benefits and/or working conditions, assistance or domination of the anti-union committee, and discharges or layoffs for union activity—the survey results suggest that unions file ULP charges in fewer than half the elections where serious labor law violations occur.

TABLE 5

Total number and percent of allegations filed in returned surveys and full election sample

Allegations	Total allegations in returned surveys	Percent in allegations in returned surveys	Total allegations in sample	Percent allegations in sample
Assistance or domination	12	1%	13	1%
Coercive statements and threats	173	19	248	18
Denial of access	8	1	12	1
Destroying authorization cards	1	0	1	0
Discipline for union activity	66	7	95	7
Discharge for union activity	161	17	265	19
Disparagement	8	1	13	1
Weingarten rights	2	0	2	0
Harassment	41	4	57	4
Imposing onerous assignments	40	4	50	4
Interrogation	79	9	123	9
Lawsuits for union activity	0	0	1	0
Layoff for union activity	11	1	23	2
Misrepresentation	1	0	1	0
Other rules	20	2	31	2
Polling employees	11	1	16	1
Promise of benefits	35	4	58	4
Refusal to hire	3	0	4	0
Retaliation for board participation	21	2	30	2
Solicitation/distribution rules	44	5	66	5
Statements of futility	23	2	34	2
Surveillance	57	6	90	6
Suspension for union activity	46	5	63	5
Violence	1	0	2	0
Wages or benefits altered for union activity	54	6	79	6
Withholding promotions	2	0	2	0
Bribery	1	0	2	0
Impressions of surveillance	3	0	3	0
Refusal to furnish information	1	0	1	0
Refusal to recognize (Not Gissel)	1	0	1	0
Subcontracting unit work	0	0	1	0
Total allegations	926	100	1,387	100

SOURCE: Bronfenbrenner's analysis of NLRB ULP documents, 1999-2003 NLRB election sample.

The reasons workers and unions do not use the NLRB process to file charges every time a serious violation occurs are inherent in the process itself. As the Rugby case demonstrated, it is a process fraught with delays and risks to the worker, with extremely limited penalties for the employer, even in the most extreme cases. In a case where there are just one or two serious allegations, especially if those allegations involve serious 8(a)1 violations (such as threats, surveillance, interrogation) but have no financial penalties, then the risks and benefits of such filings must be weighed each time against the impact they could have on the election. For example, ULPs were not filed in 32% of the elections with serious anti-union tactics in units where the election was won. That is most likely because filing charges can hold up the election for many months if not a year or more. Thus, except in the case of the most egregious violations (e.g., serious harassment, threats of referral to ICE, multiple discharges, or violence), unions typically wait until after the election to file charges. And if the election is won, unions often file charges only on 8(a)3 violations that cannot be negotiated or settled with the employer as part of the first contract process.

Table 5 describes the nature and extent of the total allegations filed in both the returned surveys and the full sample of 1,004 elections.[16] It presents a wide spectrum of employer behaviors, but one that is extremely consistent between the full sample and the survey data, thus reinforcing the representativeness of the survey sample.

The most common allegations are coercive statements and threats (19% of the allegations filed in the survey sample, 18% of allegations filed in the NLRB sample) and discharges for union activity (17% of allegations in the survey sample, 19% of allegations in the NLRB sample). The threats include threats of job loss, wage and benefit cuts, transfers, referrals to ICE, violence, contracting out, sexual harassment or any other kind of coercive statement or action. Other common allegations include interrogation (9%), other disciplinary actions (7%), surveillance (6%), wages or benefits altered for union activity (6%), solicitation distribution rules (5%), suspension for union activity (5%), harassment (4%), imposing onerous assignments (4%), and the promise of benefits (4%).

Table 6 presents the final disposition of the ULPs for the full NLRB election sample.[17] Twenty-six percent of ULPs were withdrawn before merit determination, and 23% were found to have no merit. Fourteen percent were settled in whole or in part before merit determination in either formal or informal settlements. These precomplaint settlement agreements normally include some kind of posting, listing 8(a)1 violations and one or more 8(a)3 violations, and a back-pay award (though typically without reinstatement). But that does not mean they are for minor violations. In most of these agreements the postings include a recitation of the same combination of

---

TABLE 6

Disposition of unfair labor practice charges for full NLRB election sample

Disposition	Percent of allegations in NLRB election sample
Withdrew before merit determination	26%
No merit	23
Settlement in whole or in part prior to merit determination	14
Complaint issued	37
Withdrew prior to hearing	2
Settlement in whole or in part prior to hearing decision	18
ALJ decision (loss)	1
ALJ decision (Upheld in whole or in part)	1
Board Order (Upheld in whole or in part)	9
Board (loss)	3
Federal Court (loss)	0
Federal Court Order (Upheld at in whole or in part)	3

SOURCE: Bronfenbrenner's analysis of NLRB ULP documents, 1999-2003 NLRB election sample.

threats, interrogation, discharges, surveillance, and solicitation rules that make up most of the complaints. The difference is that these employers decided to settle with the union rather than have the NLRB general counsel issue a complaint, and these workers and their union representatives decided to take the settlement rather than risk either not getting a complaint or waiting a year or more for an ALJ decision.

Forty-five percent of unfair labor practice charges filed in the full sample resulted in either a settlement by the employer or a favorable decision by the NLRB or the courts.[18] In 14% of the cases, the employer settled before a compliant was issued and in 37%, the NLRB issued a complaint. Additionally, another 18% of complaints were settled before the ALJ decision. Once a complaint has been issued, a higher percentage of employers settle and a higher percentage of those settlements involve full back pay and offers of reinstatement as well as postings because, as our data show, once a case makes it past a complaint, only a very small percent lose. As a result, there is a great incentive for the employer to settle at this stage. However, there is equal pressure on the worker to settle because, as Table 6 shows, even though only 1% of ALJ decisions are lost, only 1% are enforced at the ALJ level. The remainder of filings are appealed to the NLRB or the courts, often taking as much as two to three years to be resolved. In most pre-hearing settlements, some but not all workers are offered reinstatement, or workers are offered some but not all of their back-pay. The workers' alternative is to wait the full year or more for the ALJ decision, and as these data show, in most cases to wait for the appeal to the full NLRB.

We found several cases in our sample where the ALJ recommended a Gissel bargaining order, but in each case, the NLRB reversed the decision. The most dramatic of these was Abramson LLC, where the violations committed by the employer were so severe that they led Administrative Law Judge Lawrence W. Cullen to decide that a Gissel bargaining order should be issued retroactive to when the union first obtained majority status through signed authorization cards. He found there were "hallmark violations committed by [Abramson] including threats of plant closure and job loss, and threats of loss of substantial benefits by the elimination of transportation benefits, hotels, expense money, and

per diems on out of town assignments." Furthermore, these threats and actions emanated "from the highest level of management and resulted in a substantial reduction in Union support as evidenced by the overwhelming loss of support for the Union on election day from the peak of 54 cards signed in support of the Union" (345 NLRB No.8, 23-24 (2005)).

If the company had not appealed the ALJ decision to issue the Gissel order, bargaining would have commenced within 10 days of Cullen's decision. Instead the workers waited three more years only to have the NLRB overturn the bargaining order and instead order a second election. Part of the basis for the NLRB's decision was that in three cases with "more serious and more pervasive unfair labor practices," a bargaining order was not issued and traditional remedies were used instead. The NLRB reasoned that Abramson's conduct was not bad enough to warrant a bargaining order if previous cases with worse behavior relied on traditional remedies and the running of a second election (345 NLRB No.8, 7 (2005)). The second election was lost.

The decision on which ULPs to settle and which to take to a higher level is partially determined by the type of allegation because, as shown in **Table 7**, certain types of allegations are much more likely to be found to have merit either singly or in combination with other allegations.

The job loss and wage and benefit change allegations have the highest bar to overcome in the merit determination process, most likely because they both require individual workers to come forward and testify and also because those workers have to prove two things. First, that the employer is aware of their union activity, and second, that their union activity is the reason for the discipline, layoff, benefit cut, or changed working conditions. But even if they make it past that phase, these cases tend to be pushed toward non-precedent making settlements rather than ALJ or NLRB decisions, in part because workers cannot afford to wait that long for reinstatement, and the back-pay quickly loses its value once money earned on other jobs is deducted. But the decisions also suggest that the bar to achieving a full NLRB win keeps being raised higher and higher each year, and that the NLRB is increasingly likely to dismiss the serious allegations relating

TABLE 7

Allegations by disposition for full NLRB election sample

Allegations	Pre-merit loss		Pre-merit settlement	MERIT DETERMINED—Complaint issued											Total with charges settled or upheld in whole or in part
	% Withdrew before	% No merit	% Settled before, in whole, or in part	% Withdrew after	% Settled after in whole or in part	% ALJ Loss	% ALJ upheld in whole or in part	% Board loss	% Board upheld in whole or in part	% Court loss	% Court order upheld in whole or in part	Total loss	
Coercive statements & threats	30%	17%	13%	1%	21%	1%	1%	2%	11%	0%	4%	**50%**	50%
Interrogation	26	11	14	3	29	1	0	3	7	0	5	**45**	55
Polling employees	56	13	13	6	13	0	0	0	0	0	0	**75**	25
Promise of benefits	25	18	18	4	27	0	2	2	4	0	0	**49**	51
Surveillance	25	20	16	2	17	0	0	3	8	1	7	**52**	48
Impressions of surveillance	33	0	67	0	0	0	0	0	0	0	0	**33**	67
Other rules	13	13	20	3	10	0	0	13	13	0	13	**43**	57
Solicitation/ distribution rules	13	14	14	2	27	2	2	0	14	0	14	**30**	70
Statements of futility	21	6	21	3	36	0	0	0	9	0	3	**30**	70
Bribery	50	0	50	0	0	0	0	0	0	0	0	**50**	50
Disparagement	17	8	17	0	0	17	0	8	33	0	0	**50**	50
Harassment	23	30	23	2	11	0	0	2	9	0	0	**57**	43
Assistance or domination	23	31	8	0	15	0	0	0	15	0	8	**54**	46
Discharge for union activity	27	36	10	2	14	0	1	3	7	0	0	**68**	32
Discipline for union activity	16	30	15	3	17	1	0	5	8	0	4	**56**	44
Suspension for union activity	24	33	13	3	17	0	0	2	8	0	0	**62**	38
Layoff for union activity	30	26	9	0	13	0	0	9	13	0	0	**65**	35
Wages or benefits altered	31	23	17	0	15	0	1	0	13	0	0	**54**	46
Imposing onerous assignments	33	25	17	2	13	0	0	2	4	0	4	**63**	38
Retaliation for board participation	23	30	13	7	10	0	0	10	7	0	0	**70**	30

SOURCE: Bronfenbrenner's analysis of NLRB ULP documents, 1999-2003 NLRB election sample.

The timing of employer anti-union activity

to threats of job and benefit cuts or serious interrogation, harassment, and coercion, while sustaining the accusations around more minor solicitation and distribution rules, promises, and less coercive threats.

Another indication of the increased intensity of employer opposition is the timing of when ULP charges are filed. As described in **Table 8**, 22% of all ULPs were filed before the election petition was filed, and 16% were filed more than 30 days before the petition was filed. Thus, we find

that nearly a quarter of the discharge ULPs (24%) were filed before the petition, and 16% were filed more than 30 days before the petition. Similarly, 19% of ULPs relating to threats were filed before the petition, including 14% filed more than 30 days before, while 24% of interrogation ULPs, 31% of the assistance and domination ULPs, 16% of the surveillance ULPs, 25% of the solicitation/distribution rules ULPs and 17% of the alteration of wages and benefit ULPs were filed more than 30 days before the petition was filed for the election.

Recognizing that the behaviors listed in the ULP charge had to have occurred days if not weeks before the

TABLE 8

Percent of allegations filed prior to the petition being filed

Allegations	Percent of allegations filed prior to petition	Percent of allegations filed before 30 days prior to petition	Percent of allegations filed within 30 days prior to petition
Assistance or domination	31%	31%	0%
Coercive statements and threats	19	14	5
Denial of access	25	25	0
Discharge for union activity	24	16	8
Discipline for union activity	25	18	7
Disparagement	17	17	0
Harassment	26	16	10
Imposing onerous assignments	18	13	5
Interrogation	29	24	5
Layoff for union activity	14	5	9
Misrepresentation	50	0	50
Other rules	45	41	4
Polling employees	13	13	0
Promise of benefits	14	10	4
Refusal to hire	25	0	25
Retaliation for board participation	3	0	3
Solicitation/distribution rules	30	25	5
Statements of futility	9	6	3
Surveillance	26	16	10
Suspension for union activity	24	17	7
Violence	50	50	0
Wages or benefits altered for union activity	20	17	3
All allegations	23	16	6

SOURCE: Bronfenbrenner's analysis of NLRB ULP documents, 1999-2003 NLRB election sample.

actual charge was filed, these data confirm not only that a significant amount of employer opposition is in place very early in many union campaigns, but that employer campaigning does not depend on an election petition to kick into effect.

Ultimately, this brings us back from the ULP data to the employer behavior data. For it is important to remember the difference between the extent of employer opposition documented by union organizers, and those

violations they chose to file charges on with the NLRB, and then again, what, if anything, they gained from filing those charges even when they prevailed. **Figure A** compares the most serious illegal employer behavior reported on the survey: interrogation, threats, harassment and other discipline, alterations in wages, benefits, or conditions for union activity, discharges for union activity, assistance or domination of union, promises of benefits, and all serious allegations.[19] Although as shown in Figure A,

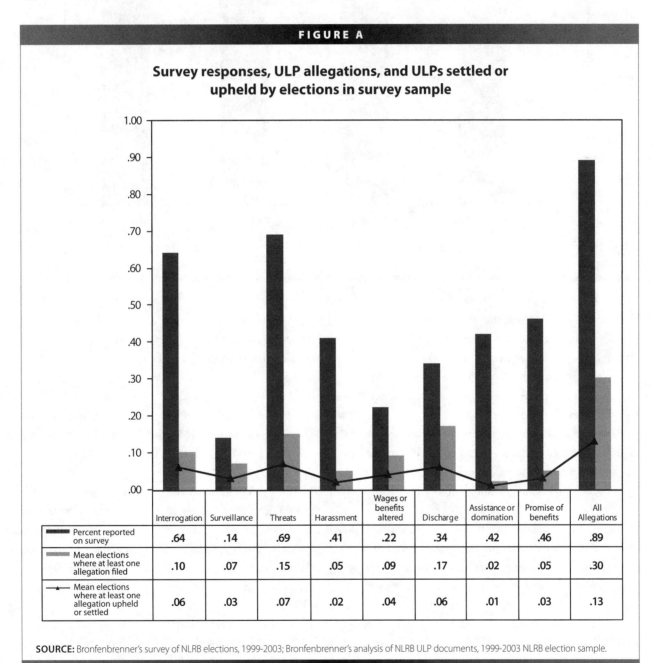

FIGURE A

Survey responses, ULP allegations, and ULPs settled or upheld by elections in survey sample

	Interrogation	Surveillance	Threats	Harassment	Wages or benefits altered	Discharge	Assistance or domination	Promise of benefits	All Allegations
Percent reported on survey	.64	.14	.69	.41	.22	.34	.42	.46	.89
Mean elections where at least one allegation filed	.10	.07	.15	.05	.09	.17	.02	.05	.30
Mean elections where at least one allegation upheld or settled	.06	.03	.07	.02	.04	.06	.01	.03	.13

SOURCE: Bronfenbrenner's survey of NLRB elections, 1999-2003; Bronfenbrenner's analysis of NLRB ULP documents, 1999-2003 NLRB election sample.

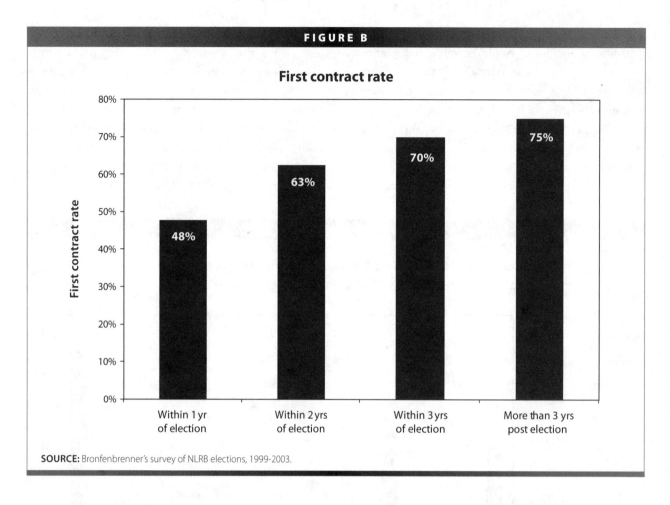

FIGURE B

First contract rate

First contract rate (y-axis)

- Within 1 yr of election: 48%
- Within 2 yrs of election: 63%
- Within 3 yrs of election: 70%
- More than 3 yrs post election: 75%

SOURCE: Bronfenbrenner's survey of NLRB elections, 1999-2003.

the employer tactics and the charges filed followed the same pattern, unions failed to file charges in more than half of the elections where they reported that employers committed serious labor law violations. The allegations were upheld or settled in whole or in part in fewer than half the ULPs that they filed.

As these data have shown, the choice not to use the NLRB process is a rational one. Already discouraged by threats, harassment, and retaliation in the organizing campaign itself, workers have good reason to believe they are at risk, yet they can expect little gain even if they do prevail.

Even if the union succeeds in making it through the hoops of fire that it takes to win the election, **Figure B** shows that it will be many years before a union ever obtains a collective bargaining agreement. Within one year after the election, only 48% of organized units have collective bargaining agreements. By two years it increases to 63% and by three years to 70%. Only after more than three years will 75% have obtained a first agreement.

Given that many workers had to wait many months—if not years—to schedule an election, they should not have to wait years to get a first contract.

For all the effort they go through, we know that fewer than 60,000 workers end up in a unit where an election is won, and fewer than 40,000 in a unit with a first contract. Worse yet, for many it is a process that can take as long as three to five years of threats, harassment, interrogation, surveillance, and, in some cases, job loss.

But it does not have to be this way. We know from the last two decades of United States public-sector organizing experience that there are alternative models in place to help us develop a framework that can make it possible for private-sector workers in the U.S. to organize without going through the trial by fire that they now endure. **Table 9** displays the stark contrast between employer behavior under the NLRB and employer behavior in state and local elections and card check certifications in the public sector (in this case New York, Minnesota, Florida,

TABLE 9

Comparison of employer opposition in public and private-sector campaigns

	Percent of elections	
	NLRB 1999-2003	Public 1999-2003
Election campaigns	100%	83%
Election win rate	45%	84%
Card check campaigns	0%	17%
Card check win rate	-	100%
No employer campaign	4.0%	48%
Hired management consultant	75%	23%
Employer use of threats, interrogation, and surveillance		
Held captive audience meetings	89%	22%
Number of meetings	10.4	9.47
Mailed anti-union letters	70%	21%
Number of letters	6.54	2.64
Distributed anti-union leaflets	74%	22%
Number of leaflets	16.2	4.1
Held supervisor one-on-ones	77%	26%
One-on-ones at least weekly	66%	2%
Used them to interrogate workers	63%	20%
Used them to threaten workers	54%	15%
Used E-mail communications	7%	14%
Attempted to infiltrate organizing committee	28%	6%
Threatened cuts in benefits or wages	47%	14%
Used electronic surveillance	11%	2%
Used anti-union DVDs/videos/Internet	41%	1%
Made plant closing threats	57%	3%
Actually closed plant after the election	15%	0%
Fear, coercion, and violence		
Used guards, put up security fencing, or cameras	14%	5%
Brought police into the workplace	21%	6%
Retaliation and harassment		
Alteration in benefits and working conditions	22%	3%
Discharged union activists	34%	3%
Other harassment and discipline of union activists	41%	13%
Laid off bargaining unit members	5%	1%
Number laid off	32.6	5
Contracted out bargaining unit work	3%	5%
Number of jobs contracted out	34	1

cont. on page 24

TABLE 9 (CONT.)

Comparison of employer opposition in public and private-sector campaigns

	Percent of elections	
	NLRB 1999-2003	Public 1999-2003
Promises, bribes, and improvements		
Established employee involvement program	15%	9%
Made positive personnel changes	27%	9%
Made promises of improvement	48%	12%
Granted unscheduled raises	18%	7%
Promoted pro-union activists	11%	2%
Used bribes and special favors	23%	2%
Held company social events	16%	1%
Other tactics		
Assisted anti-union committee	30%	8%
Used media campaign	12%	7%
Involved community leaders/politicians	6%	8%
Intensity of employer campaign		
Number of tactics used by employer	10.9	2.7
Employer used no tactics	6%	53%
Employer ran a weak campaign (1-4 tactics)	10%	25%
Employer ran a moderate campaign (5-9 tactics)	30%	14%
Employer ran an aggressive campaign (10 or more tactics)	54%	7%

SOURCE: Bronfenbrenner's analysis of Public Sector Survey data 1999-2003.

New Jersey, California, Illinois, and Washington). Five of the states in our sample—New York, New Jersey, California, Illinois, and Washington—have both card check and election certification of ballots.

In 48% of the public-sector campaigns, the employer did not campaign at all—no letters, no leaflets, no meetings. The entire decision was left up to the workers and the union. The remaining 52% of public employers did use some of the same tactics as private employers, but on an entirely different scale. Three percent discharged workers for union activity or made unilateral changes in wages and benefits, 22% held captive audience meetings, and 2% held supervisory one-on-ones at least weekly. Not surprisingly, both win rates and first contract rates continue to remain much higher in the public sector, averaging 84% overall. But in the few cases where unions are faced with moderate or aggressive employer opposition, the win rate plummets, suggesting that they are ill-prepared for the kind of opposition that has become routine under the NLRB.

Conclusion

When examined in combination, the survey data and the ULP data confirm what many U.S. workers already know: Our labor law system is broken. Polling consistently shows that a majority of workers believe they would be better off if they had a union in their workplace (Teixeira 2007), but they also feel that they would be taking a great risk if they were to try to organize (Hart 2005). They know intuitively what our data show—that the overwhelming majority of U.S. employers are willing to use a broad arsenal of legal and illegal tactics to interfere with the rights of workers to organize, and that they do so with near impunity. The data show that:

- 57% of employers threaten to shut down all or part of their facilities;

- One-third of employers fire workers for union activity during NLRB certification campaigns;

- 47% threaten to cut wages or benefits;

- 28% attempt to infiltrate the organizing committee;

- 14% use surveillance;

- 22% offer bribes and special favors;

- 89% of employers require their workers to attend captive-audience meetings during work hours;

- 77% had supervisors regularly talk to workers one-on-one about the union campaign, with a focus on threats of plant closings, wage and benefit cuts, and job loss; and

- More than 60% use one-on-one meetings to interrogate and harass workers about their support for the union.

This combination of threats, interrogation, surveillance, and harassment has ensured that there is no such thing as a democratic "secret ballot" in the NLRB certification election process. The progression of actions the employer has taken can ensure that the employer knows exactly which way every worker plans to vote long before the election takes place. In fact, as our data show, many of the employer campaigns were in full swing more than a month before the petition was even filed. Although most of these actions are illegal, the penalties are minimal, usually a posting of a notice, at worst back-pay (maybe with interest and reinstatement for a fired worker), and a re-run election. Even the most serious penalties—reinstatement for fired workers, or Gissel bargaining orders—are all too often recommended by the ALJ and the General Counsel only to be reversed by the full NLRB. There are no punitive damages or criminal charges, and no extra penalties for repeat offenders. The most serious penalty—a bargaining

order—simply gets the union to the first contract process, in which the anti-union campaign often continues unabated or even escalates.

Social scientists study patterns. As a researcher who has closely examined the NLRB organizing process for more than 20 years, I find the patterns of employer behavior appear deeply carved into our legal framework and employment practices. They have become so deeply engrained that we as a society have begun to accept illegal behavior as the norm, and for a long time now many workers have become resigned to the fact that no branch of government was going to listen to their pleas that the system was not just broken, but that it was operating in direct violation of the law.

In recent years, however, there seems to be a growing awareness of the failings of the law. In the three years we spent doing the work to collect and analyze data, Congress has begun considering far-reaching legislative reforms. We believe that our findings can help inform that debate and support policies that could make the NLRA once again a labor law regime private-sector workers can rely on to exercise their right to organize.

The first reform is the passage of the Employee Free Choice Act (EFCA). EFCA would provide a means to streamline the burdensome and terrifying obstacle course that the organizing and first contract process has become, while also offering more substantive penalties for the most egregious employer violations. Under EFCA, the NLRB would be required to automatically certify the union if the majority of the employees in a unit signed authorization cards designating the union as their bargaining representative. It would also establish a process for at least 30 days of mediation and then arbitration if one of the parties feels that continued bargaining is futile after at least 90 days of trying to reach an agreement.

EFCA would also create stronger penalties for labor law violations during organizing and first contract campaigns. These include making it a priority for the NLRB to seek federal court injunctions for discharges, discrimination, threats, and other interference with workers rights during organizing and first contract campaigns. It also triples back-pay awards and provides for civil fines of up to $20,000 per violation for willful or repeat violations.

But EFCA is just a first step in putting in place a labor policy that reestablishes workers' rights to organize. We had a labor law on our books for the last 20 years that U.S. employers have violated with impunity. And the same employers who are violating the NLRA are often in violation of health and safety, wage and hour, civil rights, and other employment and labor law standards. EFCA is a start to giving workers back their rights and protections under our labor and employ- ment laws, but it will be up to Congress, policy groups, scholars, unions, concerned citizens, workers, and, yes, employers, to make sure that our regulatory agencies and the laws they enforce are once again living up to their legislative and historical mission to protect the rights of U.S. workers. Our country cannot afford a system where the only unionized workplaces are where workers are tough, brave, and lucky enough to make it through the campaign.

Appendix: source and methodology overview

The prior research that informs and shapes this report includes four in-depth national studies of NLRB certification elections in 1986-87, 1994, 1993-95, 1998-99, and research on elections, card checks, and voluntary recognitions in state and local units in the public sector in a national sample covering all states in 1991-92 (see below). Combined, this research makes up the only extant national data on legal and illegal employer behavior during union election campaigns over time, controlling for election environment, company characteristics, union tactics, and bargaining unit demographics. By examining the effectiveness of the NLRB in enabling workers to exercise their rights to organize and in restraining illegal employer and union behavior during the organizing process, my research found that employer opposition has reduced the ability of workers to organize under the NLRB. For comparative purposes I also conducted similar research looking at state and local elections in the public sector.

This report is the product of my most recent study, which set out both to update my earlier work and expand on it by doing a full Freedom of Information Act Request (FOIA) from the NLRB for all unfair labor practice documents relating to the elections in our sample. In combination these data allow us to provide an in-depth examination of the nature and extent of employer opposition to worker efforts to organize under the NLRB, and the functioning of the unfair labor practice charge process in dealing with that behavior. I conclude that both the intensity and changing character of employer behavior, as well as the fundamental flaws in the NLRB process, have left us with a system where workers who want to organize cannot exercise that right without fear, threats, harassment, and/or retribution.

For the 1986-87 data and analysis, see Bronfenbrenner (1994; 1997a). For 1993-95, see Bronfenbrenner (1997b), and for 1994, see Bronfenbrenner and Juravich (1998). For data and analysis of 1998-99, see Bronfenbrenner (2000) and Bronfenbrenner and Hickey (2004). For the public-sector study of 1991-92 data, see Juravich and Bronfenbrenner (1998) and Bronfenbrenner and Juravich 1995. For the purposes of this paper I will be focusing on data from the 1993-95 study rather than the 1994 study because they overlap, and the 1993-95 study was more comprehensive.

Endnotes

1. See Bronfenbrenner (1994) for the 1986-87 study, Bronfenbrenner (1997b) for the 1993-94 study, and Bronfenbrenner (2000) and Bronfenbrenner and Hickey (2004) for the 1998-99 study.

2. Order Consolidating Cases, Consolidated Complaint, and Notice of Hearing. The Earthgrains Company and BCTWGM, 9-CA-3872; 9-CA-33901, October 27, 2007.

3. See this paper's Appendix for details.

4. The other parts of the study look at organizing under the Railway Labor Act (RLA), private-sector elections, voluntary recognitions, and card check campaigns that occur outside the NLRB process, and state and local elections and card check certifications in the public sector for seven states: Minnesota, Illinois, Florida, Washington, California, New Jersey, and New York. The RLA and non-board data analysis will be completed later this year, while the data analysis for the public sector has been completed and we will include some of those findings in this paper for comparative purposes.

5. See Bronfenbrenner (2005) at http://works.bepress.com/kate_bronfenbrenner/14 for summary statistics on the population and a complete discussion on how the data for the population were compiled. We chose 1999-2003 to include some years before the economic downturn and to allow at least three years for the parties involved in all elections in the sample to process election objections and attempt to bargain a first contract. We limit the sample to units with 50 or more eligible voters so there would be enough data to analyze the full spectrum of variables we are examining. A question might be raised as to whether that would impact on the representativeness of the ULP data for the overall population. We did examine the relationship between unit size and number of ULPs, and did not find any consistent pattern between the size of the unit and the number or nature of the ULPs filed.

6. The only unions underrepresented in the returned surveys were independent unions, in particular local independent unions (23% return rate for local independents, 33% for national and state independents). This was because, for quite a few of the local independents, the only listing we had from the NLRB was simply "LIND," so we had no contact information. Even for those with contact information, many of the small independents went out of existence after losing the election, and there was no listing or person to contact. We do believe, however, that for the national independents that we did get a representative sample, since such a high percentage all come out of the same occupations and cluster of unions, and we were able to get returned surveys from a representative cross section of the major national independent unions operating during that period, including the nurse unions, United Electrical Workers (UE), and the various security guard unions, several of which affiliated with each other during the period of our study.

7. Although we did not receive all the documents for every case, we did get complete documents for 69% of the cases with ULPs in our full sample and 74% of the returned surveys. For the remaining 29% of the total sample and 24% of the survey cases with ULPs, where the full official records would normally have been destroyed by the NLRB because more than six years had gone by, we received at least a charge sheet and a letter describing the disposition of the case, or a letter describing the charges and disposition of the case, except for eight cases in the survey sample and two additional cases in the full sample where the NLRB was unable to find any record of the case. For the 21% of those cases where the NLRB was only able to send us a charge sheet because the other records were destroyed, we then used the CA number to conduct an "Unfair Labor Practice (Complaint Case) Advanced Search" on the http://mynlrb.nlrb.gov Web site hosted by the NLRB to find out the disposition for the case. This left us only with at most 22% of the survey cases and 22% in the total ULP sample that we were missing ULP data, and of those 11% of the survey cases and 14% of the full ULP sample cases had been confirmed by the NLRB as ULPs, but they reported to us all records had been destroyed.

8. In addition to reporting out the findings from these data in this report, summary data from these documents have been entered into a searchable database that will be made available to other scholars and researchers, making this the first ever dataset of ULPs occurring during NLRB campaigns that is based on a national random sample.

9. My estimates for the number of workers organizing in the public-sector and non-board campaigns came from the data we collected to create our population for the public-sector and non-board survey sample. For the public-sector survey we collected complete data from a cross section of five states (later adding data from two other states). I used the data from the five states that are representative of the types of public-sector elections from across the country and the range of election activity to estimate that the number of new workers organized averages 400,000 a year. Similarly, I used the numbers coming in to us from the non-board survey in our sample to come up with an estimate of 250,000-300,000. NMB election numbers average between 10,000 and 25,000 per year. Thus the total number of workers organized should range between 600,000-800,000 depending on the year. My numbers are consistent with those reported by the federations.

10. Just as this report went to press, the BNA released its 2008 election update. It showed that the total number of NLRB elections increased from 1,510 to 1,579, and the win rate increased from 61% to 67%. However, the total number organized under the NLRB remained quite small at 70,511. This represents less than 20% of the estimated 400,000 workers who organize each year in the private sector.

11. The actual percentage of employers who issued solicitation/distribution rules is likely much higher than 10% because we did not include a question about solicitation/distribution under the employer behavior section of the survey, but 10% of the respondents reported on their surveys that they had filed unfair labor practice charges regarding solicitation/distribution rules that were settled or upheld by the NLRB.

12. Although the data don't show up in the table, we also found an increase in interrogation, threats of benefit cuts, harassment, and more onerous assignments, overtime, etc. We did not include specific questions in the surveys, but we did have a column for other and for comments on why the union lost the election in each of the four surveys. In addition, we had copies of primary employer campaign documents, unfair labor practice documents, and the detailed case summaries for the NAALC Trade Secretariat for the 1993-95 study (Bronfenbrenner 1996) and the U.S. Trade Deficit Review Commission for the 1998-99 study (Bronfenbrenner 2000). In combination, these data suggest a dramatic increase in interrogation, threats, discipline, harassment, and alteration of benefits and working conditions.

13. Rugby Manufacturing and USW, ALJ Decision, Paul Bogus, August 30, 2002, 18-CA-15-802; 18-CA-16154; 18-CA16475; 18-CA16008: 3.

14. Settlement Correspondence Letters dated January 22, 2003, Rugby Manufacturing, 18-CA-15802 et al.

15. The number of allegations filed per election for the survey sample ranged from 1 to 27 with a mean of 3.97 and a median of three, while the number of allegations per election for the full NLRB election sample ranged from 1 to 52 with a mean of 4.49 and a median of three. Thirty percent of all elections in both the survey sample and the full NLRB election sample had only one allegation filed, and 9% of the elections in the survey sample and 7% of the full NLRB election sample had 10 or more ULP allegations. However, two serious discharge allegations can lead to an election being overturned, while 10 vague threats would easily be dismissed. Thus, it is content rather than number of allegations that matters the most.

16. These percentages are not percent of elections but percent of the 1,387 allegations filed that we have documented records for in the 1,004 elections in our total sample and the 926 allegations filed that we have documented records for in our survey sample. The handful of allegations that appear to be relating to a contract rather than election campaign are tied to organizing campaigns that occurred in units where employers had withdrawn recognition in previously organized units, and unions were litigating those cases while simultaneously running new organizing campaigns in the same units. This table does not include cases where we know ULPs were filed but do not know the specific nature of the allegations because the records were destroyed.

17. We also ran the same data for the survey sample and compared it against the disposition numbers for the NLRB election sample and found them to be consistent across every category.

18. MIT researcher John-Paul Ferguson collected ULP data for a similar time period for his study on ULP charges from 1999-2004. Using the CATS data he made FOIA requests to the NLRB and received data confirming ULPs for 20% out of more than 22,000 ULPs (2008). The difference is not surprising given that we had a random sample of 1,004 elections rather than his much larger study, and we had full information to include with our FOIA requests on employer name, address, certification date, election date, number of eligible voters, and election outcome. In addition, we allowed enough time to send two FOIA requests to the region and then a follow up FOIA request to both the Region and NLRB Headquarters. Most important, our response rate from the NLRB was 98% from our sample, thus suggesting that our numbers more accurately capture current ULP rates. Still, despite the difference in percentages, our overall findings about the adverse impact that ULPs have on the election process serve to complement rather than contradict each other's work.

19. The term "Threats" includes all elections in which the employer made threats of plant closing, benefit cuts, and threats to report workers to INS/ICE. It also includes employer threats of filings for bankruptcy and threats made in supervisor one-on-ones. "Assistance" or "Domination" included cases in which employers assisted with the anti-union committee or used an NLRB-like front group.

References

Ahearn, Richard. 2000. "Letter and attachments Re: The Earthgrains Company Case 9 CA-37901-1" From NLRB Region 9 Regional Director Richard Ahearn to John J. Price, BCTWGM, September 6. (docketing consolidated charges)

Associated Press. 2000. Earthgrains strike spreads to 21 plants. The Associated Press State & Local Wire. Dateline, Birmingham, Alabama. September 12, State and Regional Section. (Accessed LexisNexis.com, December 26, 2008)

BNA Plus. 2003. Database of NLRB certification elections 1999-2003. Prepared specifically for the Cornell Office of Labor Education Research by BNA PLUS, the research division of The Bureau of National Affairs. Washington, D.C.: BNA

BNA Plus. 2004. Database of NLRB certification elections 2004. Prepared specifically for the Cornell Office of Labor Education Research by BNA PLUS, the research division of The Bureau of National Affairs. Washington, D.C.:BNA

Bronfenbrenner, Kate. 1994. "Employer Behavior in Certification Elections and First-Contract Campaigns: Implications for Labor Law Reform," in Friedman, Sheldon et al., eds., *Restoring the Promise of American Labor Law*. Ithaca, N.Y.: ILR Press, pp. 75-89.

Bronfenbrenner, Kate. 1996. "Lasting Victories: Successful Union Strategies for Winning First Contracts." Proceedings of the Forty-Ninth Annual Meetings (San Francisco, January 5-7, 1996). Madison, Wisc.: IRRA.

Bronfenbrenner, Kate. 1997a. The role of union strategies in NLRB certification elections. *Industrial and Labor Relations Review*. Vol. 50, No.2: 195-221.

Bronfenbrenner, Kate. 1997b. "The Effects of Plant Closing or Threat of Plant Closing on the Right of Workers to Organize." Supplement to *Plant Closings and Workers Rights: A Report to the Council of Ministers by the Secretariat of the Commission for Labor Cooperation*. Dallas, Texas: Bernan Press, 1-56.

Bronfenbrenner, Kate. 2000. "Uneasy Terrain: The Impact of Capital Mobility on Workers, Wages, and Union Organizing." Commissioned Research Paper and Supplement to *The U.S. Trade Deficit: Causes, Consequences and Recommendations for Action*. Washington, D.C.: U.S. Trade Deficit Review Commission.

Bronfenbrenner, Kate. 2005. *Union Organizing Among Professional Women Workers: A Research Study Commissioned by the Department for Professional Employees, AFL-CIO*. http://www.ilr.cornell.edu/profiles/upload/Bronfenbrenner_Professional-Women.pdf

Bronfenbrenner, Kate, and Robert Hickey. 2004. "Changing to Organize: A National Assessment of Union Organizing Strategies," in Ruth Milkman and Kim Voss, eds., *Organize or Die: Labor's Prospects in Neo-Liberal America*. Ithaca, N.Y.: Cornell University Press/ILR Press.

Bronfenbrenner, Kate, and Tom Juravich. 1995. *Union Organizing in the Public Sector: An Anlaysis of State and Local Elections*. Ithaca, N.Y.: Cornell University Press/ILR Press.

Compa, Lance. 2004. *Unfair Advantage: Workers' Freedom of Association in the United States under International Human Rights Standards*. Ithaca, New York: Cornell University Press.

Freeman, Richard B. 2007. *Do Workers Want Unions? More than Ever*. EPI Issue Brief #182. Washington, D.C.: Economic Policy Institute.

Hart, Peter D., and Research Associates. 2005. "AFL-CIO Union Message Survey." Study No. 7518. Unpublished.

Juravich, Tom, and Kate Bronfenbrenner. 1998. "Preparing for the Worst: Organizing and Staying Organized in the Public Sector," in Kate Bronfenbrenner and Sheldon Friedman et al. (eds.), *Organizing to Win: New Research on Union Strategies*. Ithaca: N.Y.: ILR Press, pp. 263-82.

Lee, Thomas. 2001. Earthgrains Co. finds strong partner in acquisition by Sara Lee. *St. Louis Post-Dispatch Knight Ridder/Tribune Business News*. August 21, 2001. Accessed LexisNexis.com. December 26, 2008.

Lichtenstein, Nelson. 2008. How Wal-Mart fights unions. *Minnesota Law Review*. Vol. 5, No. 2, pp. 1462-1501.

Luce, Stephanie, and Kate Bronfenbrenner. 2007. "Capital Mobility and Job Loss: Corporate Restructuring, Productions Shifts, and Outsourcing," in Tom Juravich, ed., *The Future of Work in Massachusetts*. Amherst, Mass.: University of Massachusetts Press.

NLRB. 2003. "NLRB Election Report: Cases Closed June 2001." Washington, D.C.: National Labor Relations Board. www.nlrb.gov/nlrb/shared_files/brochures/rpt_june2001.pdf Accessed December 20, 2008.

NLRB. 2007. "NLRB Election Report: Cases Closed July 2007." Washington, D.C.: National Labor Relations Board. www.nlrb.gov/nlrb/shared_files/brochures/Election%20Reports/July2007.pdf. Accessed March 23, 2009.

Pavy, Gordon. 1994. "Winning NLRB Elections and Establishing Collective Bargaining Relationships" in Sheldon Friedman et al., eds., *Restoring the Promise of American Labor Law*. Ithaca, N.Y.: ILR Press. pp. 110-21.

Rugby. 2002. Rugby Manufacturing and USW, ALJ Decision, Paul Bogus, August 30, 2002, 18-CA-15-802; 18-CA-16154; 18-CA16475; 18-CA16008.

Rundle, James R. 1998. "Winning Hearts and Minds in the Era of Employee Involvement Programs," in Kate Bronfenbrenner and Sheldon Friedman et al. (eds.), *Organizing to Win: New Research on Union Strategies*. Ithaca: N.Y.: ILR Press. pp. 213-31.

Schmitt, John, and Ben Zipperer. 2009. *Dropping the Axe: Illegal Firings During Union Organizing Campaigns, 1951-2007*. Center for Economic and Policy Research. Washington, D.C.: CEPR. March.

Scott, Robert. 1996. *North American Trade After NAFTA: Rising Deficits, Disappearing Jobs*. EPI Briefing Paper #62. Washington, D.C.: EPI. http://www.epi.org/publications/entry/epi_virlib_briefingpapers_1996_northa/ Accessed December 26, 2008.

Smith, Robert Michael. 2003. *From Blackjacks to Briefcases: A History of Commercialized Strikebreaking and Unionbusting in the United States*. Athens, Ohio: Ohio University Press.

Teixeira, Ruy. 2007. *Labor Day Special! What the Public Really Wants on Unions*. Center for American Progress. Washington, D.C.: CAP. Accessed April 2009.

Verst, Edward C. 2001. Letter to R. Slaton Tuggle, III. Re: The Earthgrains Company Case 9-RC-171431 and attached Notices of Second Election. From Acting Region 9 Regional Director, the National Labor Relations Board, April 1, 2001.

Weiler, Paul. 1983. Promises to keep: Securing workers' rights to self-organization under the NLRA. *Harvard Law Review*, Vol. 96., No. 8, June, pp. 1769-1827.

Acknowledgements

This research and publication of this report would not have been possible without the dedication and support from a large group of committed colleagues, project staff, unions, foundations, and support organizations for the nearly three years that it has taken since we first started in the summer of 2006.

First, I want to thank the more than 500 organizers involved in the project for their participation in our survey collection and their patience in filling out the survey, responding to the numerous phone calls, and supplying us with the supporting documents, particularly during the extremely busy election year. For some of you who were responsible for multiple campaigns this meant literally giving us hours of your time, and you gave it without complaint. Along with the organizers we want to thank the union support staff who spent many months and numerous calls working with us to track down organizer addresses, contracts, and archived documents. Without their continued cooperation this project could never have been realized.

This project could also not have been completed without the generosity and financial support of numerous foundations, labor federations, and their affiliate unions. I would like to thank: American Rights at Work, Berger-Marks Foundation, Discount Foundation, Economic Policy Institute, Panta Rhea Foundation, Poverty & Race Action Council, Public Welfare Foundation, Union Privilege; and the following unions and federations: AFL-CIO, AFSCME, AFT, AFTRA, BCTGM, CNA, CTW, CWA, IAMWA, IATSE, IBEW, IBT, IFPTE, IUOE, LIUNA, NEA, SAG, SEIU, UAW, UFCW, UMWA, UNITE HERE, USW, UTU, UWUA, WGAW. EPI and ARAW get special mention for their effort in producing this report.

I especially need to acknowledge Dorian Warren, Assistant Professor in the Department of Political Science and the School of International and Public Affairs at Columbia University who acted as the co-principal investigator of this project for the first year and a half of this work. His expertise, enthusiasm, and support were instrumental in overcoming the many hurdles we faced through the initial phases of research design, data collection, and fund raising. This study would not be what it is without the benefit of his scholarship, values, and vision.

I want to express my never-ending gratitude to the large group of staff and research assistants who worked on this project for long hours, poring over data, doing organizer interviews, sorting through ULP documents, week after week, month after month. Mostly undergraduates, they are some of the most hard working, dedicated, and committed research assistants I have ever had the privilege to work with. These include administrative support staff Kirstine Armstrong, Diana Denner, Tamara Lovell, and Sara VanLooy and the research team: Aly Blum, Meryl Bursic, Joey Cronen, Edan Dhanraj, Chris Duni, Jeremy Dussolliet, Kassandra Frederique, Richard Getzel, Jason Georges, Puja Gupta, Wes Hannah, Nischit Hegde, Jenny Ho, Tim Judson, Stephanie Knight, Tamara Lee, John Carlos Metidieri, Sarai Narvaez, Danielle Newsome, Perry O'Brien, Troy Pasulka, Marlene Ramos, Bryn Roshong, Michael Snyder, Benjamin Traslaviña, Donna Ugboaja, Jordan Wells, Robert Woods, Karen Zapata, and Austin Zwick. These staff and students were invaluable for their intellectual contributions to the research, but no less for their focus and dedication in working under often stressful conditions and tight deadlines. In particular I need to thank Wes Hannah, Tim Judson, Bryn Roshong, Troy Pasulka, and Austin Zwick who took on the extra responsibility of lead researchers. They each worked their hardest to take some of the burden off my shoulders and ultimately worked as true partners in leading this project through each stage of the process. I could not have done it without them.

And I would like to express my appreciation to my colleagues, Professor Robert Hickey from Queens University and Professor David Van Arsdale from Hartwick College, along with ILR MS/PhD student Chad Gray for the sound advice and continuous support they have given me throughout this project.

I would also like to thank to Mark Brenner from the University of Massachusetts for his invaluable, sage, and very patient work spent as a project statistical consultant on the final stages of our analysis and to thank Shane Seger, Serge Isaacson, and Christine Brouwer from Zanzinato, and Christian Vanek and the staff from Survey Gizmo for their help in designing and maintaining the on-line survey. I especially want to thank Christian for his hard work and generous support throughout the downloading process. I also want to thank all of the staff in the ILR Fiscal, CIT Technical Support, and Cornell Sponsored Programs offices who have helped our outlier of an office overcome each of the obstacles that came along.

I also want to thank the National Labor Relations Board (NLRB) and National Mediation Board (NMB), BNA PLUS, the California Agricultural Labor Board, as well as the State Labor Boards of California, Florida, Illinois, Minnesota, New Jersey, New York, and Washington for their cooperation in providing us with election data and unfair labor practice (election interference) documents relating to the cases in our four samples. We know that you are underfunded and understaffed, which makes us appreciate your efforts all the more.

Finally and most importantly, I want to express my appreciation toward the countless workers who participated in the campaigns we studied in this research project. Their stories of struggle for the right to union representation, collective bargaining, and dignity and justice in their workplace are the real purpose behind our work. My hope is that this research will help serve as one small step in helping them finally achieve the justice on the job they have fought so bravely against such great odds to achieve.

7. Grievance Procedures

1. Define grievance.

2. In airline collective bargaining, the process of ratification of the collective bargaining agreement is typically lengthy because_____.

3. Procedures for handling grievances are usually found in the _____.

4. The applicable collective bargaining agreement does not contain specific penalties for specific employee violations of the rules. One day, an employee is an hour late arriving for work, and the company suspends him/her for a week without pay. The union files a grievance on his/her behalf. Can the outcome set precedent for other similar cases in the future?

5. The employee in the previous question is a jerk, and nobody likes working with him/her. The union steward knows that the general sentiment among the other union members in the shop is that they'd be happier without the grievant around. If the union declines to pursue the grievance, does the employee have any recourse? If so, describe.

6. What is meant by the authors saying that when a company and union seek an arbitrator to rule on a grievance, "the arbitrator becomes an instrument of the contract"?

7. Circle the correct answer. In the airline industry, arbitration of grievances is mandatory/optional.

8. How many grievances have been taken to the National Air Transport Adjustment Board (NATAB)?

9. Who decides grievances in the airline industry?

10. Is that group's decision enforceable in the courts?

11. Who pays the costs in an airline grievance proceeding?

12. True or False. In the aerospace manufacturing and non–air carrier general aviation industries, arbitration of grievances is mandated by law.

13. True or False. In the aerospace manufacturing and non–air carrier general aviation industries, most collective bargaining agreements contain a provision to resolve grievances by binding arbitration.

14. In the aerospace manufacturing and non–air carrier general aviation industries, if the collective bargaining agreement does not specifically provide for arbitration of grievances, can a court compel the company and the union to submit the issue to arbitration?

15. In an airline grievance, if either the union or the company disagrees with the decision of the System Board of Adjustment, can it challenge the decision in the courts?

16. In the aerospace manufacturing and non–air carrier general aviation industries, who pays the costs of arbitration of a grievance?

17. How are federal-employee grievances resolved and by whom?

18. Who pays the costs of the process for resolution of a federal-employee grievance?

Online Assignment

For an aviation, aerospace, or other company or agency that you or the instructor selects, identify an appropriate decision in a grievance case and describe:

    a. The issue(s) involved in the grievance

    b. The procedure by which the grievance was handled

    c. The outcome

    d. Reasons given for the outcome

    e. URLs of all online sources

Supplemental Readings

FedEx–ALPA Collective Bargaining Agreement,
October 30, 2006, Excerpt: Sections 19, 20, and 21

Sections 19–21

Investigation and Discipline

19 A. Preliminary Matters

1. Discipline is defined as Letters of Warning, Suspensions, Terminations, and any other action taken by flight management resulting in a loss of pay or benefits to which the pilot would otherwise be entitled.

2. Counseling sessions and Advisory Letters do not constitute disciplinary action and may not be grieved. An Advisory letter is a non-disciplinary form letter issued to a pilot to communicate policy, procedures, or work rules, which if violated in the future, could lead to discipline. Documentations of verbal counseling issued prior to the effective date of this Agreement shall be treated as Advisory letters.

Intent: Advisory letters serve two purposes: In cases where there is some question as to whether the pilot knew the policy, procedure, or work rules, the Advisory letter can be used to communicate the rules to that particular pilot.

3. Standard for Discipline

a. The discipline standard for non-probationary pilots shall be "just cause."

b. Probationary pilots shall be considered to be employed on an "at will" basis for purposes of administering and reviewing discipline.

19 B. Documentation

1. The Company shall provide a pilot with a copy of any written record of disciplinary action or advisory letter within 10 days after that record is placed in his personnel file.

2. A pilot shall have 60 days from the date on which the written record is received or reasonably should have been received, to place a written response concerning that action in his personnel file.

3. A pilot may examine his personnel file on any business day during normal business hours with adequate notice to his Chief Pilot.

19 C. Consideration of Prior Disciplinary Action

A letter of warning or suspension shall not serve as a basis for discipline after a period of 1 year during which the pilot receives no further letters. However, the letter may be considered in assessing future discipline involving similar

misconduct for up to 2 years after the receipt of the most recent letter of warning. This paragraph does not apply to Last Chance Letters during their effective period as described in Section 19.E.2.e.

19 D. Investigation Process

1. The Company shall investigate and understand a pilot's performance and conduct before taking any disciplinary action against that pilot. Part of a proper investigation may include management talking or meeting with a pilot or group of pilots to determine the facts and circumstances surrounding a situation. Depending on the circumstances of the particular case, some or all necessary fact gathering may occur prior to or without the need for a hearing of any type. A pilot may request Association representation at a Company investigatory interview/meeting that may reasonably result in discipline. When a pilot makes such a request, the Company shall either:

a. afford the pilot the opportunity to secure Association representation before initiating or continuing the interview/meeting;

b. refrain from or discontinue the interview/meeting immediately; or

c. offer the pilot the choice of either continuing the interview/meeting without Association representation or having no interview/meeting with the pilot before a decision is made on proceeding.

2. Under no circumstances shall flight management require a pilot to submit to a psychological or psychiatric examination. However, a pilot may be required to undergo a psychological/psychiatric examination if directed by the Company's aeromedical advisors, in accordance with Section 15.

3. If a pilot is removed from flying during an investigation, prior to any disciplinary action being taken, his access to Company communications systems (e.g., e-mail, VIPS, etc.) shall not be restricted or eliminated, and he shall continue to accrue all pay and benefits (e.g., seniority, longevity, retirement, vacation, sick leave), as if he had not been held out of service. During an investigation, if a pilot's use of Company jumpseats has been restricted by the Company, the Company shall provide him with travel to and from the disciplinary hearing, if necessary.

4. The Association has the right to have a representative present at any disciplinary hearing. The Association shall be given notice prior to any disciplinary hearing in accordance with Section 19.F.5.

19 E. Administration of Discipline

A pilot shall not be disciplined without first being afforded the opportunity for a hearing.

1. Hearing

a. Notice of Hearing

    i. The Company shall send the pilot and the Association a Notice of Hearing setting forth the date, time, and place of the hearing, together with a statement of facts and specific subject matter(s) to be addressed. The Notice of Hearing shall be sent to the pilot and Association a reasonable amount of time prior to the hearing considering the time needed to prepare as well as the interest in concluding the matter without undue delay.

    Intent: The following example applies to Section 19.E.1.

    Example: The Company believes a pilot may have falsified his employment materials by significantly overstating his flight hours and by indicating that he had never received any discipline from a former employer. The following notice would satisfy this paragraph: "You are directed to attend a hearing on April 2 at 10:00 in my office. It has been alleged that you may have falsified your employment materials. If true, these allegations could warrant discipline."

    ii. Accompanying the Notice of Hearing, the Company shall attach the relevant document(s), excluding witness statements and notes, which prompted the flight manager to send the original notice of hearing.

b. The hearing shall be conducted by a Regional Chief Pilot or an Assistant Chief Pilot. A written decision shall be issued within 15 days following the close of the hearing. If the decision is to discipline the pilot, the decision shall state the discipline and specific grounds for that discipline.

c. After an initial discussion in which the Company may ask questions and receive answers from the pilot, if requested by the pilot or the Association, the Company shall produce documentary information (including written witness statements and information in electronic format), known and in its possession, but excluding notes except to the extent that the notes contain information from fact or expert witnesses, and names of witnesses excluding confidential witnesses. Disputes whether a witness shall be considered confidential shall be resolved by referring the issue to the arbitrator hearing the underlying case, or an arbitrator selected from the panel of arbitrators by mutual agreement. The parties shall present the issue to the arbitrator so that the System Board hearing on the underlying dispute is not delayed. Information provided along with the Notice of Hearing, as provided in Section 19.E.1.a.ii., need not be reproduced under this paragraph.

d. The pilot shall be afforded the opportunity to respond to information described in Section 19.E.1.c. (above) before a decision is rendered. If necessary, the hearing shall be delayed or continued in order to provide the pilot with adequate time to prepare and/or respond. The Company shall be able to continue to investigate the circumstances of a particular case and to gather additional documentation after the close of the hearing.

e. If a pilot is unavailable due to his arrest and detainment by government officials, the Company shall notify the Association, and shall take reasonable steps to notify the pilot of the hearing and to accommodate his participation to the extent permitted under the circumstances. After those prerequisites have been met, the pilot's unavailability shall not prevent the Company from conducting a hearing regarding the pilot.

2. Internal Appeal

a. If the decision is to terminate the pilot, the case shall automatically be appealed to the Vice President, Flight Operations. The appeal hearing shall be conducted by the Vice President, or his designee, within 15 days after the decision to terminate the pilot.

b. If the decision imposes discipline less than termination, the pilot or the Association may appeal the decision to the System Chief Pilot. Appeals shall be in writing and shall be filed within 15 days after the pilot receives notice of the decision. The appeal hearing shall be conducted by the System Chief Pilot, or his designee, within 15 days after his receipt of the appeal.

c. The hearing officer for the appeal shall be different from the hearing officer for the initial hearing.

d. After an initial discussion in which the Company may ask questions and receive answers from the pilot, if requested by the pilot or the Association, the Company shall produce documentary information (including written witness statements and information in electronic form but excluding notes maintained by management personnel) gathered since the close of the hearing.

e. Last Chance Letters

i. After the appeal hearing, the Vice President, Flight Operations may offer a terminated pilot a last chance letter as a basis for reinstatement. The maximum duration of a last chance letter is 2 years.

ii. If the pilot rejects the last chance letter, he shall remain terminated and he may appeal to the System Board of Adjustment as provided in Section 21. The fact that the Company offered a last chance letter shall not be admissible, and shall not be referred to, at the System Board of Adjustment.

iii. If the pilot accepts the last chance letter, he shall be bound by the terms stated therein, none of which shall extend beyond the maximum duration.

iv. After a pilot has served the term of his last chance letter, its use in subsequent proceedings shall be limited as provided in Section 19.C (Consideration of Prior Disciplinary Action), in the same manner as other disciplinary events.

v. Last chance letters, whether accepted or rejected, shall be non-precedential, and shall be inadmissible and non-referable in disciplinary proceedings involving any other pilot(s).

f. The hearing officer shall issue a written decision within 15 days following the close of the hearing. If the decision is to discipline the pilot, the decision shall state the discipline and specific grounds for that discipline. If the hearing officer fails to issue a written decision in a timely manner, the pilot and/or Association shall not be deemed to have waived any arguments to the System Board regarding any claim for relief based on the untimely decision. Nothing in this paragraph diminishes the Company's obligation to issue a timely decision.

3. Appeal to System Board of Adjustment

If the pilot disagrees with the decision at the internal appeal level, the pilot may appeal the decision, through the Association, to the System Board of Adjustment as described in Section 21. The appeal shall be in writing and shall be made within 15 days following the date on which the pilot received notice of the decision. Copies of the appeal shall be sent to the Association and the designated Company officials.

19 F. General

1. If, as a result of any hearing or appeal, the original discipline imposed on a pilot is reduced or rescinded, the pilot's pay, benefits, seniority, and longevity shall be restored consistent with the hearing officer's decision, and the pilot's file shall reflect such resolution.

2. Time limits and hearing/appeal dates may be modified, orally or in writing, by agreement of the parties. Oral agreements shall be confirmed in writing as soon as practicable. Requests for modifications shall not be unreasonably denied.

3. For the purpose of computing the time limits stated herein, an appeal shall be deemed "filed," and a decision shall be deemed "issued," on the day in which the appeal or decision is postmarked, or if Federal Express is used, on the day in which the appeal or decision is submitted to the Company for shipment.

4. For the purpose of Section 19, the term "day" means calendar day. However, if the last day of a time limit falls on a weekend, or on a Corporate or ALPA Holiday (currently including New Year's Day, Martin Luther King Jr. Day, President's Day, Memorial Day, Independence Day, Labor Day, Columbus Day, Thanksgiving Day and the following Friday, Christmas, or the day on which such holiday is observed by the Company or ALPA), the time limit shall be extended through the first business day following the weekend or holiday. The parties shall advise each other expeditiously of any changes to ALPA or Corporate holidays.

5. Delivery of all notices, advisory letters, decisions, and appeals pursuant to Section 19 shall be made in person, by Federal Express Overnight Letter, by certified mail, return receipt requested, or by other methods which provide verification of receipt. Such correspondence shall be sent to a pilot's bid pack mailing address, or other address as the pilot may designate. Such correspondence shall also be sent to the MEC Representation Department and the MEC Grievance Committee Chairman.

6. If the first attempted delivery of a notice is unsuccessful, the Company shall send a second notice to the same address. The second notice shall be sent by two methods, one of which shall be first-class mail. A pilot shall be deemed to have received notice upon the earlier of the pilot's actual receipt of notice or 20 days after postmark of the second notice.

7. Every participant in disciplinary proceedings shall be free to discharge his duty without fear of retaliation by

the Association or the Company. No participant shall be coerced or harassed by the Association or the Company.

8. Copies of tape recordings or other transcriptions made at any meeting conducted pursuant to this Section shall be provided to all parties, upon request, without undue delay, after it has been finalized. Failure to respond to a request without undue delay shall render that tape or transcript inadmissible until the requesting party has had sufficient time to review the tape or transcript.

9. Grievants and a reasonable number of witnesses and Association representatives involved in the resolution of disputes pursuant to Section 19 may be released from Company duty, if necessary, as provided in Section 18 of this Agreement. Expenses and flight pay loss, if any, for line pilot witnesses called by any party, shall be borne by the party who called the witness or otherwise incurred the expense.

10. Nothing in this Section shall be construed so as to waive or limit any privilege, provided under applicable law, that would protect information from disclosure, including the attorney-client privilege.

Section 20
Grievances: Administrative
Definitions:

File/Issue

A document shall be deemed "filed" or "issued," as applicable, on the day in which the document is postmarked, or if Federal Express is used, on the day in which the document is submitted to the Company for shipment.

20 A. Application

Section 20 applies to grievances, which are defined as disputes growing out of the interpretation or application of agreements between the parties hereto concerning rates of pay, rules, or working conditions. Any pilot, group of pilots covered by this Agreement or the Association on behalf of such pilot(s) who has a grievance concerning any action of the Company affecting the pilot(s), except matters involving discipline, shall have such grievance handled in accordance with the following procedures, provided that such grievance is properly and timely filed in the manner set forth below.

20 B. Filing of Grievance

1. A grievance under Section 20 shall be filed in writing with the Vice President, Flight Operations, within 60 days following the date on which the pilot acquired knowledge,

or reasonably should have acquired knowledge, of the fact(s) or event(s) giving rise to the grievance. The 60-day filing period for a grievance shall be extended to 90 days in cases where there is written evidence within the 60-day period that a pilot (or the Association on behalf of a pilot) notified either FedEx Contract Administration or a member of flight management of the underlying issue in an attempt to resolve the matter within the 60-day filing period. A grievance shall contain a statement of the facts and circumstances from which it arises, a citation to the provision(s) of the agreement that has allegedly been violated and the relief or remedy requested.

2. Notwithstanding the time limitation in Section 20.B.1. (above), grievances arising out of clerical or bookkeeping errors may be filed outside the 60-day period provided that they:

   a. do not involve a dispute of the Company's interpretation or application of agreements between the parties hereto; and

   b. can be definitively resolved by reference to Company records.

3. The Company may take corrective action at any time upon the discovery of clerical or bookkeeping errors, and the pilot shall be given notice of such change.

4. Copies of grievances shall be provided to the Association, and the designated Company officials.

20 C. Discovery

In response to a request by the other party for specific information, and if known and directly relevant to a grievance, a party shall produce names of witnesses and documentary information (including information in electronic format) but excluding notes except to the extent that the notes contain information from fact or expert witnesses. The party shall produce such information as soon as practicable. If necessary, the grievance hearing shall be delayed or continued in order to provide the parties with adequate time to prepare and/or respond. This paragraph shall not be construed to waive any privilege, provided under applicable law, that would protect the information from disclosure, including the attorney-client privilege.

20 D. Hearing with Vice President

1. Within 15 days following receipt of a grievance, the Vice President, Flight Operations, or his designee, shall conduct a hearing to establish the facts of the case and, if possible, to resolve the dispute.

2. A pilot shall be entitled to Association representation, or the pilot may elect to be represented by another pilot, at any hearing conducted under Section 20.

3. The Association has the right to be present during any hearing conducted under Section 20.

4. The hearing may be conducted telephonically if mutually agreeable to the grievant(s), the Association and the Vice President, Flight Operations, or his designee. Within 15 days after the close of the hearing, the Vice President, Flight Operations, or his designee, shall issue his decision in writing to the signatory of the grievance, with a copy to the named grievant(s), the FedEx MEC Representation Department, and the designated Company officials. If the FedEx MEC Grievance Chairman is not the signatory of the grievance, then a copy shall be distributed to the Grievance Chairman as well.

20 E. Appeal of Decision

If the decision of the Vice President, Flight Operations, or his designee, is not satisfactory to the pilot or the Association, such decision may be appealed by the Association to the System Board in the manner set forth in Section 21. Such appeal shall be in writing and shall be filed within 15 days following the date on which the signatory of the grievance received the decision. Copies of the appeal shall be sent to the FedEx MEC Grievance Committee Chairman, and the designated Company officials.

20 F. General

    1. Time Limits

    a. Time limits and meeting dates set forth in this Section may be modified, orally or in writing, by mutual agreement of the parties. Oral agreements shall be confirmed in writing as soon as practicable. Requests for modifications shall not be unreasonably denied.

    b. When any hearing or appeal afforded a pilot(s) by this Section is not requested within the respective time limits prescribed herein, including any extension mutually agreed upon, the decision of the Company shall be final and binding.

    c. If the Company fails to schedule or conduct a hearing in a timely manner, or to issue a timely decision as required by this Section, the grievance shall be deemed denied on the deadline for the hearing or decision, provided, however, that:

        i. the Company's obligations under Section 20.D.1. or D.4. shall not be diminished by this provision; and

        ii. the Association shall not be deemed to have waived any arguments to the System Board regarding any claim for relief based on the untimely hearing or decision.

2. For purposes of Section 20, the term "day" means calendar day. However, if the last day of a time limit falls on a weekend, or on a Corporate or ALPA Holiday (currently including New Year's Day, Martin Luther King Jr. Day, President's Day, Memorial Day, Independence Day, Labor Day, Columbus Day, Thanksgiving Day and the following Friday, Christmas, or the day on which such holiday is observed by the Company or ALPA), the time limit shall be extended through the first business day following the weekend or holiday. The parties shall inform each other expeditiously of any changes in Corporate or ALPA holidays.

3. Delivery of all notices, appeals, and discovery requests and responses pursuant to this Section shall be made by Federal Express Overnight Letter, by certified mail, return receipt requested, in person, or by other methods which provide verification of receipt. Company decisions shall be issued by FedEx Overnight Letter. Such correspondence shall be sent in the same manner to the FedEx MEC Representation Department, and to the FedEx MEC Grievance Committee Chairman.

4. The release from Company duty of the grievant(s) and a reasonable number of witnesses and Association representative(s) involved in the resolution of disputes pursuant to Section 20 shall be as provided in Section 18 of this Agreement. Expenses and flight pay loss, if any, for line pilot witnesses called by any party, shall be borne by the party who called the witness or otherwise incurred the expense. Pilots participating as a witness or representative in a Section 20 hearing shall be authorized round trip business jumpseat status to prepare for and attend such hearing.

5. If the first attempted delivery of a notice is unsuccessful, the Company shall send a second notice to the same address. The second notice shall be sent by two methods, one of which shall be first class mail. A pilot shall be deemed to have received notice upon the earlier of the pilot's actual receipt of notice or 20 days after postmark of the second notice.

Section 21
System Board of Adjustment

Definitions:

File/Issue

A document shall be deemed "filed" or "issued," as applicable, on the day in which the document is postmarked, or if Federal Express is used, on the day in which the document is submitted to the Company for shipment.

Case in Chief

The evidence presented by a party in the primary presentation of its case. The term does not include evidence used on cross examination or in rebuttal. As provided in Section 204, Title II of the Railway Labor Act, a System Board of Adjustment is established for the purpose of adjusting and deciding grievances which arise under the terms of this Agreement and have been processed under Section 19 or Section 20 of this Agreement which are properly brought before it in a timely fashion. The System Board of Adjustment shall be known as the Federal Express Pilots' System Board of Adjustment (hereinafter referred to as "the System Board").

21 A. Jurisdiction

1. The disciplinary System Board shall have jurisdiction over disputes between a pilot(s) or the Association and the Company growing out of grievances, or out of the interpretation or application of any of the terms of the Agreement, which are processed under Section 19 of this Agreement and which are submitted to the System Board as provided in Section 21.B. A neutral arbitrator from the disciplinary panel shall hear such disputes as the sole member of the Board unless either party elects to proceed before a 3-person board. Any such election must be made at least 45 days prior to the System Board proceeding.

2. The non-disciplinary System Board shall have jurisdiction over disputes between a pilot(s) or the Association and the Company growing out of grievances, or out of the interpretation or application of any of the terms of the Agreement, which have been processed under Section 20, and which have been submitted to the System Board as provided in Section 21.B. Such disputes shall be heard by a 3-person System Board unless either party elects to proceed before a 5-person System Board. Any such election must be made at least 45 days prior to the System Board proceeding.

3. Retirement and Benefit disputes which are referred to the Pilot Benefit Review Board, as provided in Sections 27 and 28, are handled as set forth in those Sections.

4. The jurisdiction of the System Board shall not extend to proposed changes in hours of employment, rates of pay, or working conditions covered by agreements between the parties in existence at the time the System Board decision is rendered.

21 B. Submissions to the System Board

1. At least 60 days prior to a System Board proceeding, the Company and the Association shall confer and designate the case(s) to be heard during that session. Copies of the appeal(s) for the case(s) designated to be heard shall be promptly provided to the neutral member. If the parties cannot agree, the oldest case(s) shall be selected first, except that under the disciplinary System Board, termination cases shall take precedence over non-termination cases.

2. Disputes shall be appealed to the System Board by filing an Appeal with the System Board Chairman as provided herein.

3. Appeals to the System Board shall contain the following:
a. Statement of facts and circumstances.
b. A citation to the portions of this and/or related Agreements which gave rise to the Grievance.
c. A statement of the issue(s) and/or questions to be decided.
d. Position of the party submitting the appeal.
e. Position of the other party or parties.
f. The relief sought (optional).

4. Copies of appeals shall be sent to the FedEx MEC Grievance Committee Chairman, the FedEx MEC Representation Department, and the designated Company officials.

5. If any party disagrees with the statement of its position contained in an appeal filed by another party, the objecting party may submit its own statement to the System Board and all other parties.

6. Pre-hearing briefs may be submitted only to the System Board by agreement of the parties, or by order of the arbitrator.

21 C. System Board Composition and Proceedings

1. Composition
a. The Company and the Association, when applicable, shall each appoint an equal number of members to serve on the System Board. Such members shall be employees of the Company or regular employees of the Association. The neutral member of the System Board shall be the arbitrator.
b. Each member of the System Board shall have one vote.
2. Proceedings before the System Board
a. System Board proceedings shall take place in person, unless all parties agree to conduct the hearing telephonically.
b. Disputes between pilots or the Association and the Company which are processed under Section 19 of this Agreement and which are submitted to the System

Board as provided in Section 21.B., may be consolidated by mutual agreement of the Company and the Association.

21 D. Arbitration

1. The 3-person System Board, when elected by one of the parties for disciplinary cases, shall hear disputes submitted under Section 19 of this Agreement. Otherwise, the neutral member shall decide disciplinary cases alone. The non-disciplinary System Board shall hear disputes submitted under Section 20 of this Agreement.

2. Each member of the System Board shall have one vote. If one member of a 5-person System Board is absent, he may give his proxy to another member. Proxies must be in writing.

a. The System Board may not reach a decision without a vote by all members. No member may refuse to vote in order to prevent a decision from being rendered.

b. If the System Board reaches a decision by majority vote, that decision shall be final and binding on all parties and the System Board shall issue a written decision within 30 days after the vote.

3. The neutral member shall serve as the chairman of the System Board and shall preside at all hearings of the System Board.

4. 15 Day Evidentiary Exchange. Each party shall exchange all documents they intend to enter in their case in chief, in support of their respective positions, and make available, in writing, the names of all witnesses they intend to summon whom they deem necessary to the dispute 15 days prior to the date set for the hearing. Nothing herein shall require the parties to present the aforementioned documents or summon the aforementioned witnesses during the course of the hearing. The parties shall not be restricted from entering documents or summoning witnesses who become known subsequent to the 15-day exchange, provided timely notice is given to the opposing party.

21 E. Panels of Arbitrators

1. The Association and the Company shall maintain 2 separate panels of 6 arbitrators each: one with arbitrators for disciplinary cases and the other with arbitrators for non-disciplinary cases.

2. Impaneling of Arbitrators

a. At least 180 days prior to the amendable date, the Association and the Company shall meet to determine whether to retain either of the current panels of ar-

bitrators. If either of the parties decides to replace a panel(s), the parties shall simultaneously exchange a list of 15 arbitrators for each panel to be replaced. An incumbent arbitrator(s) on a panel that is being re-selected may be submitted on a party's 15 arbitrator list.

b. Within thirty days following the exchange, the parties shall meet in order to select the subsequent panel(s) of arbitrators.

c. The selection of arbitrators shall be accomplished as follows:

i. If an arbitrator(s) appeared on both exchanged lists described in Section 21.E.2.a., such arbitrator(s) shall be accepted as a member of the respective panel. If the panel is not complete, then;

ii. the parties shall examine each other's lists and determine whether there are any arbitrators on the other party's list that are acceptable to both parties. Any such arbitrator(s) shall be accepted as a member of the respective panel. If the panel is not complete, then;

iii. within 15 days following the meeting, the parties shall simultaneously exchange a second list, containing 7 different arbitrators, and repeat the process described in Section 21.E.2.b., and E.2.c.i., and E.2.c.ii. If a panel still is not complete, then;

(a) the parties shall jointly request the NMB to provide a single list containing 7 arbitrators for each remaining vacancy on that panel (e.g., a list of 14 arbitrators to fill 2 vacancies on a panel).

(b) following receipt of the list(s), the parties shall examine the list(s) and determine whether any arbitrators are acceptable to both parties. Any such arbitrator(s) shall be accepted as a member of the respective panel. If the panel still is not complete, then;

(c) any remaining vacancies shall be filled using the alternate strike method based on the list(s) provided by NMB. A coin toss shall determine which party has the first strike. If the alternative strike method is necessary for both panels, then the party losing the coin toss regarding the administrative panel shall have the first strike on the disciplinary panel.

3. Vacancies on a Panel of Arbitrators

a. Should vacancies occur on either panel of neutral members, other than by operation of Section 21.E.5., the parties shall attempt to agree on a replacement within 30 days after the vacancy occurs. If the parties are unable to agree on a replacement, the vacancy shall remain unfilled.

b. If there are too few arbitrators to hear scheduled arbitrations, the parties may select an arbitrator to hear a scheduled arbitration on an ad hoc basis. This arbitrator shall be selected by the alternate strike method from a list of 7 arbitrators provided by the National Mediation Board. A coin toss shall determine which party has the first strike.

4. Scheduling of Neutral Members of the System Board

a. In September of each year, the Company and the Association shall schedule mutually agreeable dates on which the neutral members of the System Boards shall conduct System Board proceedings during the following calendar year. The slotting of neutral members into the scheduled dates shall be done by mutual agreement. If by September 20 of each year, the parties have been unable to agree upon such slotting, then on the first business day thereafter, the parties shall meet to determine such slotting by drawing the panel members' names (first draw determined by coin toss) and slotting them in the order drawn.

b. If necessary, additional dates for System Board proceedings will be scheduled by mutual agreement of the Company and the Association.

5. Removal of Neutral

a. Bilateral

The Association and the Company may, by mutual agreement, remove an arbitrator from a panel(s). Within 30 days after the arbitrator's removal, the parties shall meet to determine whether the vacancy should be filled or left vacant. If either party wishes to fill the vacancy, then the following shall apply:

    i. The Association and the Company shall simultaneously exchange a list of 7 arbitrators within 10 days after the removal.

    ii. Thirty days following the exchange, the Association and the Company shall meet in order to select the arbitrator. The selection of the arbitrator shall be accomplished as follows:

        (a) If a single arbitrator appeared on both exchanged lists, such arbitrator shall be accepted as a member of the panel.

        (b) If more than one arbitrator appeared on both exchanged lists, the replacement arbitrator shall be selected by an alternative strike method among the arbitrators appearing on both lists, with a coin toss to determine which party has the first strike.

        (c) If no arbitrator appeared on both lists, the parties shall determine whether either party is willing to accept an arbitrator from the other party's list. If a mutually acceptable arbitrator is found, such arbitrator shall be impaneled. If not, then the parties shall use the process described in Section 21.E.2.c.iii.(a)–(c) to fill the vacancy.

b. Unilateral

Each party shall have the opportunity to remove a total of three arbitrators during the term of the Agreement, but no more than one in any period of 12 months. A party exercising a unilateral removal shall inform the other party, in writing, of its removal.

    i. The arbitrator shall be considered removed as of the date of the notice of removal, provided, however, that a System Board for which an appeal has been filed shall continue to retain jurisdiction over the dispute(s).

    ii. If the removed arbitrator originally appeared on both parties' list, then his replacement shall be accomplished as provided in Section 21.E.5.a.i. and ii.

    iii. If the removed arbitrator originally appeared only on one party's list, then, within 30 days following the removal, that party shall submit a list of 7 arbitrators. Within 15 days following receipt of the list, the parties shall determine whether there is a mutually acceptable arbitrator. If not, then the parties shall use the process described in Section 21.E.2.c.iii.(a)–(c) to fill the vacancy.

6. Unless otherwise agreed, all arbitrators, whether on lists submitted by the parties or obtained from the NMB, shall be members of the National Academy of Arbitrators experienced in airline arbitrations.

21 F. General Provisions

1. Time limits and meeting dates may be modified, orally or in writing, by mutual agreement of the parties. Oral

agreements shall be confirmed in writing as soon as practicable. Requests for modifications shall not be unreasonably denied. When any appeal to the System Board is not requested within the respective time limits prescribed herein, including any extension mutually agreed upon, the decision of the Company shall be final and binding.

2. For purposes of Section 21, the term "day" means calendar day. However, if the last day of a time limit falls on a weekend, or on a Corporate or ALPA Holiday (currently including New Year's Day, Martin Luther King Jr. Day, President's Day, Memorial Day, Independence Day, Labor Day, Columbus Day, Thanksgiving Day and the following Friday, Christmas, or the day on which such holiday is observed by the Company or ALPA), the time limit shall be extended through the first business day following the weekend or holiday. The parties shall inform each other expeditiously of any changes in Corporate or ALPA holidays.

3. The Association, the Company and, if applicable, the individual grievant pilot are parties to all System Board proceedings.

4. Every participant in System Board proceedings shall be free to discharge his duty without fear of retaliation by the Association or the Company. No participant shall be coerced or harassed by the Association or the Company.

5. The reasonable expenses and fees of neutral members and any line pilot witnesses summoned by the System Board, and the cost of facilities selected for System Board proceedings shall be borne equally by the Company and the Association. A party may order a transcript or other record of a System Board proceeding. A copy of such record shall be made available to a party upon request, provided the requesting party agrees to pay a pro-rata share of the cost of making such record. All other costs associated with System Board proceedings, including, but not limited to, expenses and, if applicable, flight pay loss for line pilot witnesses called by any party, shall be borne by the party who called the witness or otherwise incurred the expense.

6. If applicable, a schedule for submission of post-hearing briefs shall be established immediately prior to the close of the hearing.

7. Proceedings of the System Board shall be conducted at locations selected by agreement of the Company and the Association. In making such selections, the Company and the Association shall endeavor to minimize costs. In the absence of an agreement, proceedings shall be conducted in Memphis, Tennessee.

8. The grievant(s) and a reasonable number of witnesses and Association representatives involved in the resolution of disputes pursuant to this Section may be released from Company duty pursuant to the provisions of Section 18 of this Agreement. The arbitrator hearing the underlying dispute shall resolve disputes regarding whether the number of Grievants and witnesses to be released from Company duty is disruptive to Company operations. The Parties shall present the issue to the arbitrator so that the System Board hearing on the underlying dispute is not delayed by disputes regarding the number of grievants or witnesses to be released from Company duty. Pilots participating as a witness, representative or member in a System Board proceeding shall be authorized round trip business jumpseat status to prepare for and attend such proceeding.

9. Delivery of all notices, decisions and appeals pursuant to Section 21, and any other documentation pursuant to Section 21 shall be made in person, by Federal Express Overnight Letter, by certified mail, return receipt requested, or by other methods which provide verification of receipt. Such correspondence shall be sent to a pilot's bid pack mailing address or other address as the pilot may designate. Such correspondence shall also be sent to the FedEx MEC Representation Department, and the FedEx MEC Grievance Committee Chairman. Whenever a party sends correspondence or other documentation to an arbitrator related to a case under this Section, the other party shall be copied on such correspondence or documentation using the same delivery method by which the arbitrator was sent his copy. Correspondence by email is acceptable among System Board members unless the neutral provides otherwise.

10. If the first attempted delivery of a notice is unsuccessful, the Company shall send a second notice to the same address. The second notice shall be sent by two methods, one of which shall be first-class mail. A pilot shall be deemed to have received notice upon the earlier of the pilot's actual receipt of notice or 20 days after postmark of the second notice.

11. By mutual agreement between the Company and the Association, a neutral from the disciplinary panel may hear a non-disciplinary case, and vice versa.

12. At any System Board proceeding, the Company and ALPA may be represented, respectively, by an employee or agent of the Company or a representative or agent of ALPA.

Grievance Procedure between the Communications Workers of America and Southwestern Bell Telephone Company, 2004

Article XIX.
Grievances

Section 1.

The Union shall be the exclusive representative of all the employees in the bargaining unit for the purposes of presenting to and discussing with the Company grievances of any and all such employees arising from such employment; subject always, however, to the provisions of this Agreement, the current Agreement of General application between the Union and the Company and of any applicable law.

Section 2.

a. Any employee complaint (except those which contemplate treatment or proceedings inconsistent with the terms of a collective bargaining contract or agreement then in effect including proposals for the modification of, or addition to, any such contract or agreement) which is reduced to writing and delivered by a Union representative in accordance with Section 2.b following, within 45 days of the action complained of shall be considered and handled as a formal grievance.

b. The grievance procedure shall normally consist of three successive steps. Notice of grievances and appeals of decisions made at the first and second steps shall be forwarded in accordance with the following:

Step 1. Company Representative Designated to Receive Grievance

1. General Management level manager having supervisory authority over the conditions or circumstances which gave rise to the grievance. (In the absence of a General Management level, the Company shall inform the Vice President, CWA, District 6, in writing of the appropriate Company representative who is designated to hear grievances.)
or
Vice President–Labor Relations if the grievance involves employees in more than one General Management level organization. If the grievance is initially filed at this level, there shall be no successive steps.
2. Vice President–Labor Relations.

c. If the grievance involves or affects only employees reporting to a single immediate supervisor, a copy of the notice shall also be forwarded at the same time to such supervisor.

Section 3.

a. The decision made at either of the first two levels of the grievance procedure may be appealed to the next higher level of the grievance procedure provided such appeal is submitted within two weeks of the date the decision is communicated to the Union.

b. A decision at the second level of the grievance procedure or default on the Company's part to meet with the Union, as explained in Section 7, at the second level shall be construed as full completion of the "Formal Grievance" procedure.

c. The decision of the Company as to grievances submitted shall be confirmed in writing to the Union.

Section 4.

So that the Union may present formal grievances to the appropriate Company representative, the Company will notify the Union of changes in Company organization that require a change in the then existing manner of presentation.

Section 5.

After a notice as set forth in Section 2.b. above has been received by the Company, the Company will not attempt to adjust the grievance with any employee or employees involved without offering the Union an opportunity to be present.

Section 6.

At any meeting held pursuant to Section 2 above, the Company will designate its representative(s) to meet with the aggrieved employees(s), the representative(s) designated by the Union, or both.

Section 7.

Meetings at each level of the grievance procedure shall be arranged promptly. If, due to the Company's actions, a mutually agreeable meeting date is not arranged within two weeks of either the Company's receipt of the initial notification or the appeal of the grievance, the Union may present its original grievance to the next higher level of the formal grievance procedure.

Section 8.

The place of the meeting at each level of the grievance procedure shall be mutually agreed upon, with each party giving due consideration to the convenience of the other.

Section 9.

Those employees of the Company including the aggrieved employee(s) and the employee representative(s) designated by the Union, who shall suffer no loss in pay for time consumed in, and necessarily consumed in traveling to and from, grievance meetings shall not be more than three at any level of the grievance procedure.

Section 10.

At any meeting held under this Article for the adjustment of a grievance or complaint, any party present (including Union or Company representatives) shall be afforded full opportunity to present any facts and arguments pertaining to the matter or matters under consideration. The decision made upon such facts and arguments shall be made as promptly after conclusion of the presentation as may be reasonably and effectively possible.

Section 11.

Any complaint which is not delivered in writing by the Union as specified in Section 2 above, shall be handled by the Company as an informal complaint on an informal basis; provided, however, that nothing in this Article shall preclude the Union and the Company from using any other mutually satisfactory and proper method of presentation, discussion, and disposition of grievances.

Part Three. The Changing Labor Relations Environment

8. The Airline Industry

1. What federal agency had jurisdiction over airline consolidations, mergers, and acquisitions between 1938 and January 1, 1985?

2. What federal agency has had jurisdiction over airline consolidations, mergers, and acquisitions since January 1, 1985?

3. What happened on January 1, 1985, that caused this power shift?

4. Does it appear that Congress was concerned about possible adverse consequences to airline workers or collective bargaining agreements in the airline industry when it enacted the Airline Deregulation Act of 1978?

5. The Airline Deregulation Act of 1978 included labor-protective provisions that would provide financial support to airline employees who lost their jobs or whose employer filed bankruptcy as a result of deregulation. How much money did Congress appropriate to fund that program? How much was actually paid out?

6. How many separate unions are certified in the airline industry?

7. Before airline mutual aid pacts were outlawed by the Airline Deregulation Act of 1978, how much had they paid to struck airlines?

8. What was the condition of the U.S. economy and the U.S. airline industry when airline deregulation took effect?

9. Compare the condition in question 8 to that of today.

10. Did the government's firing of thousands of air traffic controllers in response to the PATCO strike have any significant effect on private-sector labor relations? Explain.

11. What are the three major topic areas in airline labor negotiations?

12. What, if any, major U.S passenger airlines are now operating entirely with nonunion labor?

13. Define *furlough*. As used in the airline industry, how is this different from a layoff?

14. Define *double-breasting*.

15. Give an example of double-breasting in the airline industry.

16. Define *snapback provisions* in a collective bargaining agreement.

17. Have many airline industry collective bargaining agreements been negotiated in recent years that included concessions (give-backs) from labor included snapback provisions? Why?

18. Explain how a two-tier wage agreement works.

19. Define *fence agreements*. Are they still in use in the airline industry?

20. What is the "Gordian knot"? (This term is not in the text. Try your dictionary, encyclopedia, or the Internet.)

21. Some legal scholars have referred to the perpetuity of airline collective bargaining agreements under the

RLA as the "Gordian knot" of airline labor relations. How did Continental Airlines owner Frank Lorenzo legally cut that Gordian knot following airline deregulation?

22. Were any other airlines able to follow Continental's lead (discussed in question 21)? Why?

23. Identify current trends affecting the U.S. airline industry and its labor force.

24. Identify looming issues that may affect the U.S. airline industry and its labor force.

Online Assignments

1. Identify all U.S. airline mergers that have occurred since 2008, if any.

2. Identify all U.S. airline bankruptcies that have occurred since 2008, if any, and the final outcome of each.

3. With respect to an airline you or your instructor selects, compare:

    a. Most recent total employment data to the company's year-end total employment data for the previous year

    b. Most recent annual revenue to the company's previous year annual revenue

    c. Most recent profits/losses to the company's previous year profits/losses

Supplemental Reading

US Airline Bankruptcies since Deregulation, 1979–2011

Date	Air Carrier	Bankruptcy Chapter
5/18/79	New York Airways	11
11/19/79	Aeroamerica	11
1/24/80	Florida Airlines	11
3/3/80	Indiana Airlines	11
12/15/80	Air Bahia	11
12/31/80	Tejas Airlines	11
3/6/81	Mountain West	11
9/11/81	Pacific Coast	11
9/18/81	Swift Air Line	11
10/9/81	Golden Gate	11
1/26/82	Pinehurst Airlines	11
3/3/82	Silver State Airlines	11
3/26/82	Air Pennsylvania	11
4/2/82	Air South	11
4/16/82	Cochise Airlines	11
5/12/82	Braniff International	11
7/8/82	Astec Air East	11
8/19/82	Will's Air	11
10/5/82	Aero Sun International	11
10/19/82	Aero Virgin Islands	11
11/9/82	Altair	11
12/9/82	North American	11
2/1/83	Inland Empire	11
2/14/83	State Airlines	11
4/22/83	Golden West	11
9/24/83	Continental Airlines	11
12/2/83	National Florida	7
1/30/84	Air Vermont	11
2/2/84	Pacific Express	11
2/8/84	Dolphin	11
4/9/84	Combs Airways	11
7/3/84	Air Florida	11
7/17/84	Excellair	7
7/19/84	American International	11
8/21/84	Emerald	11
8/29/84	Hammonds Commuter	11
9/4/84	Air North	11
9/27/84	Wright Air Lines	11
10/2/84	Oceanaire Lines	7
10/10/84	Atlantic Gulf	11
10/10/84	Connectaire	7
10/26/84	Air One	11
11/23/84	Capitol Air	11
11/28/84	Wien Air Alaska	11
1/8/85	Northeastern International	11
1/22/85	Pompano Airways	11
2/22/85	Far West Airlines	11
3/8/85	American Central	11
3/13/85	Provincetown Boston	11
3/19/85	Sun West Airlines	11
5/1/85	Wise Airlines	11
8/19/85	Cascade Airways	11
10/7/85	Wheeler Airlines	11
12/2/85	Pride Air	11
1/21/86	Southern Express	11
1/30/86	Imperial Airlines	11
2/11/86	Arrow Airways	11
4/9/86	Sea Airmotive	11
8/19/86	Trans Air	11
8/28/86	Frontier Airlines	11
2/19/87	Chicago Airlines	11
2/23/87	McClain Airlines	11
2/27/87	Rio Airways	11
3/6/87	Air Puerto Rico	11
3/10/87	Gull Air	11
3/12/87	Royal West Airlines	11
4/3/87	Air Atlanta	11
6/17/87	Air South	11
9/9/87	Royale Airlines	11
1/5/88	Sun Coast Airlines	11
1/14/88	Air New Orleans	11
1/15/88	Air Virginia	11
1/20/88	Mid Pacific Airlines	11
3/4/88	Exec Express	11
5/6/88	Caribbean Express	11
5/25/88	Pocono Airlines	11
6/20/88	Virgin Island Seaplane	11
8/11/88	Princeton Air Link	7
9/14/88	Qwest Air	11

US Airline Bankruptcies since Deregulation, 1979–2011 (continued)

Date	Air Carrier	Bankruptcy Chapter
9/27/88	Southern Jersey Airways	11
3/9/89	Eastern Air Lines	11
3/14/89	Big Sky Airlines	11
7/19/89	Air Kentucky	7
9/28/89	Braniff International	11
10/26/89	Presidential Airways	11
11/17/89	Resort Commuter	11
1/23/90	Pocono Airlines	11
5/10/90	SMB Stage Lines	11
7/5/90	CCAir	11
12/3/90	Britt Airways	11
12/3/90	Continental Airlines	11
12/3/90	Rocky Mountain Airways	11
1/8/91	Pan Am Express	11
1/8/91	Pan Am World Airways	11
1/9/91	L'Express	11
1/18/91	Eastern Air Lines	7
1/20/91	Bar Harbor Airlines	11
1/22/91	Virgin Island Seaplane	11
1/29/91	Northcoast Executive	7
3/25/91	Midway Airlines	11
3/26/91	Grand Airways	11
4/1/91	Metro Airlines	11
5/20/91	Jet Express	11
5/30/91	Metro Airlines Northeast	11
6/27/91	America West Airlines	11
8/12/91	Mohawk Airlines	11
11/27/91	Midway Airlines	7
12/31/91	Flagship Express	11
1/31/92	Trans World Airlines	11
2/28/92	L'Express	7
6/8/92	Hermans/Markair Express	11
6/8/92	Markair	11
12/15/92	States West Airlines	11
5/1/93	Key Airlines	11
9/20/93	Evergreen International Aviation	11
9/21/93	Hawaiian Airlines	11
10/11/94	Florida West Airlines	11
2/3/95	Crescent Airways	11
4/14/95	Markair	11
6/30/95	Trans World Airlines	11
11/28/95	Grand Airways	11
1/10/96	GP Express	11
1/22/96	Business Express	11
1/23/96	Conquest Airlines	11
9/30/96	Kiwi International Airlines	11
7/25/97	Mahalo	11
8/28/97	Air South	11
10/5/97	Western Pacific Airlines	11
11/6/97	Mountain Air Express	11
2/26/98	Pan American World Airways	11
7/29/98	Euram Flight Centre	11
3/23/99	Kiwi International Airlines	11
6/25/99	Sunjet International/ Myrtle Beach Jet Express	11
9/30/99	Eastwind Airlines	7
11/29/99	Access Air	11
2/29/00	Tower Air	11
5/1/00	Kitty Hawk	11
9/19/00	Pro Air	11
9/27/00	Fine Air Services	11
12/3/00	Legend Airlines	11
12/6/00	National Airlines	11
12/13/00	Allegiant Air	11
1/10/01	Trans World Airlines	11
8/13/01	Midway Airlines	11
1/2/02	Sun Country Airlines	7
7/30/02	Vanguard Airlines	11
8/11/02	US Airways	11
12/9/02	United Airlines	11
3/21/03	Hawaiian Airlines	11
10/30/03	Midway Airlines	7
1/23/04	Great Plains Airlines	11
1/30/04	Atlas Air/Polar Air Cargo	11
9/12/04	US Airways	11
10/26/04	ATA Airlines	11
12/1/04	Southeast Airlines	7
12/30/04	Aloha Airlines	11
9/14/05	Comair	11

US Airline Bankruptcies since Deregulation, 1979–2011 (*continued*)

Date	Air Carrier	Bankruptcy Chapter
9/14/05	Delta Air Lines	11
9/14/05	Northwest Airlines	11
9/29/05	TransMeridian Airlines	7
10/13/05	Mesaba Airlines	11
11/7/05	Independence Air	11
12/28/05	Era Aviation	11
1/6/06	Independence Air	7
2/21/06	Florida Coastal Airlines	11
10/15/07	Kitty Hawk Aircargo	11
12/24/07	MAXjet Airways	11
1/7/08	Big Sky	7
3/31/08	Aloha Airlines	7
3/31/08	Champion Air	11
4/2/08	ATA Airlines	11
4/7/08	Skybus Airlines	11
4/11/08	Frontier Airlines	11
4/26/08	Eos Airlines	11
5/14/08	Air Midwest	7
6/18/08	Gemini Air Cargo	11
7/18/08	Vintage Props & Jets	11
8/12/08	Gemini Air Cargo	7
10/6/08	Sun Country	11
10/15/08	Primaris Airlines	11
1/5/10	Mesa Air	11
6/30/10	Arrow Air	11
11/4/10	Gulfstream International Airlines	11
11/29/11	American Airlines	11

SOURCES: ATA Research; company reports; DOT records; "The Bankruptcy Virus in the U.S. Airline Industry: Causes and Cures," Aviation Forecasting and Economics and The George Washington University; Lehman Brothers Equity Research, BankruptcyData.com, *Chicago Tribune.*

9. The Aerospace Industry

1. Identify four major unions in the aerospace industry.

2. True or False. A substantial majority of aerospace jobs is in subcontractor plants employing fewer than one hundred workers.

3. True or False. A majority of workers in the aerospace industry are union members or are covered by union contracts.

4. True or False. Production workers in aerospace earn about twice as much as in other U.S. private and manufacturing industries.

5. True or False. The aerospace industry is the largest manufacturing contributor to the U.S. balance of trade.

6. Identify five trends the aerospace industry, like the airlines, is facing.

7. What have aerospace manufacturers attempted to accomplish through mergers and acquisitions?

8. Which major aerospace companies have tended to be more stable: those diversifying across civil products and military products or those focusing on one or the other?

9. How has lean manufacturing affected productivity and job security?

10. Identify two factors that may lead a manufacturer to outsource component production.

11. In your opinion, does outsourcing component production overseas compromise aviation safety? Explain, giving an example.

12. In the aerospace industry, worldwide revenues from aircraft sales are in what currency, while costs of production are paid in what currencies?

13. In February 2008, the President's Interagency Aerospace Revitalization Task Force characterized what as a "demographic cliff" the aerospace industry was about to fall off?

14. What factors does that report identify as component causes of the problem?

15. What are the implications of that problem for the U.S. aerospace industry and U.S. economy?

16. Why can some jobs in the U.S. aerospace industry not be outsourced overseas?

17. What is your institution of higher learning doing to address the challenges identified in the report of that presidential task force?

18. What more do you think your institution could be doing to help solve these problems?

19. What more do you think the aerospace industry could be doing to help solve the problem?

20. What more do you think labor unions in the aerospace industry could be doing to help solve the problem?

21. Identify two areas of opportunity for the aerospace industry presented by environmental challenges.

Online Assignments

1. Identify a recent merger of aerospace companies. Give the names of the companies, nature of work performed by each, and your opinion, with your reasoning, of the wisdom of the merger.

2. Identify a current example of outsourcing of work formerly performed by unionized employees of a U.S. aerospace company. Give the URLs for all online sources used.

3. Identify a current or recent labor dispute in the U.S. aerospace industry, giving the names of the company and union involved, the craft of workers involved, the main issues, and your opinion of the relative merits of the company and union positions. Give the URLs for all online sources used.

10. General Aviation

1. Define general aviation.

2. Why has union organizing of the general aviation workforce been slow, as compared to the airlines and aerospace manufacturing?

3. What trend is making this workforce a more attractive target for union organizing?

4. True or False. All general aviation labor relations are governed by the National Labor Relations Board.

5. True or False. All general aviation labor relations are governed by the National Mediation Board.

6. Should it make any difference to a general aviation company or union whether the NMB or NLRB has jurisdiction? Explain.

7. True or False. Some general aviation operators fall under NLRB jurisdiction, while others fall under NMB jurisdiction.

8. What test does the NMB apply to determine whether it has jurisdiction over a general aviation business?

9. Under which labor regulatory agency's jurisdiction do air taxi operators fall? Why?

10. Under which labor regulatory agency's jurisdiction do fractional aircraft operators fall? Why?

11. Under which labor regulatory agency's jurisdiction do general aviation businesses providing ground services such as fueling, ground handling, storage, and maintenance fall? Why?

12. Under which labor regulatory agency's jurisdiction do general aviation businesses providing flight training fall? Why?

13. In your opinion, does the present division of jurisdiction over general aviation labor relations make good sense? Explain.

14. Do you foresee consolidation of any areas of general aviation business other than air taxi, fractional, and flight training operations within the next decade? Explain.

15. Do you foresee growth or contraction in the general aviation industry over the next decade? Explain.

16. A company is in the business of providing training for aviation maintenance technicians. Assuming the company has no other source of income, what federal agency has jurisdiction over its labor relations? Explain.

17. A company is in the business of managing corporate business jets, providing aircraft, crew, and maintenance-scheduling services, along with flight crew and insurance-selection advice. Under the agreement between the company and aircraft owner, the company is completely responsible for operational control of the aircraft and all pilots and maintenance personnel or employees of the aircraft owner. No aircraft in the program may be used for common carriage by air. Assuming the company has no other source of income, what federal agency has jurisdiction over its labor relations? Explain.

18. If the company in the preceding question also provided management services and flight crewmembers to on-demand air charter operators, would that change your answer to the preceding question? Explain.

19. Under which federal labor-relations agency's jurisdiction would a company in the business of building, selling, leasing, installing, and servicing flight simulators and having no other aviation-related source of income fall? Explain.

20. United Air Lines currently operates a major flight training facility where it provides recurrent training and testing to its own flight crews and under contract to those of other airlines. What federal agency has labor relations jurisdiction over that facility? If United sells that facility to a company specializing in flight training, and United outsources to the buyer the work formerly provided by United, would that affect agency jurisdiction? Explain.

Online Assignment

With respect to a general aviation business that you or your instructor selects, determine:

a. The full legal name of the company

b. Nature and scope of the company's business

c. Operating locations

d. Total number of employees and approximate number at each operating location

e. Extent of union representation of the company's workforce

f. Federal agency responsible for overseeing labor relations at the company

g. URLs for all online sources used

Supplemental Reading

COLLECTIVE BARGAINING AGREEMENT
By and Between
AIR METHODS CORPORATION
and
OFFICE AND PROFESSIONAL EMPLOYEES
INTERNATIONAL UNION, LOCAL 109
Term:
January 1, 2006 through April 30, 2009

TABLE OF CONTENTS

PARTIES TO AGREEMENT

This Agreement is entered into between *Air Methods Corporation*, hereinafter called the "Company," and the *Office and Professional Employees International Union*, and its *Local 109* hereinafter jointly called the "Union" or the "OPEIU."

ARTICLE 1
Purpose of Agreement

Section 1.1

The purpose of this Agreement is, in the mutual interest of the Company and its Pilots, to provide for the operation of the services of the Company under methods which will further, to the fullest extent possible, the safety of air transportation and the efficiency of operation.

Section 1.2

No Pilot covered by this Agreement will be interfered with, restrained, coerced or discriminated against by the Company or the Union, its officers, or its agents because of membership or non-membership in the Union, or any lawful activity under the Railway Labor Act not in violation of this agreement.

Section 1.3

It is understood, whenever in this Agreement, Pilots or jobs are referred to in the male gender, it shall be recognized as referring to both male and female Pilots.

ARTICLE 2
Recognition

Section 2.1

This Agreement is made and entered into in accordance with the provisions of Title II of the Railway Labor Act, as amended, by and between Air Methods Corporation (the "Company") and the Office and Professional Employees International Union (the "Union") representing employees composed of the craft and class of Flight Deck Crew Members (hereafter called "Pilots") as certified by the National Mediation Board in Case Number R-6949, September 16, 2003.

The Company hereby recognizes the Union as the sole collective bargaining agent and authorized representative for those employees described in Section 1 above, to represent them and, on their behalf, to negotiate and conclude agreements with the Company as to hours of work, wages, and other conditions of employment in accordance with the provisions of the Railway Labor Act, as amended. This Collective Bargaining Agreement and any formal letters of agreement between the Company and the Union may be collectively referred to as the "Agreement."

Section 2.2

This Agreement covers all revenue flying performed by the Company with Pilots on its payroll. All revenue flying covered by this Agreement shall be performed by Pilots whose names appear on the Air Methods Corporation Pilot's System Seniority List.

Section 2.3

In the event the Company sells all or part of its helicopter operations to another carrier during the term of this Agreement, in advance of such sale, the Company shall give notice of the existence of this Agreement to such successor carrier and shall make reasonable effort to persuade such successor carrier to agree to the continuation of the terms set forth in this Agreement. In the event the Successor Carrier does not adopt the terms of this Agreement the Company shall not be liable for any differences (in hours, wages, benefits, or all other working conditions) after the effective date of the change of ownership.

Section 2.4

In the event the Company acquires all or substantially all of the assets or equity of another carrier, or another air carrier acquires all or substantially all of the assets or equity of the Company, the Company will meet promptly with the Union to negotiate a possible "Fence Agreement" to be in effect during the period, if any, the two carriers are operated separately without integration of the Pilot work force. These discussions shall not be pursuant to Section 6 of the Railway Labor Act, and reaching an agreement with the Union shall not be a prerequisite for closing, or any other aspect of the transaction or operations pursuant to the transaction.

ARTICLE 3
Agency Shop & Dues Check Off

Section 3.1

Membership in the Union is not compulsory. Pilots have a right to join, not join, maintain, or drop their membership in the Union as they see fit. Neither party shall exert any pressure on or discriminate against any Pilot as regards such matters.

Section 3.2

Each Pilot covered by this Agreement who was hired prior to or after the execution of this Agreement shall become a member or an agency fee payer within sixty (60) days after his/her date of hire or the effective date of this agreement and shall be required as a condition of continued employment by the Company to pay an equivalent agency fee, so long as this agreement remains in effect. The agency fee referred to in this Section shall be equal to the Union's regular and usual initiation fee and its regular, uniform and usual monthly dues. Notwithstanding the foregoing, nothing herein shall be construed to be in violation of or in conflict with the provisions of the Railway Labor Act.

Section 3.3

During the life of this Agreement, the Company agrees that upon receipt of a properly executed Authorization of Payroll Deductions, voluntarily executed by a Pilot, it will make bi-weekly deductions from the Pilot's earnings after other deductions authorized by the Pilot or are required by law have been made, to cover this current standard bi-weekly assessments and/or initiation fees or agency fees uniformly levied in accordance with the Constitution and bylaws of the Union as set forth in the Railway Labor Act. Any authorizations for payroll deductions under this Article shall be effective the first day of the month following its receipt by the Payroll Department and shall apply to the next pay check for which dues deduction or agency fees is made.

Section 3.4

The Company remittance to the union will be accompanied by a list of the Pilots names and employee numbers of the Pilots for who the deductions have been made in that particular month and the individual amounts deducted. Deductions shall be remitted to the designated Financial Officer of the Union not later than ten (10) days after the deductions are made.

Section 3.5

Collection of dues or agency fees not deducted because of insufficient current earnings missed because of clerical error or inadvertent error in the accounting procedures, agency fees missed due to delay in receipt of the Authorization for Payroll Deductions, shall be the responsibility of the Union and shall not be the subject of payroll deductions from subsequent paychecks, and the Company shall not be responsible in any way for such missed collections. It shall be the Union's responsibility to verify apparent errors with the individual Pilot prior to contacting the Payroll Department. The total or balance of unpaid dues, assessments and/or initiation fees or agency fees due and owed the Union at the time a Pilot terminates his employment shall be deducted from the final paycheck in accordance with applicable law.

Section 3.6

An Authorization for Payroll Deduction under this Article shall be irrevocable for the term of this Agreement or for a period of one (1) year from the date the Authorization is first executed, whichever occurs sooner. Revocation shall become effective when the Pilot serves written notice on the Payroll Department to revoke such Authorization for payroll deductions. An Authorization for Payroll Deduction shall automatically be revoked if:

A. The Pilot transfers to a position with the Company not covered by the Agreement;
B. The Pilot's service with the Company is terminated;
C. The Pilot is furloughed; or
D. The Pilot is on an authorized leave of absence.

Section 3.7

Upon written demand from the Union, the Company shall terminate any employee within the bargaining unit who fails to tender the sum due the Union under Section Two of the Article within thirty (30) days from the date such sum is due provided the Union informs the Company and the employee in writing and allows him/her an additional fifteen (15) days after the 30th day of delinquency. If the employee fails to resolve his/her dues delinquency with the Union during this fifteen (15) day period and after notification to the Company by the Union, the Company will terminate the employee effective the end of that payroll period.

Section 3.8

Any dispute between the Company and the Union arising out of the interpretation or application of this Article, when reduced to writing as a grievance, shall be subject to the Grievance Procedure by initially referring the grievance to Step Three. The grievance thereafter may be processed in accordance with the provisions of Articles 6 and 7 in this Agreement.

Section 3.9

The Union agrees to hold the Company harmless and to indemnify the Company against any suits, claims, liabilities, and reasonable and customary attorney's fees which arise out of or by reason of any action taken by the Company under the terms of this Article.

Section 3.10

It is further agreed between the parties that the Union shall notify each Pilot of their Beck rights as provided by law.

ARTICLE 4
Management Rights

Section 4.1

The Union recognizes that the Management of the business of the Company and the direction of the working force are vested exclusively with the Company, subject to the expressed provisions of this Agreement.

Section 4.2

Except as restricted by an express provision of this Agreement, the Company shall retain all rights to manage and operate its business and work force, including but not limited to the right to sell, or discontinue or diminish in whole or part to determine where and when to operate scheduled or unscheduled flights; to determine its marketing methods and strategies; and to determine the type of aircraft it will utilize to negotiate customer contracts consistent with their requirement, to determine the number of workover hours to be worked, the qualifications of Pilots it may employ and to adopt, modify and rescind reasonable work and safety rules.

Section 4.3

The exercise of any right reserved herein to manage in a particular manner, or the non-exercise of such right, shall not operate as a waiver of the Company's rights hereunder, or preclude the Company from exercising the right in a different manner or at a future date.

Section 4.4

It is further agreed that the rights specified herein may not be impaired by an arbitrator or arbitration even though the parties may agree to arbitrate the issue involved in a specific manner as provided in the grievance and arbitration procedure set forth elsewhere in this Agreement.

Section 5

Under any contract of services or joint venture agreement/arrangement where the Company's Operating Certificates are utilized the flight deck crew members will be covered by this contract.

ARTICLE 5
Non Discrimination

There shall be no discrimination by the Company or the Union in the application of the terms of this Agreement because of race, color, religion, national origin, age, sex or handicap. The Company and the Union will comply with applicable laws prohibiting discrimination.

ARTICLE 6
Grievance Procedure

Section 6.1

Disputes relating to the interpretation or application of the specific provisions of this Agreement may be the subject of a grievance. Any such grievance shall be processed in the following manner:

Step 1. The Pilot shall first attempt to resolve the grievance with his immediate supervisor within seven (7) calendar days from the date of the occurrence of the event giving rise to the grievance, or within seven (7) calendar days of the date the Pilot knew or should have known of such event. The supervisor shall give his answer within seven (7) calendar days from that date, after receiving permission to resolve said grievance from either the applicable Operations Manager, Program Director or Designee.

Step 2. If the grievance is not resolved at Step 1 to the satisfaction of the grievant, the grievance shall be reduced to writing and presented to the designated representative of the Company within seven (7) calendar days after the receipt of the immediate supervisor's answer. The written grievance must state the nature of the grievance, the circumstances out of which it arose, the remedy or correction requested and the specific provisions of the Agreement alleged to have been violated. The Company representative will give his answer to the grievant in writing with a copy to the Union within seven (7) calendar days after the receipt of the grievance.

Step 3. In the event the decision by the Company representative is unacceptable to the aggrieved employee or union, it may be appealed in writing to the designated representative of the Company within seven (7) calendar days of the receipt of the decision. The appeal must include a statement of the reasons the grievant believes the decision was erroneous. The Company's representative shall render a decision on the appeal in writing within seven (7) calendar days of receipt of the appeal. In the event the decision at Step 3 is unacceptable to the grievant, the Union may appeal to the System Board of Adjustment in accordance with Article 7 of this areement.

Section 6.2

In the event a non-probationary Pilot who has been discharged wishes to grieve such discharge, the grievance must be presented at Step 2 within seven (7) calendar days after the termination.

Section 6.3

All provisions of this Article shall apply to Union grievances except such grievances shall be presented to the designated Company representative at Step 2. Any grievance not presented and processed in the manner, and within the time limits set forth above, shall be waived and deemed null and void provided, however, at any time in advance of the expiration of such time limit the parties may agree, by mutual written consent, to extend any time limit for a specified period of time. Compliance with all time limits specified in this Article shall be determined by the date of mailing as established by postmark.

Section 6.4

No grievance, the basis for which occurred prior to the execution of this Agreement, shall be considered.

Section 6.5

The Company and the Union agree to furnish to the other party the names of their designated representatives charged with administration of the grievance procedure within thirty (30) calendar days after the execution of this Agreement. Any changes in these representatives shall be furnished to the other party in writing.

Section 6.6

The Union and the Company may, by mutual agreement in writing, elect to bypass any or all steps in this Article and proceed to the System Board of Adjustment in accordance with Article 7 of this Agreement.

Section 6.7

All grievances resolved at any step of the grievance procedure prior to the Systems Board of Adjustment shall be on a non-precedent basis unless mutually agreed otherwise.

Section 6.8

If a grievant is exonerated, his personnel file shall be cleared of all references to the incident in question, consistent with applicable Federal regulations and may not be used in future disciplinary actions against the Pilot. A grievant that is cleared of all charges shall be made whole in every respect.

ARTICLE 7
System Board of Adjustment

Section 7.1

In compliance with Section 204, Title II of the Railway Labor Act, as amended, this Agreement establishes a System Board of Adjustment, which shall be called the Air Methods Pilots' System Board of Adjustment, hereinafter called "the Board."

Section 7.2

The Board has jurisdiction over timely filed and appropriately processed grievances arising out of the interpretation and application of the specific provisions of this Agreement relating to rates of pay, rules, working conditions, discipline and discharge. The procedures set forth in this Article are the exclusive and mandatory forum for all such disputes.

Section 7.3

The Board does not have jurisdiction over any dispute unless all of the procedures required by the Grievance Procedure provided for in this Agreement have been timely and completely exhausted in the dispute, and the dispute has been properly submitted to the Board pursuant to the provisions of this Article.

Section 7.4

Neither the Systems Board or Arbitrator shall have any jurisdiction to modify, add to or otherwise alter or amend any of the terms of this Agreement or to make any decision that has such an effect.

Section 7.5

The Board shall consist of four members, two of whom shall be selected and appointed by the Company and two of whom shall be selected and appointed by the President of the Local Union. A Board member appointed by the Union shall serve as chairman and a Board member appointed by the Company shall serve as vice-chairman in even years, and a Board member appointed by the Company shall serve as chairman and a Board member appointed by the Union shall serve as vice-chairman in odd years. The Vice-chairman shall act as chairman in his absence. Each Board member has a vote in connection with all actions taken by the Board. In the event the four Board members cannot reach a decision with respect to a particular dispute, the Board will select a neutral member who will decide the dispute. In the event the Board cannot agree on a neutral member, within seven (7) calendar days thereafter either party may request that the American Arbitration Association (AAA) submit a list of seven (7) arbitrators, all of whom are members of the National Academy of Arbitrators. The Arbitrators shall be selected in accordance to the rules of AAA. The Board hearing before the third party neutral member shall be conducted in accordance with the AAA rules.

Section 7.6

The Board will meet quarterly in a location determined by mutual agreement, provided that at such time there are cases on file with the Board for its consideration.

Section 7.7

Any expenses incurred by Board members appointed by one of the parties to this Agreement will be paid by that party. The fees and expenses of any neutral member of the Board shall be borne equally by the Company and the Union.

Section 7.8

Disputes may only be submitted to the Board by the President of the Local Union or a duly designated officer of the Union or the Company's Vice President of Human Resources.

Section 7.9

Decisions by the Board are final and binding on the Company, the Union and the affected Pilots, provided they conform to Section 7.4 above.

Section 7.10

The party appealing a final decision under the Grievance Procedure in this Agreement shall submit the dispute for consideration by the Board within fourteen (14) calendar days of that decision, including all papers and exhibits, and a list of potential witnesses known to the appealing party at that time shall be submitted by each party seven (7) days prior to a scheduled Board of Adjustment. Neither party will intimidate or coerce any witness so identified. If the appeal is not made within this fourteen (14) day period, the Board does not have jurisdiction over the dispute.

Section 7.11

All disputes referred to the Board shall be sent to the Vice President of Human Resources for the Company and his/her office shall assign a docket number according to the order in which the dispute is received. However, grievances involving suspension or discharge shall be given preference for disposition.

Section 7.12

The appealing party will ensure that a copy of the petition is served on the members of the Board. Each case submitted to the Board must state:

A. The question or questions at issue;
B. a statement of the facts with supporting documents;
C. a reference to the applicable provisions of the Agreement alleged to have been breached;
D. the position of the aggrieved party; and
E. the remedy requested.

Section 7.13

Decisions by the Board shall be rendered no later than thirty (30) calendar days after the close of the hearing or receipt of post-hearing briefs.

Section 7.14

The Company and the Union shall, in good faith, attempt to make a joint submission of their dispute to the Board. If the parties are unable to agree on a joint submission, the appealing party shall file a submission with the Board containing all of the information described in Article 6, Section 1, and the responding party may do the same. Any party filing a submission with the Board pursuant to this Article shall serve a copy of its submission with the other party.

Section 7.15

The parties agree that each Board member is free to discharge his duties in an independent manner without fear of retaliation from the Company or the Union because of any action taken by him in good faith in his capacity as a Board member.

ARTICLE 8
No Strike/No Lockout

Section 8.1

Neither the Union or any of its agents (stewards) nor any of its members will collectively, concertedly, or in any manner engage in a strike, sick-out, boycott, sympathy strike, slow down or work stoppage of any kind during the term of this Agreement. During the term of this Agreement, the Company agrees not to lock out any of the employees covered by this Agreement. It is further understood that the duly-authorized representatives of the Union shall use their best efforts on behalf of the Union to actively encourage the employees engaging in a violation of this Section to cease such conduct. If the Company knows one of its Customers will have a primary picket line, the Company will notify the Pilot before dispatching the Pilot to the location. A Pilot may refuse to take an assignment to cross a picket line if he has reasonable safety concerns based on verifiable incidents of picket line misconduct at the site. In such cases, the Company reserves the right to meet Customer needs however it deems appropriate.

Section 8.2

Employees found to be in violation of the terms of this Section shall be subject to discharge. Such discharge shall not be subjected to the grievance procedure and System Board of Adjustment provisions of this agreement, except as to the question of whether the Pilot engaged in such a violation.

ARTICLE 9
Discipline and Discharge

Section 9.1

Pilots may be subject to disciplinary action, up to and including discharge for just cause including violation or infraction of company rules or policies, or for violating this Agreement. The Company will continue to use a system of progressive discipline. The Company may suspend a Pilot with pay prior to notifying him of the nature of the charge against him. Within seven (7) calendar days of the date of suspension the Company will inform the Pilot in writing, with a copy to the Union, of the nature of the charge and its decision on the type of discipline that should be imposed.

Section 9.2

In a case where a Pilot is called into a meeting where as a result disciplinary action could be taken against him, the Pilot may request to be accompanied by his Steward, and such a request will be granted by the Company. Request for a steward or alternate shall be honored if they are available within a reasonable time not to exceed forty-eight (48) hours, provided the Company incurs no workover or travel costs whatsoever. If a Pilot at the base, while on duty, is selected to attend such meeting as a representative of the Pilot being investigated, he shall suffer no loss in pay. If called to take a mission, the Pilot and the one being investigated shall reschedule said meeting at the earliest possible time. The parties agree that there shall be no delay in the duty Pilot taking the mission.

Section 9.3

Upon his request, a Pilot's personnel file shall be open for his inspection during normal office hours in the presence of a Company representative, upon reasonable notice. Nothing of a derogatory nature will be placed in a Pilot's file unless a copy is sent to the Pilot. Upon receipt of such report, the Pilot shall have the option of responding by returning his explanation or comments to be included with the report in his file or by challenging the accuracy of the report. If the Company determines the challenge to be justified, the report will be removed from the Pilot's file and destroyed. If the Company determines otherwise, it shall notify the Pilot he may then appeal this decision through the normal grievance procedure.

Section 9.4

Customer complaints or correspondence of a derogatory nature shall not serve as the basis for discipline after twelve (12) months from the date of issuance unless within the twelve (12) month period there has been a recurrence of the same or similar nature.

Section 9.5

Disciplinary records involving safety matters shall not serve as a basis for any disciplinary action after five (5) years from the date of issuance.

Section 9.6

A Pilot may be immediately removed from the payroll and suspended or discharged without pay if he violates the FAA Drug/Alcohol policy or commits other acts of serious misconduct.

Section 9.7

In the event the Pilot feels he has been unjustly disciplined or discharged, the Pilot or Union may appeal in writing the Company's decision to the Company designee within seven (7) calendar days of the adverse action against the Pilot. Such appeal will be taken at Step 2 of the grievance procedure and must set forth the facts giving rise to the appeal and state the remedy or relief requested.

Section 9.8

The parties recognize that flight safety is paramount to the well-being of the business, patients and employees. The Pilots acknowledge it is essential to abide by all applicable FAR's. The parties further agree that neither will rely upon any discipline administered prior to the execution of this agreement.

ARTICLE 10
Union Representation

Section 10.1

In the event it is necessary for a Union representative to enter the premises owned or leased by the Company to discuss the application of this Agreement, the Union representative shall notify the manager for the particular location, and they shall arrange a mutually satisfactory time, date and place for the visit within a *five (5) day* period thereafter. The Union representative shall not take any action that would interrupt or in any way interfere with the Company's operations or the job duties of any employee. Such visits shall comply with customer or base entrance requirements.

Section 10.2

The Company will not be obligated to deal with any Union representative who has not been designated in writing to be an authorized representative of the Union.

Section 10.3

The Union may elect or appoint Pilots to be primary job steward(s) and alternate(s) to conduct Union business and shall notify the Company, in writing, of their election, appointment or removal. Pilots who have been designated as primary stewards (and the alternate steward in the absence of the primary steward) shall be granted reasonable time to investigate, present and process grievances during their normal duty hours without loss of pay, provided it does not cause a delay in meeting mission requirements. Stewards or alternates who serve their fellow Pilots shall be considered Union representatives.

Section 10.4

The Company and the Union desire that complaints and grievances shall be settled whenever possible with supervisors at the location where the complaint or grievance originates. It is understood and agreed that a steward's activities shall fall within the scope of the following functions:

> A. To consult with a Pilot(s) regarding a presentation of a complaint or grievance that the Pilot(s) desires to present. Stewards shall be permitted to present grievances to management and attempt to resolve any grievance.

B. To present a grievance or complaint to a Pilot's immediate supervisor in an attempt to settle the matter. Stewards shall be granted the right to consult with Pilots at their base for the purpose of enforcing the provisions of this agreement.

C. To investigate a complaint or grievance as defined in the grievance Procedure.

Section 10.5

The Company and the Union agree that a minimum amount of time shall be spent in the performance of steward duties.

ARTICLE 11
Seniority List

Section 11.1

The Air Methods Corporation Pilot System Seniority List shall consist of the seniority number, name, and seniority date of all Pilots covered by this Agreement. The Company will post the seniority list on its web page. Thereafter Pilots may post the seniority list on the bulletin boards, where permitted, and/or in the Union information book. Copies of the seniority list will be furnished to the Union.

Section 11.2

When two or more Pilots are employed on the same date, they shall be placed on the seniority list according to the last four digits in their social security number. The Pilot with the lowest last four digits will be awarded the most senior position. A. In the event more than one Pilot is hired from a newly acquired contract such Pilots shall be placed at the bottom of the seniority list in order of their time in service with the previous company.

Section 11.3

The Company agrees to update the seniority list each six (6) months, beginning with the effective date of this Agreement with a copy to the Union. A Pilot shall have a period of thirty (30) days after the posting of the seniority list to protest to the Company any omission or incorrect posting affecting his seniority. Pilots on vacation, leave of absence, or furlough shall be permitted thirty (30) days after their return to duty to make any protest concerning his seniority. Once the thirty (30) day period has expired without a protest, the posting will be considered correct and shall not be subject to further protest, unless the omission or incorrect posting was the result of a clerical error on the part of the Company.

ARTICLE 12
Seniority

Section 12.1

Seniority of a new hire Pilot shall begin on the date the Pilot is entered on the Company's payroll.

A. It is understood and agreed Pilots who are employed by AMC at the time of this Agreement shall be placed on the Company seniority list using their original date of hire with AMC or, if applicable, their original date of hire from a previously acquired Company.

B. In the event of future acquisitions or mergers, the Company will meet promptly with the Union for the purpose of integrating the Pilot groups.

Section 12.2

There shall be two (2) types of seniority, Company seniority and Bidding seniority.

A. Company Seniority – Company Seniority shall be defined as a Pilot's length of service with the Company or present customer, regardless of location, and except as provided for elsewhere in this agreement, shall govern pay rates, and accrual or granting of paid days off pursuant to Vacation - Article 27 of this Agreement. Company Seniority shall be adjusted for leaves of absence as provided for in Leaves of Absence - Article 23 of this Agreement.

B. Bidding Seniority – Bidding Seniority shall be defined as a Pilot's length of uninterrupted Pilot service with the Company less all time spent outside of the bargaining unit as defined in Section 12.3 of this Article. Bidding Seniority shall govern all Pilots covered by this Agreement in bidding for job assignments and vacancies as provided for in this Agreement.

Section 12.3

A Pilot who is promoted to a non-flying or supervisory position shall stop accruing bidding seniority, unless they return to flying duties within twelve (12) calendar months. Such Pilot shall continue to accrue Company Seniority and retain his Bidding Seniority. If said Pilot returns to flying duty, it shall be in accordance with his Bidding seniority. In the event there is no vacancy, he shall be assigned to other duties if they exist and such Pilot chooses to accept them, or placed on layoff status until a bid opportunity becomes available and the Pilot is awarded the job. If a Pilot is terminated while in a supervisory or non-flying position, such Pilot shall have no rights under this Agreement.

Section 12.4

A Pilot's seniority shall be nullified and his/her employment shall be terminated if any of the following occur:

A. Resignation or retirement;

B. Discharge for cause;

C. Failure to inform the designated Company representative in person or by certified mail of his intention to return to work as provided for in the Reductions in Workforce - Section 13.5 (A);

D. Failure to return to work on or before a date specified in the notice of recall from the designated Company representative after a layoff as provided for in the Reductions in Workforce - Section 13.5 (B);

E. A Pilot's seniority and recall rights shall terminate after being on furlough for a period of three (3) calendar years.

Section 12.5

Disputes arising over seniority shall be handled in accordance with Grievance Procedure and System Board of Adjustment outlined in this agreement.

ARTICLE 13
Reductions in Workforce
Section 13.1

If there is a loss of a contract, base closure, or other reduction in the workforce, a Pilot's seniority, pursuant to Seniority - Article 12 of this Agreement, shall govern the layoff. Pilots with the least seniority shall be laid off first. The Company shall give at least fourteen (14) days notice of an impending layoff unless prevented from doing so due to causes beyond its control, or two (2) weeks pay in lieu thereof.

Section 13.2

Pilots will be recalled from furlough in seniority order, with the most senior laid-off Pilot being recalled first. At the point of being placed on furlough status the Pilot shall avail himself of all available job postings on the Company web site. The Pilot shall bid on the postings and indicate his order of preference. Provided the Pilot possesses the requisite credentials he shall be offered the positions in order of his preference before the position is filled by outside applicants. The Company shall not be permitted to hire a new Pilot until all furloughed qualified Pilots are recalled.

Section 13.3

Pilots shall continue to accrue Bidding Seniority and Company Seniority while on furlough.

Section 13.4

Laid off Pilots are required to file their proper mailing address, email address, and telephone number(s) with the Human Resources Department at the time of the layoff and will promptly notify the Company of any address changes. Failure to do so will forfeit that Pilots' rights under this Article.

Section 13.5

In the event no positions are available laid off Pilots shall be notified of a recall in order of their seniority by e-mail with confirmed response, telephone or certified mail to the most recent telephone number and address provided by the Pilot. Notification by telephone must be accomplished by positive telephone contact with the Pilot and the call must be followed up with official notification by certified mail. The date of recall notification shall be the earlier of the date on which telephone contact was made or the recall letter was mailed. Notices sent to the last address of record shall be considered conclusive evidence of notice to that Pilot.

A. Each Pilot accepting recall shall answer his recall notice no later than three (3) business days after receipt of such notice in e-mail with confirmed response, telephone, or by certified mail.

B. A laid off Pilot will not be allowed more than twenty one (21) calendar days after the date of recall notification to report to duty from layoff.

C. Pilots who fail to respond to a recall notice within the time limits set forth above, Pilots who refuse recall, or Pilots who reject a recall notice shall forfeit all recall rights and have their name removed from the seniority list.

D. The offer of recall shall be made in order of seniority status from the furloughed Pilots. However, if the senior furloughed Pilot declines on the offer of recall it shall be made in descending order to the remaining furloughed Pilots with the understanding that the junior qualified Pilot shall be obligated to accept the offer. If such Pilot refuses the offer of recall he shall forfeit all rights under this article. In such circumstances the offer shall be made in ascending order to the remaining Pilots. If no opening exists within the Company such Pilot may displace the least senior Pilot in the Company consistent with the hospital based Customer approval, if applicable, provided he is qualified (as defined in Job Posting and Bidding Section 14.2 F (1), or accept a furlough until such time a position becomes available within the timeframe outlined in Section 13.5 (E) of this Article.

E. Seniority and recall rights shall terminate if a laid off Pilot is not recalled within three (3) years from the commencement of his layoff.

ARTICLE 14
Job Posting and Bidding

Section 14.1

A Pilot may bid when a new job or permanent vacancy occurs, or when a new job or crew position is created. All vacancies will be posted on the Company Web Page within seven (7) calendar days after the vacancy occurs. The notice shall provide as much information as is available regarding the vacant position, including the job location and closing date for bid application. This Article does not allow a senior Pilot to bid a job that is already filled or to displace a junior Pilot from a job he is currently filling. The parties agree that a vacancy does not exist if the Customer changes aircraft type and requests that the assigned Pilots remain on the job.

A. Vacancies resulting from LOA's will be considered temporary and will be posted and assigned as such. Pilots accepting such temporary positions will be subject to replacement by the returning LOA Pilot, at which time the displaced Pilot will be eligible to bid on any other job opening within the Company.

Section 14.2 Bidding procedures are as follows:

A. Pilots will be given fourteen (14) calendar days from the initial posting to bid on any vacant position. The fourteen (14) days shall commence from the time of notification.

B. The Company will make the awards within seven (7) calendar days after the bidding has closed or the last hospital based customer interview, if required, is conducted.

C. The senior qualified Pilot, as defined in Section 14.2, Paragraph F of this Article that bids on the vacancy, who successfully completes the hospital based customer interview, if required, shall be awarded the job, except those positions covered in Section 14.4 of this Article.

D. A Pilot responding to more than one (1) vacancy shall indicate his order of preference on the bid and shall be awarded his highest available preference.

E. In the event that a Pilot voluntarily bids on and is awarded a new position, the Company reserves the right to require a Pilot to remain in that new position for a period of twelve (12) months; or eighteen (18) months if company paid relocation or training costs are incurred.

F. The term "qualified" as used in this Article means that a Pilot has been trained in an aircraft type, or holds the necessary Airman Certificate and endorsements and has the aeronautical experience to meet customer and Company requirements to be trained by the Company in that aircraft type. Training shall be provided in accordance with Article 18.

Section 14.3

A Pilot will be assigned to his new position within ninety (90) days of the position being awarded to him, unless the Company and Pilot agree otherwise.

Section 14.4

The following positions shall be posted at the base where they occur and not be subject to the bidding procedure described above; Lead Pilot, Aviation Services Manager (ASM), Aviation Base Manager (ABM), Safety Representative/ Officer, Check Airman, and Training Captains. Such positions shall be filled at the sole discretion of the Company. The Company shall interview Pilots who have signed the bid and all other applicants who have done likewise thereafter to determine their qualifications. In the event the Company selects a person other than a Pilot to fill the ASM position, it will then designate, at its discretion, one of the Pilots at the base as the Lead Pilot or ABM.

Section 14.5

For the purposes of this article, "awarded" shall be defined as being determined to be the successful bidder to fill a vacancy, "assigned" shall be defined as being transferred to the new base and commencing a work schedule.

ARTICLE 15
Training

Section 15.1 Recurrent Training

A. In accordance with applicable Federal Aviation Regulations (FAR's), the Company will develop and maintain a computerized training system whereby a Pilot can complete the classroom portions of his required recurrent ground training at his normally assigned work location at his convenience. In addition and in accordance with subpart G of FAR 135, the Company will utilize a system of written or oral examinations to accomplish the testing required where written or oral exams are required. The Company's training will provide adequate computerized or base resource materials that clearly detail the information upon which the Pilot will be tested for recurrent ground training. In no circumstances will the Pilot be tested on materials or information that is not reasonably available for the Pilot to study at his normally assigned base. The Pilot will be required to successfully complete recurrent ground training by the assigned completion deadline.

B. In circumstances where the Company requires training away from the Pilot's normally assigned base, the Company will make a reasonable effort to schedule recurrent training during a Pilot's work schedule. If for unusual operational reasons recurrent training cannot be scheduled during a Pilot's work schedule, then training may be scheduled during a Pilot's off duty time. The Company will make every effort to schedule training immediately before or after the Pilot's work schedule.

C. The Aviation Service Manager, Aviation Base Chief, Lead Pilot, or other aviation base management representative shall submit to the training department at least two months prior to scheduled recurrent flight training a list of two possible sets of dates that training is requested and can be accommodated by all Pilots. The Training Department will attempt to accommodate training on the dates submitted by the base to the fullest extent possible. If a Pilot is unable to attend training during the scheduled training dates due to illness, injury, or a reasonable unforeseen absence the Pilot and the Training Department will agree to alternate dates to compete the training.

D. Internet training sites will list all available recurrent ground training classes and deadlines.

Section 15.2 Upgrade/Transition/Special Training

The Company will schedule such training consistent with customer service requirements and the availability of qualified training personnel. The Company will make a reasonable effort to schedule such training during the Pilot's normal work period, but if unable to do so applicable work-over will be paid to the affected Pilot. The Company will make every effort to schedule training immediately before or after the Pilot's work schedule.

Section 15.3 Training Failures

It is recognized that not all Pilots reach the required level of proficiency in the same amount of time. Therefore, when it becomes apparent to the Company that a Pilot will require time in excess of that usually required to reach proficiency the Company Training Department will, in consultation with the Pilot, determine the cause of his inability to reach the required proficiency level and establish a plan for correcting the problem.

A. A Pilot who fails any portion of training, written exam, oral exam or flight check will be removed from line duty, with pay, until he has commenced retraining and has been successfully retested by the Company.

B. A Pilot who fails training, an oral exam, or flight check may request a change of instructor/check airman. However, if a Pilot elects to request a change of instructor/check airman the Pilot will be removed from the payroll, but permitted to use unused vacation until such time that the Pilot successfully completes retraining, an oral exam or flight check. Such re-training or re-testing shall be conducted within fourteen (14) days.

C. In the event a Pilot fails a subsequent written exam, oral exam, or flight check the Company will make a determination as to his/her continued employment. If the Company determines that retraining is inappropriate the Company reserves the right to terminate said Pilot.

D. If a Pilot is unable to successfully complete upgrade or transition training the Pilot will be allowed to return to their previous position, if that position still exists. If the Pilot's previous position has been filled or no longer exists the Pilot will be offered the opportunity to apply for any position for which they are currently qualified to perform, Company wide.

E. A Pilot who fails any portion of his new hire training will be subject to termination by the Company.

Section 15.4 Travel and Accommodations

A. In the event a Pilot is based away from home during training or special assignment, the Company shall in all cases provide single hotel room accommodations to each Pilot.

B. All travel expenses shall be paid by the Company. All travel will be performed in accordance with Company travel policy.

Section 15.5 Training Pay and Per Diem

A. All Pilots shall be paid while attending Training, including travel days, at their normal rate of pay. Training conducted on a Pilot's normal off duty day will be compensated at the applicable work-over rate.

B. All Pilots shall be paid per diem while Training, including travel days, at the rate of $36.00 per day.

ARTICLE 16
Schedules of Service

Section 16.1

Pilots at each base shall determine the appropriate schedules of service consistent with Company and customer service requirements. They shall forward their schedule to the appropriate Company official. A normal scheduled shift shall not exceed twelve (12) hours. This section will not relieve any Pilot from accepting any flight that may extend the shift beyond the scheduled twelve (12) hours as long as the flight can be conducted in accordance with the applicable FAR's and Company duty time policies.

Section 16.2

The parties to this agreement will maintain schedules of service which provide for one (1) day off for each day scheduled. Example: (7 days on – 7 days off; 4 days on – 4 days off) The Pilot's salary is based upon 182 ½ work shifts per year.

Section 16.3

Other work schedules will be discussed between the parties. However, both parties recognize schedules of service will meet customer requirements.

Section 16.4

The schedule in Section 16.2 of this Article shall be considered standard. Any other schedules shall be considered non-standard. Non-standard schedules shall be filled on a voluntary basis. Vacancies in a standard schedule resulting from temporary Pilot absences caused by illness, injury, vacation, holidays, training or leaves of absences shall not be considered a non-standard schedule.

Section 16.5

Pilots shall be allowed to trade or swap standard schedules provided it is approved by the appropriate Manager and a copy of the revised schedule is submitted to the Human Resources Department. Under no circumstance shall a trade or swap result in a workover shift for either Pilot.

16.6 Customer Requested Work Schedules

In the event a customer or prospective customer requires the Company to operate on a non-standard schedule, other than one (1) day scheduled for each day off, the parties shall meet to agree upon an applicable rate of pay. In the event the parties are unable to reach an agreement, the Company shall not assume the work in question.

ARTICLE 17
Workover

Section 17.1 Workover Assignment Procedure

The Union recognizes the importance of the Company's ability to provide 24/7 coverage to remain competitive in the marketplace and will use their best efforts to achieve this. A workover is defined as being scheduled for and reporting to work on a regularly-scheduled day off. Before offering workover to Pilots at a particular base, the Company reserves the right to utilize Relief or Part-time Pilots. If no Relief Pilots or Part-time Pilots are available, workover shall be offered as follows:

1. The workover will be offered to the Pilots at the base where it occurs. If more than one (1) Pilot volunteers for the workover it will be offered to the senior Pilot first and rotated thereafter among the other volunteers, at that base, in the descending order of seniority.

2. In the event there are insufficient Pilots stationed at the base where the workover occurs the Company will solicit volunteers from bases in close proximity to fill the workover shift, using the same method described above.

3. In the event there are no volunteers from bases in close proximity, the Company may use Pilots from other bases who have volunteered to work additional shifts.

> a) Pilots who would like to be contacted for such assignments will be required to post their name on a list maintained on the Company Web Site.

> b) The Pilot who volunteers for the largest number of consecutive shifts shall be awarded the assignment.

4. The Company reserves the right to limit Pilots to twenty-one (21) shifts per calendar month, and the number of shifts shall also be limited by applicable FAR's. This provision is designed to assure an equitable distribution amongst the applicable Pilots.

5. If the previous options do not provide a solution to the vacancy, the Company may utilize qualified management personnel to fill these open shifts.

Section 17.2 Emergency Workover Assignment

A. Emergency workover shall be defined as an unplanned vacancy for which the Company did not have seven (7) days advanced notice of (i.e. injury, illness, and bereavement). In which case, absent volunteers, the following procedures shall be utilized to fill such vacancies.

B. In any calendar year in which the number of uncovered Pilot duty shifts does not exceed two (2) at a location, due to a lack of volunteers, the Company will not have the ability to require workover at that location.

C. In the event such uncovered shifts exceed two (2) in any calendar year at a location, required workover may be assigned in an emergency situation on the basis of reverse seniority and rotated thereafter. The Company may only use this option to cover vacancies where less than seven (7) days advance notice of the vacancy was received.

D. For the purposes of Emergency workover, the Company shall not require any Pilot to perform more than two (2) Emergency workover shifts or more than twenty one (21) total shifts in any calendar month.

E. The Company will report to the union the number of uncovered shifts each month.

F. No Pilot can be forced on an emergency workover at a base other than his assigned base. Pilots who are forced to perform a workover shall be reimbursed for any verifiable non-refundable expenses they incurred on the day of the workover only.

Section 17.3 Workover Pay

Effective January 1, 2006 Pilots shall receive one-and-one-half times (1 ½ X) their normal daily rate, excluding supplemental pay and ACCRA. A workover shift is defined as being scheduled for and reporting for work on a regularly scheduled day off that was not the result of a trade or swap.

Section 17.4 Overtime

All work performed in excess of twelve (12) hours in a duty shift up to fourteen (14) hours shall be paid at the straight time hourly rate. Thereafter the Pilot's shall be paid at the Workover rate. Such payment shall be based on the actual termination time of the flight plus 15 minutes.

Section 17.5 Company Meeting Pay

Pilots who are required by the Company to attend meetings on their scheduled time off shall be compensated at the workover rate for all actual time in attendance. Pilots shall be paid a minimum of two (2) hours for attending such meetings.

ARTICLE 18

Pilot Status

Section 18.1

A newly employed Pilot shall be on a 180 calendar day probationary status during which time such a person may be discharged by the Company without recourse. After accumulating 180 calendar days, such employee shall be considered a non-probationary employee and his/her hire date shall revert back to the most recent date of hire.

Section 18.2

A newly employed Pilot shall be entitled to all the rights and benefits as any other Pilot of the terms of this Agreement, except that the Company shall retain the right to discharge a probationary Pilot at any time within their probationary period, without recourse to the grievance procedure and/or System Board of Adjustment.

Section 18.3

Once a month, the Company will provide the local Union office with a list of Pilots who have been hired, terminated, resigned, transferred or promoted to a management position, and/or on a military leave of absence during the prior quarter. This listing shall include the home address and phone number of said Pilots.

Section 18.4

A Union representative, if available, will be introduced to a new Pilot once they are assigned to a base for the purposes of explaining the obligations and benefits of this agreement.

ARTICLE 19
Pilot Classifications

Section 19.1

A full-time Pilot is a Pilot who is assigned to a regular work schedule at a specific base or program.

Section 19.2

A Relief Pilot is a full time Pilot who fills vacancies at any base as directed by the Company.

Section 19.3

A Temporary Full Time Pilot is a Pilot temporarily assigned to cover a specific vacancy arising due to a Full Time Pilot's leave of absence. Such Pilots will be allowed to bid for any open position after serving for six months as a Temporary Full Time Pilot. A Temporary Full Time Pilot's status shall coincide with the reinstatement rights of the Full Time Pilot returning from his/her Leave of Absence. A newly hired Temporary Full Time Pilot shall not qualify for benefits under the Severance pay provisions of this Contract.

Section 19.4

A Part Time/Per Diem Pilot is a Pilot who is offered work consistent with the Company's Customer Service or operational requirements. Such Pilots shall not have a regular work schedule, nor be eligible to participate in Company benefit programs as defined elsewhere in this Contract, unless provided for under either State or Federal statute, to include the Severance pay provision, nor shall they have any job bidding rights. Such Pilots shall be paid on a per diem basis in accordance with the published pay scale. Such Pilots shall have no rights under the Grievance and System Board of Adjustment procedures until having completed ninety (90) work schedules. Any Part Time/Per Diem Pilot who works twelve (12) or more work schedules per month for three (3) consecutive months shall become full-time. At no time shall the total number of Part Time/Per Diem Pilots exceed four percent (4%) of the full time Pilot staff.

Section 19.5

The Company shall not use Temporary Full Time or Part Time/Per Diem Pilots to avoid filling Full Time Pilot positions. The Company shall not use Part Time/Per Diem Pilots to cover vacant shifts when a current and qualified Full Time or Relief Pilot is available.

ARTICLE 20
Fees and Physical Examinations

Section 20.1

It shall be the responsibility of each Pilot to maintain an appropriate and current FAA medical certificate, and to provide a copy of this certificate to the Company by the 20th of the month in which it is due, if possible. If a Pilot is unable to provide the Company with a copy of their current FAA medical certificate by the 20th of the month in which it is due, the Pilot will coordinate with the training department/flight records clerk to communicate the delay. Under all circumstances it shall be the Pilots' responsibility to provide the training department/flight records clerk with their current FAA medical certificate no later than the last business day of the month in which the medical certificate is due.

Section 20.2

It shall be the responsibility of each Pilot to maintain the appropriate FAA Pilot certificate(s) required for his duty position. The Pilot shall provide the most current certificate(s) to the Company, and immediately report any changes that affect the validity of those certificates.

Section 20.3

It shall be the responsibility of each Pilot to arrange his required medical examinations by a qualified aero medical examiner of the Pilot's choice, as required by the Federal Aviation Regulations. Examinations will be scheduled while the Pilot is off duty. The Company will reimburse a Pilot for the cost of the class I or class II medical examination. Any additional physical exams and/or tests required by the Company or a customer beyond those required as provided for in Section 20.4 of this article shall be paid for by the Company.

Section 20.4

When the Company believes that there are grounds to question a Pilot's physical or mental condition to remain on flight status, the Company may require that such Pilot be examined by a FAA designated Aero Medical Examiner (AME) selected by the Pilot. The Company shall pay for this medical examination or tests required by the Company pursuant to this Article. The Pilot agrees to sign a medical release to allow a copy of the results to be given to the Company and the Pilot shall also be provided a copy of this report. A Pilot who fails to pass such an examination may have a review of the case. Such review will be conducted by the Medical Certification Branch of the FAA. The Pilot may, at his expense, have a second medical examination conducted and submitted along with the Company's medical examination to this branch of the FAA.

Section 20.5

A Pilot who is medically unable to perform his duties shall be placed on a leave of absence as described elsewhere in this Agreement.

Section 20.6

In the event the Company adopts an identification card or badge system, the Company shall provide the identification card or badge at no cost to the Pilot. However, if the Pilot loses the identification card or badge he/she shall be obligated to replace it at the cost of $10.00.

ARTICLE 21
Moving Expense

Section 21.1

The Company shall provide a paid move to Pilots whom are required to move as a result of being assigned to a base other than where the Pilot has established his residence, provided that the Pilot moves within a fifty (50) mile radius of his new base and the new base is at least fifty (50) miles away from the previously assigned base.

Section 21.2

In order to receive a Company paid move, Pilots must complete such move within six (6) months from the date of the new assignment and shall be entitled to the following reimbursement upon presentation of reasonable documentation:

A. Actual moving expenses, including insurance, for normal household effects, including normal packing charges, up to a maximum of $3500.00.

Section 21.3

Pilots shall be allowed the following en route expenses when properly substantiated by receipts during the period of en-route travel:

A. For Pilot only - $36.00/day

B. For Pilot and family - $72.00/day

The period of en-route travel shall continue after arrival until the day the household effects arrive or until the end of the fifth day, whichever comes first.

Section 21.4

For the purpose of determining necessary travel time, the Company will allow one (1) travel day for each five hundred (500) miles or fraction thereof, to a maximum of five (5) travel days when driving a vehicle. The Pilot is expected to move during his days off and be prepared to work on his regular hitch. The most direct AAA mileage between the two (2) cities will determine travel time.

Section 21.5

In addition to moving expenses, such Pilot will be reimbursed at the rate established by the IRS for one vehicle driven to the new location.

Section 21.6

To be eligible to obtain reimbursement from the Company, a Pilot must meet the requirements of Section 21.1 of this Article and have completed his probationary period.

ARTICLE 22
Travel Pay

Section 22.1

Mileage shall be paid to the Pilot at the applicable rate established by the Internal Revenue Service under the following circumstances:

a. Use of a personal vehicle when requested by the Company to relocate to another base or a location other than a Pilot's normal base for purposes of assignment on a temporary basis. The mileage will be calculated from the point of departure to the next base and not the Pilot's home.

b. In the event a Pilot is required to report to a base other than his assigned base, mileage will be calculated from the assigned base to the new work location.

c. Pilots shall not be required to use their personal vehicles when distances between the Pilots' home to the temporary assigned base are in excess of one hundred (100) miles.

Section 22.2

Pilots shall be paid at their regular rate of pay for travel on a scheduled duty day. In the event a Pilot travels on an off work day, such Pilot will be compensated at the applicable workover rate.

Section 22.3

When transportation or lodging are not provided by the Company, reasonable and actual expenses will be allowed. Within five (5) calendar days after returning to his home base or at the close of each week in the event the Pilot is away for a period longer than one (1) week, the Pilot shall submit expense receipts for payment. The per diem shall be consistent with Company policy.

ARTICLE 23
Leaves of Absence

Section 23.1

A Leave of Absence (LOA) is intended to account for a reasonable period of time that a Pilot may be required to be absent from the job for reasons other than vacation or paid bereavement leave. A LOA may fall into one of the following categories:

A. Personal LOA – (a reasonable time not to exceed 30 calendar days) without pay may be granted to a Pilot for urgent personal matters. Except as approved by the applicable operational official, a Pilot may be granted no more than one (1) personal LOA in a 2-year period. To be eligible for such a leave a Pilot has to have completed six (6) months of service. Approved personal LOA start and end dates shall be in writing. Such leaves may be extended for additional periods, if approved by the Company.

B. Pregnancy Disability Leave (PDL) – PDL shall be granted consistent with the applicable statute requirements for Pilots who reside in California and the Company's separate policy on same.

C. Military LOA – Military leaves of absence and reemployment rights upon return from such leave shall be granted in accordance with applicable laws. All orders for military duty, including National Guard and Reserve duty, shall be provided to the Human Resources Department in accordance with applicable laws.

D. Family & Medical LOA, and California Family Rights Act (CFRA) – Leave granted under the Family and Medical Leave Act or the California statute, will be granted to eligible Pilots as required by law.

    1. A Pilot on a medical leave of absence due to a serious non-occupational health condition of the Pilot, who does not return to work during the twelve (12) week period provided for under the Company's short term disability benefit, shall be granted an additional medical leave for the duration of the illness or injury, up to twelve (12) months, if the Company and Physician agree there is a reasonable expectation for the Pilot to return to duty within twelve (12) months from the expiration of short term disability. At the end of the first twelve (12) month leave of absence an additional twelve months shall be granted if the Company and Physician agree there is a reasonable expectation for a Pilot to return to duty within twenty four (24) months from the expiration of short term disability.

    2. Pilots who are unable to work as a result of a non-job related illness or injury shall be placed on Medical LOA. Such Pilot shall retain insurance coverage for a period of six (6) months. During this period the Company shall continue to provide disability and life insurance coverage at no cost to the Pilot. The Pilot's portion of medical, dental, and vision premiums will continue to be the responsibility of the Pilot. If a Pilot who is on Medical LOA is not receiving compensation from Air Methods or if the compensation received does not fully cover the Pilots portion of medical, dental, and vision premiums, the Pilot will be required to remit their portion of said premiums, on a monthly basis, no later than the fifteenth day of the month following commencement of Medical LOA. Failure to provide payment by the fifteenth of the month following the commencement of

Medical LOA will result in the termination of medical, dental, and vision benefits and the initiation of offering medical insurance under COBRA. Once the applicable time period has been exhausted, the Pilot will be eligible for medical insurance under COBRA.

E. Union Leave of Absence - A Pilot who accepts a temporary position with the Union (up to one (1) month) will be permitted to return to his original position upon release from such temporary assignment. At no time will the Company authorize the release of more than two (2) Pilots under this provision.

1. When requested by the Union, one (1) Pilot who is elected or appointed to a full-time position with the Union shall be granted an indefinite leave of absence. A Pilot leaving full-time service of the Union, for any reason, must return to duty within thirty (30) days or be terminated. Such Pilot upon returning to work with the Company will be entitled to return to his previous position at his last assigned base or apply for any open position for which the Pilot is qualified.

2. By mutual agreement, the Company may grant up to three (3) Pilots an unpaid leave of absence for a one (1) week period of time so that Pilots selected by the Union may perform work for the Union, such as attendance at Union conventions and conferences.

Section 23.2

A Pilot who wishes to apply for a Leave of Absence must submit his request in writing to his supervisor. This written request must include the expected duration of the leave, the purpose of the leave (if it does not violate any applicable statutes) and where the Pilot may be contacted during the leave. It is the Pilot's responsibility to keep Human Resources informed of any changes in his contact information for the duration of the approved leave.

Section 23.3

All requests for leaves of absence must be submitted in writing and must be approved by the applicable operational official. Except as approved by the applicable operational official, a Pilot will not be granted a leave of absence (except a Military LOA, Workers Compensation LOA, or Union LOA) without first using all vacation.

Section 23.4

Prior to returning to duty from medical leave, a Pilot may be required to present a physician's statement to the Company verifying that he is medically fit to perform all Pilot duties.

Section 23.5

In the event of a reduction in force, a Pilot on a leave of absence who would otherwise be furloughed will have his leave of absence cancelled. The Pilot will be notified that his rights under this article have been changed to those of a furloughed Pilot.

Section 23.6

A Pilot returning from a leave of absence will be returned to his duty position if it still exists, or any other vacant position where his qualifications permit. Any Pilot returning from a leave of absence who requires training prior to returning to flying will be scheduled for required training prior to return to flight duty *not to exceed three* (3) *weeks.* Pay shall resume when the Pilot commences training.

Section 23.7

All leaves of absence shall specify the date on which the Pilot will return to duty unless mutually agreed otherwise or by operation of law.

Section 23.8

All leaves of absence shall be without pay unless otherwise specified in this agreement or required by statute.

Section 23.9

Failure of any Pilot to return to active status at the end of any leave of absence shall be deemed a voluntary resignation and his name will be removed from the seniority list.

Section 23.10

Any Pilot on a leave of absence who enters the services of another Company or who enters into a business of his own without first obtaining written permission from the Company will be terminated and will forfeit his seniority rights.

Section 23.11

During any approved leave of absence, a Pilot will retain and accrue Company and Bidding Seniority.

ARTICLE 24
On-the-Job Injury (OJI) Leave

Section 24.1

A Pilot is eligible for all state and federal workers compensation benefits with respect to injuries or illnesses arising out of and in the course of employment with the Company.

Section 24.2

A Pilot must report the occurrence of an OJI to his supervisor as soon as possible, depending upon the nature of the accident or resulting injuries.

Section 24.3

All health, accident and life insurance benefits shall continue to be available to an injured Pilot on the same basis as an active employee.

Section 24.4

The Company may require an injured Pilot to submit to a physical examination in accordance with the provisions of Article 20.

Section 24.5

Prior to returning to duty from an OJI leave, a Pilot shall be required to present a physician's statement to the Company verifying that he is medically fit to perform all Employee duties. In the event there is a dispute concerning the Employee's fitness for duty, the procedures of Article 20 shall be utilized to resolve the dispute. Upon return from an OJI leave, a Pilot shall be returned to his former position if the position still exists, or to any other position where his seniority permits.

Section 24.6

All Pilots are entitled to a copy of any and all accident reports and any and all written or recorded statements made or taken with regard to an OJI within seventy-two (72) hours of a written request.

Section 24.7

All Pilots are entitled to a copy of any and all medical records, maintained by the Company at no cost, resulting from OJI's within five (5) days of a written request.

Section 24.8

Employee shall not be terminated or otherwise discharged from employment, except for cause, while recovering from OJI injuries.

Section 24.9

A Pilot has the right to select his own Vocational Rehabilitation Counselor while recovering from an OJI consistent with State regulations.

ARTICLE 25
Holidays

Section 25.1

Air Methods recognizes the following holidays:

New Years Day
Presidents Day
Memorial Day
Independence Day
Labor Day
Thanksgiving Day
Friday after Thanksgiving
Christmas Day

Section 25.2

To be eligible for Holiday pay a Pilot must work on a Holiday. The Pilot will be paid for the shift worked on the Holiday.

Section 25.3

The Pilot will receive their normal pay plus their annual base pay divided by 182.5 for each Holiday worked. For shifts worked that are less than twelve (12) hours the amount of holiday pay shall be prorated for each full hour worked.

ARTICLE 26
Sick Leave

Section 26.1

Sick Leave is granted to a Pilot to provide him an opportunity to recover from a non-job related illness and/or injury.

Section 26.2

Each Pilot shall earn up to sixty (60) hours of sick leave each calendar year. Sick leave shall be earned at the rate of 2.3076 hours per pay period. Sick leave shall be earned on all hours worked on workover, vacation, sick leave used, holidays, jury duty, and bereavement leave. Unused sick leave shall be earned up to a maximum of one hundred twenty (120) hours.

Section 26.3

Effective on the execution of the Contract any accrued sick leave beyond 120 hours may be used during a transition period up to 24 months for a bona fide medical need.

ARTICLE 27
Vacations

Section 27.1 Vacation Schedule

All Pilots shall be eligible to receive vacation on the following schedule:

Vacation Hours	Months of Service	Hourly Accrual Rate
84 Hours/Year	0 thru 60	*.0383562*
126 Hours/Year	61 thru 120	*.0575342*
168 Hours/Year	121 thru 180	*.0767123*
210 Hours/Year	181 and above	*.0958904*

• Vacation accrual will be applied to the first 2190 hours worked in a calendar year.
• Vacation balance will continue to be reported on the bi-weekly pay stub.
• Maximum Vacation Balance: 264 Hours
• Any Pilot who, at the date of ratification of the Contract, receives more vacation than the above schedule shall be grandfathered at their current vacation accrual rate.

Section 27.2

Vacation pay, when cashed out, shall be based upon the Pilot's current rate of pay.

Section 27.3

When a Pilot reaches the maximum vacation accrual according to the above schedule they shall not accrue any further vacation allowance. Once reaching the maximum accrual the Pilot will be paid seventy two (72) hours of his accrued vacation.

Section 27.4

At each Base location, Pilots will submit initial vacation requests by November 30 for desired vacations to be taken in the following year. The Company shall grant such requests in order of seniority, provided Pilots had or will have the requested time available on the books. After the initial vacation schedule has been accomplished, Pilots may submit vacation requests for any desired week/days on a first come, first served basis. Vacations may be changed/swapped by mutual agreement of the Pilot and Company. When possible, vacation requests will be submitted to the immediate supervisor at least sixty (60) calendar days in advance of the requested time off. Vacation requests received at least sixty (60) calendar days in advance of the requested time off that do not reduce base staffing levels below 75% shall be granted. The Company reserves the right to decline any vacation request when such vacation request would reduce full staffing levels to below 75%. The Company may grant vacation requests which will reduce staffing levels to below 75% provided sufficient voluntary work over from the base is assured and such allowances are consistent with all published regulatory and program rest requirements.

Section 27.5

Vacation will only be earned based upon compensable hours, which include holiday, vacation, sick leave, jury duty, or bereavement leave.

Section 27.6

Vacation pay may be cashed out based upon a quarterly schedule published by Payroll.

Section 27.7 Cancellation of Vacation

If a Pilot volunteers to cancel a scheduled vacation at the Company's request, he shall be reimbursed for all *verifiable* non-refundable expenses incurred. Such Pilot shall also have the following options:

1. Reschedule his vacation to any remaining available weeks/days in the same calendar year.

2. In lieu of the above option, the Pilot may choose to be paid the full value of his cancelled vacation period at the rate of one and one-half (1 ½) times his rate of pay. Payment for this vacation will be made by issuing a separate check to the Pilot within ten (10) days from election of this option.

ARTICLE 28
Health, Dental and Life/AD&D Insurance Benefits

Section 28.1

For the term of this Agreement, the Company shall offer Pilots health, dental, vision, LTD, STD, life and AD&D insurance as described in the summary plan descriptions furnished to the Union. In the event that the Company elects to change carriers, or administrators, it will endeavor to provide benefits that are comparable benefit value to those currently provided. The parties recognize in an effort to contain health care costs, it may be necessary to modify benefit levels, prior to doing so the Company will meet with the Union to review the proposed changes and solicit suggestions. The plans offered to the Pilots shall be the same as offered to all other non-represented employees.

Section 28.2

The Company will extend its best efforts to assist Pilots in resolving any claim disputes which do arise under the above plans after the member has followed the claims appeals process of the respective carrier or administrator. No matter relating to a claims dispute which is not the direct result of negligence by the Company shall be submitted to the grievance and/or Systems Board of Adjustment provisions of this agreement.

Section 28.3

A Pilot shall be eligible to participate in the group benefits listed above on the first day of the month coinciding with or following the date of initial hire. To be eligible for coverage in the above plans a Pilot must work or be paid consistent with the definitions in Article 19, Sections 19.1 through 19.4. Any Pilot who fails to meet the above definitions shall not have coverage in the following month.

Section 28.4

Pilots who participate in one of the Company Health and/or Dental Plans shall have the following amounts withheld from each bi-weekly pay check for the 2005-2006 plan year:

Health & Dental

Coverage	Plan 1	Plan 2	Dental
Employee Only	$36.00	$33.00	$1.50
Employee plus Spouse	$81.00	$59.00	$4.00
Employee + Children	$66.50	$56.00	$3.25
Family	$98.00	$82.00	$5.75

Future Health and Dental Plan annual rate increases for Pilots shall not exceed ten percent (10%) per year based on the 2005-2006 plan year Employee contribution schedule. In no case shall the annual percentage increase for a Pilot exceed that of the percentage increase for the Company.

Section 28.5

Pilots shall be covered at one and one-half (1 ½) times their total annual salary in Life Insurance and Accidental Death and Dismemberment Insurance under the provisions of the plan defined in the Company Benefit Plan.

ARTICLE 29
Company 401(k) Plan

Section 29.1 Plan Modifications

The Company reserves the right to amend from time to time the plan to cover the eligible Pilots to conform to the applicable State and Federal statutes. Any amendments shall be furnished to the Pilots and Union. The Company shall pay all costs associated with the administration of the plan.

Section 29.2 Enrollment

Enrollment in the plan shall be quarterly, provided that in the first year of employment said Pilot worked at least one thousand (1,000) hours.

Section 29.3 Vesting

Years   Percent of Vesting

One year	33 1/3 Percent
Two years	66 2/3 Percent
Three years	100 Percent

Section 29.4 Contribution

For those Pilots who contribute to this plan the Company shall contribute seventy percent (70%) on the first eight percent (8%) contributed by the Pilot. All Company and employee contributions shall be deposited into the respective employee's 401(k) account on the same day the wages are paid.

ARTICLE 30

Jury Duty

Section 30.1

The purpose of jury pay is to make the Pilots' pay whole while meeting their civic duty. Pilots who are required by proper court order or summoned to be absent from work in connection with jury duty will be paid the earnings he would have received for a regular scheduled shift up to a maximum of seven (7) work schedules per calendar year.

Section 30.2

Jury pay is not applicable when a Pilot is on leave of absence, vacation or layoff.

Section 30.3

In the event a Pilot is released from Jury Duty on a duty day, he shall proceed to his base or assignment the following day commensurate with his crew rest requirements.

Section 30.4

Pilots under subpoena for reasons benefiting the Company will be compensated for all lost time provided the Pilot was scheduled to work.

Section 30.5

Vacation time may be used any time a Pilot is required by subpoena to appear in a matter not benefiting the Company.

ARTICLE 31

Bereavement Leave

Section 31.1

The Company shall grant a bereavement leave for each individual for the death of a member of the Pilot's immediate family. Pilots on bereavement leave shall be paid for each duty day missed, up to a maximum of four (4) days or forty-eight (48) hours, whichever is less, per occurrence. Pilots may use accrued but unused Vacation beyond the four (4) days or forty-eight (48) hours bereavement leave. For the purposes of this Article, a Pilot's immediate family shall include his current spouse, in-laws, children, step-children, parents, grandparents, siblings and legal guardian.

Section 31.2

The Company shall grant bereavement leave for each individual for the death of a member of the Pilot's extended family of one (1) day or twenty-four (24) duty hours, whichever is less. A Pilot's extended family includes aunt, uncle, nephew and niece. Pilots may use accrued but unused Vacation beyond the one (1) day or twenty-four (24) duty hours bereavement leave.

Section 31.3

Funeral leave is not compensable when the Pilot is on scheduled days off, leave of absence, layoff, or suspension.

ARTICLE 32
Severance Pay

Section 32.1

A Pilot who is laid off and is placed on furlough with the Company shall receive severance pay according to the schedule in Section 32.2 below. Except if one or more of the following conditions exist he shall receive no severance pay.

> 1. He refuses to accept a job or assignment within his category of Pilot with the Company;

> 2. He is dismissed for cause or resigns or retires.

Section 32.2

Severance pay will be paid within seven (7) days following the Pilot's furlough based on the following schedule:

Full Years of Company Service	Calendar Weeks
One (1) full year of service but less than four (4)	Two (2) weeks
Four (4) full years of service but less than eight (8)	Four (4) weeks
Eight (8) full years of service but less than twelve (12)	Six (6) weeks
Twelve (12) full years of service but less than fifteen (15)	Eight (8) weeks
Fifteen (15) full years of service or more	Ten (10) weeks

Section 32.3

The Company will attempt to give Pilot(s) two (2) weeks advance notice of a base closure or loss of contract.

Section 32.4

Medical and Dental insurance, if any, shall continue for thirty (30) calendar days following the Pilot's layoff or furlough, provided the Pilot pays the appropriate contribution amounts. The Pilot will thereafter be eligible for COBRA coverage at that time.

ARTICLE 33
Union Bulletin Boards & Communications
Section 33.1

The Company shall permit the Union to display an unlocked bulletin board at each base that is company owned. The Union shall purchase the bulletin boards and shall be responsible for their installation. The bulletin boards shall only be placed in areas that have been agreed to by the Company in advance. The provision shall not be applicable if such bulletin boards are not permitted or authorized by a customer who owns the premises.

Section 33.2

The bulletin boards used by the Union and Pilots covered by this agreement shall be for posting notices of Union social and recreational affairs, meetings and elections.

Section 33.3

General distributions, posted notices and official business will bear the seal or signature of an officer of the Union or a Pilot representative and will not contain anything defamatory, derogative, inflammatory, negative, or of a personal nature attacking the Company or its representatives.

Section 33.4

The Company may refuse to permit any posting that would violate any of the provisions of this Agreement. Any notices posted that are not in accordance with this Article shall be removed by the Union or by the Company upon notice to the Union.

Section 33.5

If no bulletin board is permissible, the union may maintain an information book which shall remain in the Pilot's reference area or office.

ARTICLE 34
General and Miscellaneous
Section 34.1

Any deviation from this Agreement shall be made by mutual consent between the Company and the Union. Such consent must be in writing and signed by both parties.

Section 34.2

All orders or notices to Pilots covered by this Agreement involving a transfer, promotion, demotion, layoff, or leave of absence shall be given in writing to such Pilot with a copy to the Union within ten (10) calendar days.

Section 34.3

The pay period is currently fourteen (14) days (bi-weekly). If the Company wishes to change the pay period timing, it shall meet and discuss the change with the Union prior to implementation.

Section 34.4

This Agreement prohibits a Pilot from engaging in any activities that are in competition with the Company and flying activities that interfere with their service to the Company, provided, however that this provision shall not be construed to prohibit Pilots from affiliating with the Armed Forces of the United States.

Section 34.5

The Company shall make a copy of the current contract available to all Pilots on the Air Methods' website. In addition, the Company shall share in the cost of printing this Agreement up to a maximum of $1,000.00.

Section 34.6

A Pilot's primary responsibility is to ensure the safe operation of the aircraft. A Pilot may also be required to assist in minor aircraft maintenance other than that specifically authorized; washing of aircraft, couriering of parts, or other non-flying duties. In no case shall a Pilot be required to operate a ground ambulance or perform facility repairs. This provision does not restrict a Pilot from performing non-flying duties related to the promotion of the profession such as conducting educational classes, public relations presentations, or events of that nature.

Section 34.7

If a Pilot's personal items are damaged due to an aircraft accident or other unusual circumstance beyond the Pilot's control, a claim may be submitted to the Company and paid consistent with its insurance policy. However, the Company reserves the right to require proof of loss and value of the item covered in the claim.

Section 34.8

Any Pilot leaving the service of the Company shall, upon request to the Human Resource department, be provided with a letter setting forth the Company's record of his job title, stating his length of service and rate of pay at the date he left the Company.

Section 34.9

Pilots covered by this Agreement shall be governed by all reasonable Company rules, regulations and orders previously or hereafter issued by proper authorities of the Company which are not in conflict with the terms and conditions of this Agreement, and which have been made available to the Pilots and union prior to becoming effective.

Section 34.10

If the Union considers the rule to be unreasonable, it will have the right to file a written grievance challenging such rule prior to the implementation by the Company. Grievances properly filed in this respect will be subject to the normal Grievance and System Board of Adjustment procedures as set forth in Article 6 and Article 7 of this Agreement.

ARTICLE 35
Equipment and Facilities

Section 35.1

The Company shall furnish each Pilot with the following:

1. A helmet if required.

2. If a helmet is not required, effective upon execution of the Contract the Company will provide a one-time $100.00 allowance toward the purchase of an individual headset upon proof of purchase. Such allowance will not be applicable to previously purchased headsets. In either case a backup headset(s) will be provided in each aircraft as a primary means of communication.

3. An appropriate name tag, badge, embroidery, or other suitable means to identify each Pilot on their uniform.

4. A minimum of two suitable work uniforms deemed appropriate by the Company or Customer. Such uniforms shall be given to Pilots new to a program and be replaced annually as necessary.

5. One jacket, suitable for the local climate as deemed by the Company or Customer, and replaced as necessary.

6. Up to two (2) department or Customer ball caps annually if provided by the department or Customer and requested by the Pilot.

7. The Company shall reimburse, upon proof of purchase, up to one hundred dollars ($100.00) per year to each active Pilot on the payroll, for the purpose of purchasing Company or Customer required acceptable footwear.

Section 35.2

The Company will endeavor to provide reasonably quiet quarters with a rest facility for duty Pilots only.

Section 35.3

At each base the Company will provide internet access for appropriate weather source and/or required Company information. An area shall be designated for the completion of Company paperwork.

Section 35.4

Pilots who are required to spend the night away from their assigned base location shall be provided with single room hotel accommodations.

Section 35.5

The Company shall provide a VCR or DVD player, and television in an area accessible by the Pilot, if not already provided by the department or Customer. Where standard broadcast signal is not available, the Company will provide basic cable or satellite.

ARTICLE 36
Productive Work Environment Policy

Section 36.1

It is agreed that the Company, as a responsible corporate citizen, is committed to maintaining a hospitable, cooperative work environment that promotes professionalism, common courtesy and mutual respect among all levels of employees, supervisors, managers, and executives. To advance that commitment, the Company has adopted and will communicate to employees the productive work environment policy that strictly prohibits sexual and workplace harassment on the basis of race, color, creed, gender, religion, national origin, age, sexual orientation or disability or any other status protected by either Federal or State statute. This policy shall not be amended during the term of this agreement unless required by law.

Section 36.2

The Union agrees to support the provisions of the Air Methods corporate productive work environment policy. Each Pilot will be required to read, understand and sign an acknowledgement of this policy, which will be placed in his personnel file.

ARTICLE 37
Waiver and Complete Agreement

Section 37.1

This Agreement sets forth the entire understanding and agreement of the parties and may not be modified in any respect except by writing subscribed to by the parties. This Agreement supersedes all previous agreements, commitments or practices, oral or written, between the Company and the Union and/or the Pilots, and expresses all of the obligations of and restrictions imposed upon each of the respective parties during its term. The waiver of any provision of this Agreement or any breach of this Agreement by either party during the term of the Agreement shall not constitute a precedent for the future waiver of any breach or provision. Nothing in this Agreement shall prohibit the parties from bargaining on any issue they desire if both parties mutually agree to do so during the term of this Agreement.

Section 37.2

This document, together with all exhibits, memoranda of understanding, letters of agreement, and letter of interpretation incorporates the complete agreement between the parties on all issues specifically addressed herein.

Section 37.3

The parties agree that any past practices established prior to the date of this Agreement shall not create any contractual or legal obligation to continue such practices following the effective date of this Agreement.

ARTICLE 38
Savings Clause

Section 38.1

Should any part of this Agreement be rendered or declared invalid by reason of any existing or subsequently enacted legislation, act of government agency, or by any decree of a court of competent jurisdiction, such invalidation of such part or portion of this Agreement shall not invalidate the remaining portions hereof, and they shall remain in full force and effect.

Section 38.2

In the event that any provisions of this Agreement are in conflict with or are rendered inoperative or unlawful by virtue of any duly enacted law or regulation or any governmental agency or commission having jurisdiction over the Company, the Union and Company will meet and attempt to negotiate changes necessary, pertaining only to those provisions so affected or directly related thereto.

ARTICLE 39

Duration

This Agreement shall be effective from January 1, 2006 through April 30, 2009 and shall automatically renew itself from year to year thereafter, unless written notice of intended change is served in accordance with Section 6, Title I of the Railway Labor Act by either party at least sixty (60) days prior to the amendable date or any anniversary thereof.

OFFICE AND PROFESSIONAL EMPLOYEES AIR METHODS CORPORATION INTERNATIONAL UNION

APPENDIX A
Salary Schedule

Section 1. Base Pay

The Pilot in Command Base Pay Schedule listed below shall be effective on January 1, 2006. Co-Pilots shall be paid a rate equal to 75% of the Pilot in Command Pay Schedule.

Hire Year	1-Jan-06	Pay Step	1-Jan-07 3.75%	1-Jan-08 3.75%	1-Jan-09 4.00%
2006	$50,000	0-1	$51,875	$53,820	$55,973
2005	$50,813	1-2	$52,718	$54,695	$56,883
2004	$51,639	2-3	$53,576	$55,585	$57,808
2003	$52,479	3-4	$54,447	$56,489	$58,748
2002	$53,332	4-5	$55,332	$57,407	$59,703
2001	$54,199	5-6	$56,232	$58,341	$60,674
2000	$55,081	6-7	$57,146	$59,289	$61,661
1999	$55,976	7-8	$58,075	$60,253	$62,663
1998	$56,886	8-9	$59,020	$61,233	$63,682
1997	$57,811	9-10	$59,979	$62,229	$64,718
1996	$58,751	10-11	$60,955	$63,240	$65,770
1995	$59,707	11-12	$61,946	$64,269	$66,839
1994	$60,678	12-13	$62,953	$65,314	$67,926
1993	$61,664	13-14	$63,977	$66,376	$69,031
1992	$62,667	14-15	$65,017	$67,455	$70,153
1991	$63,686	15-16	$66,074	$68,552	$71,294
1990	$64,721	16-17	$67,148	$69,666	$72,453
1989	$65,774	17-18	$68,240	$70,799	$73,631
1988	$66,843	18-19	$69,350	$71,950	$74,828
1987	$67,930	19-20	$70,477	$73,120	$76,045
1986	$69,035	20-21	$71,623	$74,309	$77,282
1985	$70,157	21-22	$72,788	$75,518	$78,538
1984	$71,298	22-23	$73,971	$76,745	$79,815
1983	$72,457	23-24	$75,174	$77,993	$81,113
1982-1977	$73,635	>24	$76,397	$79,261	$82,432

Upon contract ratification all Pilots shall be placed onto the Base Pay Schedule in the 2006 year column commensurate with their year of hire. Beginning in 2007 each Pilot shall move to the 2007 year column on January 1, 2007 to the row corresponding with their years of service. At the Pilot's anniversary date with the Company, beginning in 2007, the Pilot will move to the next row corresponding with their years of service. The anniversary date is defined as the date a Pilot entered service with the Company as a Pilot in Command or Co-Pilot.

Section 2. Methodology for determining where a Pilot initially fits in the scale.

The Company reserves the right, based on previous experience of a Pilot(s), to place them on the above scale up to the five (5) year level or step. Thereafter the Pilot annually shall be advanced to the next step. Any disputes relative to that placement shall not be subject to the grievance and/or Systems Board of Adjustment provision located elsewhere in this agreement. Such placement on the scale will be made utilizing written documentation of active years in aircraft aviation experience. The Company reserves the right to determine the adequacy of the documentation.

Section 3. Base Assignment

The Pilot shall be paid based upon the applicable schedule for the base to which he/she is assigned or relocated.

Section 4. ACCRA Geographic Differential Pay

Effective with the implementation of the above schedule the Company shall determine the ACCRA impact for each current base using the most recent available quarterly ACCRA data when a Tentative Agreement is reached between the parties. The above schedule shall be considered 100% under the ACCRA system and all current bases shall be adjusted according to their respective ACCRA rating as per the table below. If no ACCRA data is available for a current or new base location, the five (5) nearest reporting cities to that base may be used to derive an ACCRA average provided that there are five (5) locations in close proximity of that base. Close proximity shall be considered within 75 miles. The Company reserves the right to develop recruitment and/or retention systems which will be paid above the schedule. Such schedules or systems will be paid to all Pilots at the base in question. In the event the Pilot voluntarily leaves his/her original base their pay will be based on their actual date of hire for purposes of step increases. The ACCRA impact rating effective at the execution of this agreement shall remain unchanged for the duration of the Contract. The ACCRA rating shall not be applicable for workover pay.

Location ACCRA rating	Pay scale adjustment
0 – 105%	100%
105.1 – 115%	110%

115.1 – 125%	120%
125.1 – 135%	130%
135.1 – 150%	140%
Greater than 150%	160%

Section 5. Initial Training

During initial training Pilots shall be paid at the starting rate commensurate with the assigned base.

Section 6. Relief Pilots

All relief Pilots shall have an ACCRA rating utilizing the Denver, Colorado ACCRA rating.

Section 7. No Reduction

No Pilot shall suffer a loss of pay due to the implementation of the above schedule. The Company will extend a one-time payment of 3% Salary Adjustment to any Pilot above the pay schedule. Such payment shall be made within forty-five (45) days of ratification. For such Pilots, in years 2007, 2008 and 2009 they shall receive on January 1 of each year a check equivalent to the amount of annual increase granted all other employees less applicable taxes. Such adjustment shall not be added to the Pilots' base pay. For those Pilots who receive less than a three percent (3%) increase in the ACCRA adjusted base pay as of January 1, 2006, the Company will extend a one-time payment that equals the difference between three percent and the total of the first year increase.

Section 8. Supplemental Pay

Pilots performing duties in the following positions shall receive the indicated annual supplemental pay (divided by 26 and paid through the normally occurring pay period cycle). Pilot(s) who receive more than the supplemental pay listed below shall receive that amount so long as they hold such position. The amount of such pay shall be determined by the actual dollars the employee received prior to the adoption of this collective bargaining agreement. Pilot(s) who currently receive IFR supplemental pay shall continue to do so for the duration of this agreement.

Check Airmen	$3,000
Training Captain/Trainer	$2,500
Aviation Service Manager	$4,200
ASM w/Multiple A/C	$5,700
ASM w/Multiple A/C Locations	$7,200
Aviation Base Manager	$1,500
Lead Pilot	$3,000

Base Safety Pilot	$800
Two to Three A/C	$1,600
Four to Five A/C	$2,400
Six or more A/C	$3,200
ATP in category assigned	$600

APPENDIX B

Base ACCRA Ratings
Revised March 1, 2006

Location	**ACCRA Formula**	
Albany NY	124.6	120.0%
Anaheim CA	156.1	160.0%
Anderson SC	94.4	100.0%
Asheville NC	99.4	100.0%
Atlanta GA	97.4	100.0%
Augusta GA	89.0	100.0%
Aurora CO	100.6	100.0%
Bakersfield CA	110.3	110.0%
Banning CA	126.4	130.0%
Bartow FL	99.4	100.0%
Bend OR	103.9	100.0%
Billings MT	98.1	100.0%
Bluefield WV	92.6	100.0%
Blueridge NC	92.4	100.0%
Boulder City NV	109.9	110.0%
Branson MO	86.7	100.0%
Brooksville FL	98.9	100.0%
Cape Girardeau MO	90.7	100.0%
Carlsbad CA	150.3	160.0%
Cartersville GA	94.4	100.0%
Champaign IL	95.9	100.0%
Charleston WV	92.6	100.0%
Charlotte NC	92.4	100.0%
Chesterfield MO	94.3	100.0%
Chicago IL	110.1	110.0%
Chinle AZ	112.4	110.0%
Clarksville TN	87.0	100.0%
Colorado Springs CO	94.7	100.0%
Columbia MO	91.6	100.0%
Columbia SC	96.4	100.0%
Columbus GA	97.4	100.0%
Conyers GA	97.4	100.0%
Cottonwood AZ	106.4	110.0%

Denver CO	100.6	100.0%
Des Moines IA	93.9	100.0%
Duluth MN	98.1	100.0%
Effingham IL	92.8	100.0%
El Cajon CA	126.4	130.0%
Elizabethtown KY	93.7	100.0%
Evansville IN	99.0	100.0%
Farmington NM	94.9	100.0%
Flagstaff AZ	112.4	110.0%
Frankfort KY	93.7	100.0%
Franklin NC	99.4	100.0%
Fredericksburg VA	125.2	130.0%
Frisco CO	100.6	100.0%
Gardnerville NV	112.1	110.0%
Glen NY	136.5	140.0%
Glendale AZ	100.4	100.0%
Greeley CO	95.4	100.0%
Greenville NC	95.2	100.0%
Griffin GA	97.4	100.0%
Gulfport MS	95.0	100.0%
Hartford CT	115.7	120.0%
Hazard KY	93.7	100.0%
Huntington WV	92.6	100.0%
Huntsville AL	89.9	100.0%
Hutchinson MN	98.1	100.0%
Imperial CA	123.6	120.0%
Iowa City IA	95.2	100.0%
Jacksonville FL	95.5	100.0%
Jefferson GA	97.4	100.0%
Joplin MO	82.4	100.0%
Kingman AZ	109.4	110.0%
Kobelt NY	136.7	140.0%
LaGrande OR	103.9	100.0%
LaMonte MO	92.9	100.0%
Las Vegas NV	109.9	110.0%
Lebanon TN	91.9	100.0%
Lincoln NE	96.7	100.0%
Litchfield IL	94.3	100.0%
London KY	93.7	100.0%
Marshfield WI	95.0	100.0%
Mason City IA	89.7	100.0%
Merced CA	159.0	160.0%
Mesa AZ	100.4	100.0%
Miami Baptist, FL	116.2	120.0%
Miami FL	116.2	120.0%
Modesto CA	159.0	160.0%

Mojave CA	118.4	120.0%
Morgantown WV	101.1	100.0%
Mt Pleasant TN	91.9	100.0%
Mt Sterling KY	93.7	100.0%
Nashville TN	94.7	100.0%
New Richmond WI	98.1	100.0%
Newark DE	108.7	110.0%
Norfolk NE	91.1	100.0%
Norwich CT	114.4	110.0%
Odessa FL	98.9	100.0%
Oklahoma City OK	91.0	100.0%
Olathe KS	91.7	100.0%
Omaha NE	89.0	100.0%
Osage Beach MO	90.1	100.0%
Oxnard CA	118.4	120.0%
Pahrump NV	109.9	110.0%
Palo Alto, CA	159.0	160.0%
Parsons KS	90.0	100.0%
Philadelphia PA	123.9	120.0%
Pueblo CO	90.3	100.0%
R Cucamonga CA	128.1	130.0%
Reno NV	112.1	110.0%
Richmond KY	93.7	100.0%
Richmond VA	105.9	110.0%
Roanoke VA	90.7	100.0%
Rockford IL	99.2	100.0%
Safford AZ	97.2	100.0%
Saginaw MI	96.4	100.0%
Salt Lake City	95.9	100.0%
San Antonio TX	91.6	100.0%
San Juan PR	97.8	100.0%
Sarasota FL	107.9	110.0%
Scottsbluff NE	98.5	100.0%
Seminole OK	91.0	100.0%
Shelbyville TN	91.9	100.0%
Sierra Vista AZ	94.0	100.0%
Sioux City IA	93.3	100.0%
Somerset KY	93.7	100.0%
Sparta IL	94.3	100.0%
Springfield MO	92.0	100.0%
Springville AZ	112.4	110.0%
St Cloud MN	100.8	100.0%
St. Joseph MO	90.1	100.0%
St. Louis MO	94.3	100.0%
Sullivan MO	94.3	100.0%
Tallahassee FL	90.7	100.0%

Tampa FL	96.0	100.0%
Texarkana AR	88.7	100.0%
Tucson AZ	97.3	100.0%
Tullahoma TN	91.9	100.0%
Tulsa OK	90.1	100.0%
Tupelo MS	87.5	100.0%
Valhalla NY	136.5	140.0%
Victorville CA	125.8	130.0%
Warrenton MO	94.3	100.0%
Waterloo IA	88.9	100.0%
Wildwood FL	98.9	100.0%
Willcox AZ	90.1	100.0%
Winslow AZ	112.4	110.0%
Winston Salem NC	89.6	100.0%
Worcester MA	118.2	120.0%
Wytheville VA	90.7	100.0%

11. The Public Sector

1. Do federal employees generally have the right to union representation?

2. What act governs Federal Employment Labor Relations?

3. List ten issues most federal employee unions are precluded from bargaining over.

4. The scope of bargaining for federal employees is generally confined to what issues?

5. How is the scope of bargaining for FAA employees different?

6. Which federal employees are permitted by law to strike?

7. Are members of the armed forces empowered to organize into unions and bargain collectively?

8. Are airport security screening officers employed by the TSA empowered to organize into unions and bargain collectively?

9. Are civilian employees of the Department of Defense empowered to organize into unions and bargain collectively?

10. In your opinion, do legitimate national-security interests justify your answers to the two preceding questions? Explain.

11. Give an example of outsourcing of union jobs in aviation in the federal public employment sector.

12. What is the "A-76 process"?

13. Is the FAA experiencing workforce-replacement challenges similar to those the aerospace manufacturing industry is experiencing? If so, why? If not, why not?

14. What are the arguments for and against privatization of the air traffic control function?

15. What agency hears appeals of federal personnel actions?

16. Is the TSA experiencing workforce-replacement challenges similar to those the aerospace manufacturing industry is experiencing? If so, why? If not, why not?

17. Are most airline and major general aviation reliever airports in the United States managed, operated, and maintained by public or private employees?

18. Give an example of outsourcing of one of those functions of managing, operating, and maintaining a public airport.

19. What is the status of privatization of air carrier airports in the United States?

20. What is the status of privatization of air carrier airports overseas?

Online Assignments

1. What is the current status of the City of Chicago's effort to privatize Midway International Airport?

2. What is the current status of TSA employees' union representation and collective bargaining?

3. Identify a group of state aviation employees in your state or a state your instructor assigns you. Are those employees represented by a union bargaining collectively on their behalf? If not, are they permitted to organize and bargain collectively under state law?

Notes

3. Major Collective Bargaining Legislation

Detailed Examination of the Events Leading to Rule 83 Decision

1. Smith, *Airways*, 224; Knowlton, *Air Transportation in the United States*, 9; Fruedenthal, *Aviation Business*, 311.
2. "What's What among Pilots!" *Aviation* 32, March 1933, 91.
3. *New York Times*, February 11, 1933, sec. 7, 10.
4. *Air Line Pilot*, January 1933, 1.
5. James M. Mead to David L. Behncke, January 10, 1933.
6. *Air Line Pilot*, February 1933, 8.
7. M. Derber, "Growth and Expansion," in *Labor and the New Deal*, ed. Milton Derber and Edwin Young (Madison: University of Wisconsin Press, 1957), 3–8.
8. ALPA, *Proceedings of the 1932 Convention*, 50, 127–29.
9. David L. Behncke to All Local Chairmen, September 2, 1932.
10. ALPA, *Proceedings of the 1932 Convention*, 84–94.
11. C. F. Roos, *N.R.A. Economic Planning*, Cowles Commission for Research in Economics, no. 2 (Bloomington, IN: Principia, 1937), 28–32.
12. ALPA, *Proceedings of the 1932 Convention*, 168–90.
13. Frederick C. Warnshuis, chairman, Aeromedical Association, to David L. Behncke, September 22, 1932.
14. ALPA, *Proceedings of the 1932 Convention*, 168–90.
15. *Air Line Pilot*, February 1933, 1.
16. ALPA, *Proceedings of the 1932 Convention*, 27–28.
17. *New York Times*, February 26, 1933, 23.
18. *Air Line Pilot*, February 1933, 6.
19. Charles A. Madison, *American Labor Leaders: Personalities and Forces in the Labor Movement* (New York: Ungar, 1950), 108–35.
20. William Green to David L. Behncke, March 2, 1933.
21. *Air Line Pilot*, (March 1933), 1.
22. Arthur M. Schlesinger Jr., *Coming of the New Deal*, vol. 2, *Age of Roosevelt* (Boston: Houghton Mifflin, 1958), 87–102.
23. Roos, *N.R.A. Economic Planning*, appendix 2, 537.
24. ALPA, *Proceedings of the 1934 Convention*, 21–27.
25. Schlesinger, *Coming of the New Deal*, 108–9; Roos, *N.R.A. Economic Planning*, 55–82.
26. Schlesinger, *Coming of the New Deal*, 107–8.
27. Minutes of the meeting of June 15, 1933, Central Executive Council, ALPA.
28. Minutes of the meeting of July 6, 1933, Central Executive Council, ALPA.
29. *Air Line Pilot*, July 1933, 1.
30. Wallace S. Dawson to David L. Behncke, September 4, 1933.
31. *Air Line Pilot*, July 1933, 1.
32. Ibid., August 1933, 6.
33. Minutes of the meeting of August 3, 1933, Central Executive Council, ALPA; Schlesinger, *Coming of the New Deal*, 126; David L. Behncke to Hugh S. Johnson, August 1, 1933.
34. William Green to David L. Behncke, August 15, 1933.
35. ALPA, *Proceedings of the 1934 Convention*, 61–64.
36. Minutes of the meeting of August 15, 1933, Central Executive Council, ALPA.
37. Minutes of the meeting of August 23, 1933, Central Executive Council, ALPA *Air Line Pilot*, September 1933, 1.
38. ALPA, *Proceedings of the 1932 Convention*, 21–22; *Air Line Pilot*, September 1933, 1. The members of the pilot committee who attended the code hearings included E. Hamilton Lee (United), Howard E. Hall (T&WA), Walter J. Hunter (American), Eugene Brown (Eastern), Sam Carson (Kohler), John H. Neale (Pacific), Mal B. Freeburg (Northwest), and John H. Tilton and C. M. Drayton (Pan American).
39. "Code for the Air Transport Industry," *Aviation* 32, September 1933, 290–91.
40. "Coding Air Transport," *Aviation* 32, October 1933, 311–12.
41. *New York Times*, August 28, 1933, 12.
42. Ibid., August 29, 1933, 16.
43. "Coding Air Transport," *Aviation* 32, October 1933, 311–12; minutes of the meeting of October 10, 1933, Central Executive Council, ALPA.
44. ALPA, *Proceedings of the 1934 Convention*, 24–26; "Blue Eagle Takes Wing," *Aviation* 32, September 1933, 369–70; *New York Times*, September 12, 1933, 15. Muir signed the code on September 11 and passed it on to the White House for presidential approval, which finally came on November 20, 1933.
45. William Randolph Hearst to M. A. Roddy, ed., *Air Line Pilot*, December 8, 1933. In a letter to the nominal editor of the union newspaper, Hearst expresses his admiration for the airline pilots. He considers them a kind of ready reserve for the defense of the country, since they would, in his opinion, need little or no training before they started manning bombers: "The next war . . . which God forbid, will be decided in the air, and some of the brave men to whom this letter comes will determine the decision. The nation owes them much now and may in the future owe them many times more." Ibid.
46. ALPA, *Proceedings of the 1942 Convention*, 70–80; ALPA, *Proceedings of the 1934 Convention*, 24.
47. ALPA, *Proceedings of the 1934 Convention*, 27–28; *New York Times*, September 22, 1933, 19. On September 21, 1933, the Big Five finally issued a public statement declaring their intention to impose the new hourly pay system. Behncke knew about it early in September, however.
48. *New York Times*, September 3, 1933, 7; minutes of the meeting of October 10, 1933, Central Executive Council, ALPA.
49. *New York Times*, September 22, 1933, 19; *Air Line Pilot*, January 1934, 1; ALPA, *Proceedings of the 1934 Convention*, 76.
50. David L. Behncke to W. M. Leiserson, secretary, NLB, September 20, 1933; "Truce," *Aviation* 32, September 1933, 297.
51. Schlesinger, *Coming of the New Deal*, 146–47.
52. ALPA, *Proceedings of the 1934 Convention*, 28–30.
53. *Air Line Pilot*, October 1933, 1; minutes of the meeting of October 10, 1933, Central Executive Council, ALPA.
54. *New York Times*, September 3, 1933, sec. 8, 7.
55. Roos, *N.R.A. Economic Planning*, 33, 56–57, 221.
56. ALPA, *Proceedings of the 1934 Convention*, 30–35.
57. *New York Times*, September 27, 1933, 9; ibid., October 1, 1933, 27.
58. National Recovery Administration, National Labor Board, *In the Matter of the Hearing between Representatives of the Air*

Line Pilots Association and Representatives of United Air Lines, American Airways, and North American Aviation Corporation (abridged transcript in the ALPA archives).

59. Ibid.

60. Ibid.

61. Ibid.; ALPA, *Proceedings of the 1934 Convention*, 37–40; *New York Times*, October 3, 1933, 15; ibid., October 5, 1933, 1; ibid., October 6, 1933, 9; "Pilots' Debate," *Aviation* 32 (November 1933), 354.

62. *New York Times*, October 28, 1933, 18; ibid., October 29, 1933, 25.

63. ALPA, *Pilots' Final Brief before a Fact Finding Committee Held by Judge Shientag, Chairman of the Committee Studying the Air Line Pilot Wage and Hour Question*, 1.

64. R. M. Cleveland, "Pilots' Pay Is Debated," *New York Times*, November 5, 1933, Sec. 8, 7.

65. ALPA, *Proceedings of the 1934 Convention*, 40–41.

66. Ibid., 41–43.

67. "Wages of Pilots," *Aviation*, 32, December 1933, 382.

68. Ibid.; *New York Times*, November 7, 1933, 24.

69. ALPA, *Proceedings of the 1934 Convention*, 45–48; "Wages of Pilots," *Aviation*, 32, December 1933, 382.

70. "Wage Scale Arbitration," *Aviation*, 33, January 1934, 26–27; ALPA, *Pilots' Report of a Conference Held at the Mayflower Hotel, December 15, 1933, between the Pilots' Subcommittee and the Operators in Compliance with a Suggestion of the National Labor Board at the Hearing of December 14, 1933*. The pilots at the meeting were David L. Behncke and Jack O'Brien for United, Eugene Brown for Eastern, Alexis Klotz for Western Air Express, and Clyde Holbrook for American. The officials representing the operators were W. A. Patterson for United, Harris M. "Pop" Hanshue for North American Aviation (which by this time controlled Eastern, T&WA, and Western), and Lester D. "Bing" Seymour for American.

71. "No Quarter in Wage War," *Aviation* 33, February 1934, 54–55; *Air Line Pilot*, January 1934, 1; minutes of the meeting of January 16, 1934, Central Executive Council, ALPA.

72. J. M. Baitsell, *Airline Industrial Relations; Pilots and Flight Engineers* (Cambridge: Harvard University Press, 1966), 32.

73. M. L. Kahn, *Pay Practices for Flight Employees on U.S. Airlines*, 23 (University of Michigan–Wayne State University, Institute of Labor and Industrial Relations, no. 23, 1961), 12, rept. President's Railroad Commission, *Report of the Presidential Railroad Commission*, appendix, vol. 4.

4. Elections, Certifications, and Procedures

Strike by Trans World Airlines Flight Attendants: Contract Continuity under the Railway Labor Act

1. C. J. Loomis, "The Comeuppance of Carl Icahn," Fortune Magazine, February 17, 1986.

2. Loomis, "Comeuppance of Carl Icahn."

3. Ibid.

4. Ibid.

5. A. Bernstein and C. Hawkins, "Icahn Ponders Dismembering His New Airline," Business Week Magazine, March 17, 1986.

6. Ibid.

7. P. Wagman, "TWA Flying at Half-Strength," St. Louis Post-Dispatch, March 8, 1986.

8. Ibid.

9. P. Wagman, "Talks between Company, Attendants to Resume," St. Louis Post-Dispatch, March 11, 1986.

10. Ibid.

11. Ibid.

12. P. Wagman, "More Than Pay at Stake for TWA Strikers," St. Louis Post-Dispatch, March 26, 1986.

13. Wagman, "Talks between Company."

14. P. Wagman, "TWA, Attendants Halt Talks," St. Louis Post-Dispatch, March 13, 1986.

15. Ibid.

16. J. Davis and J. Dauner, "TWA Says It's Quit Hiring Attendants," Kansas City Times, April 29, 1986.

17. J. Dauner, "TWA Loses Fight over Union Dues," Kansas City Times, August 2, 1986.

18. Ibid.

19. Ibid.

20. J. Dauner, "TWA Appeals Due for Flight Attendants," Kansas City Times, August 8, 1986.

21. J. Taylor, "TWA Strikers Fail in Bid to Get Their Old Jobs Back," Kansas City Times, August 26, 1986.

22. Hage and de Fiebre, "Replacing Strikers Is Growing Industry Trend."

23. C. Friday and D. Pauly, "A Fatal Flight Takes Its Toll," Newsweek Magazine, September 8, 1986.

24. Ibid.

25. D. Seligman, "Keeping Up: A Soviet Election," Fortune Magazine, July 3, 1989.

26. "Railway Labor Act Isn't Excess Baggage," letters to the editor, Wall Street Journal, June 5, 1987.

6. Unfair Labor Practices

Key Airlines, 16 NMB no. 88

1. The pay raise for pilots and flight engineers was announced the day before the IBT filed a representation application on December 22, 1988, for these employees.

America West Airlines Inc., 17 NMB no. 63

2. A Laker election involves a "yes" or "no" ballot. The majority of votes cast determine the outcome of the election.

3. In a Key election, the majority of the eligible voters must vote against representation in order to prevent certification.

4. In Laker Airways Ltd., 8 NMB 236 (1981), the board stated, ". . . it is a per se violation of the [Act] for any carrier or its officials to solicit employees to turn their ballots in to the carrier. It is, furthermore, a per se violation to provide mailing envelopes for this purpose. . . . It is a per se violation to poll employees during a representation election conducted by the Board." See also Key Airlines, 16 NMB 358 and 296 (1989), and 13 NMB 153 (1986), where the board found "egregious" such carrier actions as discharge and transfer of known union supporters.

5. Among the revised language proposed by the carrier are statements such as, "While the union's allegations of coercive threats and reprisals were not supported by the evidence, the carrier is free under the First Amendment to express its opinion regarding the union."